ACQUISTION & PROPER USE OF POWER
The Destruction of White Supremacy
WHY WE STRUGGLE
WHY WE FIGHT AS A LIFESTYLE

BY
H. KHALIF KHALIFAH

Published by
UBUS COMMUNICATIONS SYSTEMS
26070 Barhams Hills Road - Drewryville, VA 23844
434-378-2140 khalifah23844@yahoo.com
publish@khabooks.com

FIRST EDITION -- FIRST PRINTING
APRIL 29, 2010
SECOND EDITION – SECOND PRINTING
June 19, 2011

Copyright © 2010 by H. Khalif Khalifah. No part maybe legally used without the written permission of the author or the Publisher: UBUSCS P. O. Box 9, Drewryville, Virginia 23844. [434] 378-2140

KHALIFAH IS AVAILABLE FOR THE FOLLOWING
- THOUGHT POWER MEDITATION & 8 A.M. DAILY
- LECTURES, WORKSHOPS BOOKSIGNING
- PUBLISHING & PRINTING CONSULTANCY
- SELF EMPOWERMENT CONSULTANCY
- SELF EMPLOYMENT CONSULTANCY
- NAT TURNER TRAIL HISTORY TOURS

ISBN# 1-56411-611-5..........................YBBG#0620

PRINTED IN U.S.A.
THE LUMUMBA BOOK PRINTERS
P. O. Box 9 - Drewryville, VA 23844
(434) 378-2140 publish@khabooks.com

CONTENTS

Chapter 1 .... Page 9
THE ACQUSITION & PROPER USE OF POWER

Chapter 2 .... Page 20
THE CHALLENGE OF WHITE SUPREMACY

Chapter 3 .... Page 30
BRIEF OVERVIEW OF THE ENCOUNTER OF BLACK AND WHITE PEOPLE

Chapter 4 .... Page 53
SUCCESSFULLY OVERCOMING SURVIVAL REQUIREMENTS WHILE STAYING FOCUSED ON THE LIBERATION NECESSITIES OF AFRIKAN PEOPLE

Chapter 5 .... Page 75
PROPER AND IMPROPER USE OF POWER

CHAPTER 6 .... Page 87
ONE ASPECT SHOULD NOT HAVE THE POWER TO CONSUME OUR LIVES

CHAPTER 7 .... Page 97
EFFECTIVE WAYS OF POWER THAT ARE NOT CONFRONTATIONAL TO THE ENEMY

CHAPTER 8 .... Page 127
THINGS IN LIFE THAT CIRCUMVENT YOUR HUMAN POTENTIAL
-The Usage of Power-

CHAPTER 9 .... Page 164
70 YEARS OF EXPERIENCE IN OPPRESSION: LIVING IN RESISTANCE AS A DUTY

CHAPTER 10 .... Page 180
THE NATURAL DESIRE TO KNOW WHO YOU ARE AND YOUR PURPOSE

CHAPTER 11 .... page 199
THE STRUGGLE IS TO OVERCOME LIFE CHALLENGES

CHAPTER 12 .... Page 204
RAISING CHILDREN THE NATURAL WAY

SHOULD BE TAUGHT IN OUR YOUTH
CHAPTER 13..................................Page 216
THOUGHT IS THE COMMON
DENOMINATOR FOR HUMANS
CHAPTER 14..................................Page 230
THE FIRST LAW OF NATURE:
YOUR FIRST STRUGGLE
CHAPTER 15..................................Page 242
NAT TURNER AS A POSITIVE
EXAMPLE FOR EVERYONE
CHAPTER 16..................................Page 254
WHITE SUPREMACIST SYSTEM JOBS
BLUNT THE MAIN OBJECTIVE
CHAPTER 17..................................Page 266
SOMETIMES ONLY WELL PLANNED DYNAMIC ACTION
TO ACHIEVE A PHYSICAL RESULT WILL WORK
CHAPTER 18..................................Page 283
POWER IS ALWAYS WITH US:
EVEN A BABY IS BORN WITH POWER
CHAPTER 19..................................Page 318
ON RAISING CHILDREN
CHAPTER 20..................................Page 333
STOP LOOKING FOR A JOB "IN THE SYSTEM" Page 334
THE ENDING OF **THE BOOK**
THE SPIRITUAL MANUAL OF THE
MYSTIC ORDER OF UBUS 365
INDEX..................................Page 403
GALLERY OF MASTER TEACHERS & COMMUNITY ORGANIZERS, FAMILY, FRIENDS AND ACQUAINTECES WHO IMPACTED ONE WAY OR THE OTHER ON THE THOUGHT PATTERNS IN THIS BOOK.
REVIEW & PREVIEW OF ALL CHAPTERS.....Page 407
POST SCRIPT: TRIBUTE TO A GREAT MAN:
DR. IMARI ABUBARKARI OBADELE......Page 416

DEDICATION

To my grandchildren Deja, Ahyanna & other Black Youth, especially "My foster children," and others who have loved me and whom I have loved in North America: And those Present and the unborn. This book and others that I put together, this deep into my Eldership are vouchsafed to you – with the hope and expectations that you will find something of substance to support and substantiate a burning desire to be free. For there is no doubt in my own mind that in your time – toddler, puberty, young adulthood, adulthood, and in your own Eldership – if you evolve an idea for freedom, justice and equality for Afrikan people, you will, as I have and am, must maintain your resolve amid nay Sayers and other skeptics, doubters, enemies [informants] and the fearful comfort seekers in white supremacy based social systems.

Hopefully what I write here will help you to maintain your resolve and determination to not settle for anything short of Complete Freedom: the freedom that our most relevant, committed ancestors struggled for. Always remember that Uncle Brother Khalifah said: "there is a right way to do anything worthwhile." And there is nothing more worthwhile than struggling for freedom, justice and equality for Black people.

The Right Way is found by understanding the knowledge that you already have about what it is you maybe trying to do: understanding of it will give you the wisdom to both clarify the Path that you can travel at that particular level of Knowledge, which is power. Wisdom will also guide your struggle to overcome the challenges you will find on the Path. Hopefully my words, acts and deeds will help to shape and mold your character to reflect the Stellar, Spiritual Being as per your human potential.

ACKNOWLEDGEMENTS

THE SUPREME BEING: THE CREATOR
SUSTAINER & CHERISHER OF ALL CREATION

THE MESSENGE OF
THE HONORABLE ELIJAH MUHAMMAD
&
ATTY/NEPHEW OPIO SOKONI
IBN H. KHALIF KHAIFAH
MASTER PAUL GUTHRIE
AREEB MALIK SHABAZZ
NEPHEW TREAVOR JAHA
&
SOSHEN AMUNTYT KHALIFAH
NIECE MARIAN BYNOE
COUSIN LULA B. EDWARDS
'COUSIN' MARGARET HOUSE
SISTER NIECE SALAAM JAHA

Acknowledgements are duly expressed, but all conjecture, errors, mistakes, excesses, and omissions, are my own

INTRODUCTION

This book is a purpose driven document that aims to help empower Black individuals to free The Race of slavery, second-class citizenship and other forms of oppression. I have tried to empty as much of myself as possible into the pages that follow. The ideal is to share the life processes that I have engaged to acquire and properly use power to attain to the state to where I Am.

The attainments of Human Beings are reflected through the character of the Human body; and the character is shaped by various challenges and tasks that the Human must overcome to sustain life in this world. To overcome the challenges and tasks requires utilization of the power and potential power that is part of the constitution of the Human: we inculcate this within it at the time of its making.

The methodologies, ways and means, used by Humans to overcome challenges to achieve his or her aims, objectives and goals is what shapes and mold the Humans Character.

This book proposes to share methodologies, ways and means to guide the aspirant to master the processes to obtain and properly use Power, to free – first – fetters from the Human – allowing it to then engage and defeat all challenges; the number one challenge for Black humans, chattel slavery, second-class citizenship and others forms of oppression that have haunted the race for so long. Hopefully, The Book will reflect the fact that the embracing of right and rejecting of wrong shapes and makes the best character; the character that reflects the image of our Creator: The surest way to guide this methodology is the awareness of the Best Interest that is served in our every word, act and deed.

OTHER BOOKS BY KHALIFAH
IN THE ORDER OF THEIR PUBLICATION.

- Real Afro-American History, Vol 1
- The Brief Affair: Too Black My Love?
- The Legacy of The Honorable Elijah Muhammad
- The Freedom Block
- How To Distribute Your Own Newspaper, Magazine or Book
- Profusion: Whatever One May Think of It: The Impact of Shahrazad Ali Book: The Blackmans Guide to Understanding the Blackwoman
- Selective Writings: The Words, Acts and Deeds of Khalifah 1982-1992
- Rodney King and the L. A. Rebellion: Comments of 13 Independent Black Writers (Editor)
- Melanin, Conscious Attunement and the God In I
- The Revolt of Nat Turner the B.L.A. in Southampton County in 1831
- A Brief History About N'COBRA and The Reparations Movement
- The Willie Lynch Letters and the Making of a Slave (Editor)
- The Nat Turner ?Quiz Book? 101 Questions and Answers About Nat Turner and the B.L.A. of 1831
- Quotations From The Book
- The Acquisition and Proper Use of Power: Why We Struggle Why We Fight

CHAPTER ONE

THE ACQUISITION AND PROPER USE OF POWER WHY WE STRUGGLE WHY WE FIGHT AS A LIFE STYLE

In short humans struggle to acquire power. We need power to overcome life's challenges. Challenges are in our Destiny as Humans; they are lessons that we overcome while mastering the processes of life.

Our first struggle is to overcome a challenge within the destiny of our birth as humans [i.e. we were destined to be born through our parents, in the hospital, or elsewhere]. During our life, we need power to circumvent the challenges to our potential as humans. Challenges in our destiny are natural to our states of being in human bodies.

Some challenges are by fellow humans who commit crimes to steal the rights we are born with – our human rights. Such criminals use our stolen rights and our property to enrich and empower themselves at our expense. Other challenges are disasters like hurricanes and earthquakes that will physically destroy us if we are in the wrong place, at the wrong time. In either case, the Creator created us such that we must defeat challenges to realize our wonderful, satisfying, beautiful potential as free human beings: regardless to the destiny we happen to be in at any particular time.

We want to make it as clear as we possibly can that the above paragraph is referring to birth and life challenges as human beings. It is certain that our birth into life as humans in a material body is only necessary to survive and fulfill our purposes in this life. The struggle to overcome challenges is a struggle to preserve and evolve the material body. But we understand that we had an existence before this life. And we understand we will have an existence after this life. My treatise is to share my understanding about obtaining and using power to overcome our challenges in this life; to fulfill our purposes. Thoughts about what happens to us after this life is conjecture, belief and wishful thinking. Wishful thinking for places we are destined to go after this life; places that we are certain is impacted by ways and means we employ to overcome obstacles and challenges our earth/human life.

We are certain there will be places after death because of our understanding of life. Life is based on Science/Law/ Mathematics & etc: so the processes are KNOWABLE. Understanding of what is known or knowable gives us the equivalent degree of wisdom to use what is known.

A residual effect of struggling to overcome challenges, some say, is the development of our character. Others say this is the sole purpose for living in our human bodies. Of course the only One Who knows our purpose for certain is the One Who created us. So there are varying thoughts about the purpose for which we are born into life. In any case overcoming challenges are necessary to live in human, material bodies.

We KNOW overcoming challenges best prepares us for where we go when our body dies and return to the essence; or when we finally succumb to a challenge that our bodies cannot overcome in life. We say *KNOW* because of the certainty that we were born into material bodies and our material bodies will surely die one day and return to the essence. We know because of our understanding of the Science; the Universal Laws by which we were Created.

There are good reasons to support thinking that the purpose for life is the development of our character. There is an unlimited potential in the being that is in the body. Our character development determines how much of the potential is manifested, expressed and realized by us within our Human bodies.

CHARACTER DEVELOPMENT

Character development is necessary for inner relations with other beings. Character determines how well you relate to other people. It also determines in part, how others relate to you. We are saying that when we struggle to acquire the power needed to live, we not only acquire power, the struggle also helps to shape our character into what is necessary to execute, or use such power. Success in building character to become a Stellar Human/woman wherein lies the Ultimate Power that our potential portends. A Stellar Character is the surest way to replicate and reflect the Spirit of The Creation (individualized, we call The Spirit The Creator) from whence we came: this affords us the utilization of Divine Power in our words, acts and deeds as human beings.

That is why we struggle. That is why we fight. Yes, we need power to overcome challenges to the realization of our human potential.

The Black human is in more need of power and understanding about the proper use of it than any other human on earth. It is apparent that as Black people, individually and as a race, the improper use of power is what subjects us to the oppression of others.

This subjugation to others is so apparent that we'll not go into details about it at this time. Except to say since Black people live in subjection to others, much of the power we have is also in subjection to them. Besides the need to acquire more power, there is also a need to understand how to more effectively use the power we already have.

When used properly, the power we already have is used to overcome the subjection to others. When used improperly the power is used to help those you are in subjection to - thus prolonging the subjection, stunting the development of character and denying the Freedom, Justice and Equality that is inculcated as a right to every Human. To be denied Freedom, Justice and Equality is to be denied our Human Rights.

It all comes down to an understanding of what is already yours. The understanding of what is already yours will give you the wisdom to decide when you should use power in the best interest of self and when you should use your power in the best interest of others. When your power is properly and willfully used in the best interest of others, it is called service. When cruelty, brutality, or whatever is used to force one to use his or her power in the best interest of others, it is slavery, second-class citizenship and other forms of oppression.

BLACKS ARE SUBJUGATED TO ALL OTHER RACES ON EARTH

The subjection of Black people is to all other groups, or races on the earth. But the subjection to white people is where it must first be overcome. This is because white people built their system of world dominance by brutally stealing the human rights of Black people.

White people built their system of dominance by using an evil doctrine called "White Supremacy." The "system" of White supremacy is made up of institutions that suppress natural things about us in order to oppress us. When you suffer oppression you are in a position where you are forced to use your power in the interest of others. This is opposed to willfully using your power in the best interest of others. Force that willfully causes you to NOT use power in your own best interest is oppression.

The systems that are based on white supremacy enforce white control over Black people. The rulers of the "system" (catchall phrase for the organism that was established using white supremacist doctrine) use the institutions to control humans besides us: but if there was no white supremacy, there would be no means for whites, or others to suppress Black human potential and subject us to using our power, not in our own best interest, but in *their* own best interest.

Since "the system" of White Supremacy is so pervasive, there is no freedom for Black people of any status within systems that are established on the doctrine of white supremacy: There is no getting around white supremacy. There is no freedom for Black people in it. Unless white supremacy is defeated and destroyed, Black people will never be free to decide our own destiny.

THE RESULT OF THE IMPROPER
UNDERSTANDING OF OUR SITUATION

Since never is not a possibility in the battle of good vs. evil, it is simply a matter of having the proper knowledge of our situation to destroy the evil of white supremacy. When we understand the knowledge about our situation, we will understand that we are subject to an evil system. It is evil because White Supremacy is an evil doctrine. We understand it to be evil because we see the results from the use of it on Humans. It hurts all people concerned. Oddly and smartly it is especially hurtful to the perpetuator that uses the evil doctrine. His or her use of white supremacy prevents the development of their character.

Black people are also hurt, painfully so, by the practice of white supremacy. However, as we overcome the challenge of white supremacy it molds and shapes our character in wonderful ways – depending on the use of our power to struggle against it to overcome the challenge to our Human Rights of Freedom, Justice and Equality.

We are subjected to the will of others because of lack of proper understanding of our situation and condition. All Black humans have good knowledge of our situation and condition. But the degrees of our UNDERSTANDING of the KNOWLEDGE does not give us the WISDOM to effectively struggle against white supremacy. Our struggle against white supremacy is to reclaim what is rightfully ours. That is a good struggle. It is a case of good vs. evil.

The correct understanding of this knowledge will give us the depth of wisdom necessary to use our power to overcome it. If we don't have sufficient power to overcome it, we must use the wisdom to do things to get enough power. In other words properly use the power that we already have to get the amounts that we need.

KNOWLEDGE IS POWER

Knowledge, indeed, is power. But it must be used to benefit self and kind to defeat the criminal intentions of white supremacists. Understanding of proper knowledge will give us the wisdom necessary for its use to defeat white supremacy, as well as any other system that upholds domination over us. *Apparently, at the same time, the struggle to defeat white supremacy is shaping our character into strong noble humans.*

The shaping of the character of Black individuals partly explains the reasons why when give any decent chance to compete against white people, the Black man or woman of character usually wins. But the character of the human shines through only when he or she takes courage and use the power, which is the KNOWLEDGE they have about self, to overcome challenges that must be defeated, or neutralized, to obtain any particular thing, methodology, system, office – whether it is governor, senator or even president of the United States of America. *How one faces and overcome challenges also shapes his or her character.*

Clearly Black U. S. President, Barack Obama exhibited the best character of all who ran for president of the United States of America in 2008. His character had been shaped, molded and polished by his Black Experience in America. Somehow he had the fortitude and understanding that his knowledge could be used to perform the job necessary during the campaign to become president. This understanding was derived from studying the knowledge that he obtained about himself; as well as knowledge about the "system." This prepared him to overcome the challenge to be president. The understanding gave him the wisdom to use his power/knowledge. He used that wisdom to map out a plan to obtain his goal. That goal was the presidency of the United States of America. But even before he set his site on that goal, he had to overcome some of the exact same challenges that every Black man in America must confront. Some of the common things that Blacks in general must overcome to survive and thrive in white supremacy will be addressed later, maybe in this book. Of course as potential first line of defense warriors, Black men must overcome some PARTICULAR, common challenges. How we overcome the challenges shapes our character as Humans.

  The above is to make no judgment as to whether becoming president of the United States of America is in the best interest of Black people. But clearly it reflects President Barack Obama's use of his personal power to obtain his individual goal. If he is sincere, he also thinks his use of his personal power is the best way to reclaim the Freedom, Justice and Equality that was stolen from Black people. In essence, how Barack

Obama used the power he already had, was to obtain white supremacy power. That is the ultimate position of power within white supremacy. The office of President of the U.S.A.

Personally, we understand he'll not be able to reclaim the Freedom, Justice and Equality systems of white supremacy doctrine stole from Black people. Nor are we sure this is a goal of his. Time will tell in his case. **In using Barack Obama's ways and means to the presidency, time have already told about the fact that he obtained his goal, partly, because of the character he derived from his Black Experience in America.**

He will not be able to achieve Freedom, Justice and Equality for Black people as the wielder of White Supremacy Power. This is because White Supremacy Power was obtained by a criminal act: a Crime Against Humanity that established a False doctrine to govern humans. It is maintained with a system of rules and laws to enforce it; but since it is a false doctrine, regardless to how strong it is, or how long it last, since it is false, it can stand no longer that it takes to establish and enforce the Truth.

Chapter Two

THE CHALLENGE OF WHITE SUPREMACY

The 'subjection' to white people is a challenge that must be overcome to live successfully, productively and as spiritually unlimited as is our human potential. The potential of our human character is in the image of our Creator and He is Divine. *So apparently, a successful, productive spiritual human being is of a divine character.* A Stellar Human Being.

Like all challenges in life, to overcome white people and the evil doctrine they have made, you must have the requisite knowledge about them to defeat the challenge. The requisite knowledge is *correct information* about white people. While it can stop there and you will be better prepared to meet the challenge, to overcome the challenge will require a certain degree of wisdom. The degree of Wisdom needed will come when you UNDERSTAND the *correct information* to a certain degree.

White supremacy was instituted, is enforced, by and for the benefit of white people...and ultimately it is a system that was founded to only benefits white people. So we need the wisdom that is in the understanding of our proper knowledge of the white founders; this includes the systems they founded to implement the doctrine of White Supremacy. If we don't have the wisdom [understanding] of the proper knowledge about white people, we will use the power that is in the knowledge, not in our own best interest, but in the best interest of white people. This is especially not good for Black people, but it is also not good Humanity.

It is in the best interest of white people, and others who believe in White Supremacy, for us to think we can be free any place, in any system that is predicated on the doctrine. A proper understanding of who they are is necessary. The wisdom from the understanding of the knowledge will cause you to use the wisdom from your understanding of the knowledge in your own best interest. Remember, the late Great Reda Faard Khalifah told us that "Knowledge is Power Ignorance is Death." This is true.

Understanding of our knowledge about white supremacy gives us the wisdom that it is in our best interest to struggle against white supremacy.

A BRIEF LOOK AT BLACK HISTORY
Vs. WHITE PEOPLE

Let us take a very brief look at the knowledge we have about our history with white people. I don't want to burden the reader with an in-depth dissertation about this history since it is so well known. Anyone who needs detailed information should read *"Africa At the Cross Roads,"* by one of my Mentors, the late John H. Clarke, *"Before the Mayflower,"* by Lerone Bennet and *"Destruction of Black Civilization,"* by the late Dr . Chancellor Williams. And of course, *"Message to the Blackman in America"* by The Honorable Elijah Muhammad. Message to the Blackman gives detailed information about how to use knowledge/power in the best interest of self while living within white supremacy systems.

Throughout this book we will reference the historical record about Black and white history. Hopefully my briefs will engender more understanding about what you already know. You may be using the power from the knowledge that you already have, and are doing very well. The large houses, new cars, clothes, children, beautiful spouses represents your successful use of the power within white supremacy systems.

It is not our intention to present information as a challenge to the power you acquire in the "system." Our intention is to present the information in ways that will give you a better understanding about life in white supremacy. A better understanding will give you wisdom to use your power to benefit self and kind more than anyone else on the planet. After reading this book, you still may not see the practicality of consciously using your power in ways that particularly, directly, benefit self and kind. Still, my intention is not to generate any feelings of guilt about your success "in the system." What I pray you find it necessary to do is not buy into the white supremacist dictum that it is ok to hurt your fellow humans to be successful. White Supremacy is predicated on this simple statement.

AFRICANS WHO ARE NOT MATERIALLY SUCCESSFUL IN WHITE SUPREMACY

On the other hand, you may not be in possession of the material things that symbolize success. But as stated above, since you are alive, you are living in a world that is dominated by the evil doctrine of white supremacy – the system.

Perhaps the ways that are open to be successful in the confines of The System are yet to be found (by you). Or the oppression that is built into white supremacist doctrine is beating you down. In either case, if you don't give up on your human potential, success will be yours when you reach another level of understanding of that you are trying to achieve. I do not recommend rejecting the limited success that is possible within "the system" with the right intention. The right intention is to use it to struggle against white supremacy.

What I do reject is the evil things that the pressures in the system cause one to think they must do in order to succeed.

More understanding of what you are trying to achieve will render you the wisdom to do the things that will bring the success. But be mindful to always move right before left. In other words, try to do right and reject wrong in your efforts to be successful. If you develop this mindset before you are successful, you still will not act right 100% of the time, but you will never act evil close to 100% of the time. Remember, any evil that we do must be, and will be requited at some time in our life.

COMFORT IN THE SYSTEM *CAN*
LEAD TO REAL HAPPINESS

We will now discuss comforts in the white supremacist system. But before we do, I want to caution the reader to be mindful of the word "comfort." Comfort in systems built on white supremacy is akin to the ideal of a "happy slave." There can be no such animal or human for that matter. Any apparent happiness can be but for two reasons: 1) the person is genuinely happy because he or she has realized something that prepares one to wage the good fight against evil. When your success is realized for that reason, the satisfaction for having reached that level renders one happy.

2) But if one is happy because they have acquired many material possessions; and think that they now "have it made" because they are successful, we must take another look. This kind of happiness is based on ignorance of the fact that the world is laden with oppression poverty and other problems that needs your help. Also, if you are successful in an oppressed society, you maybe ignorant, or have forgotten about the pain and hurt that someone suffered as you got much more than you need. We are talking specifically about folk who earn large wealth working in "the system." But even if you "go for self" and earn abundant wealth, you are not free of scrutiny about how your wealth is used – which is the main way we can determine if you are experiencing real happiness.

There are many who need the excess that you have as a possession. Find a good way to share the wealth. That is a good thought. If you devote some study to the knowledge of the thought, you will find the wisdom to experience real happiness. Real happiness is working in service to please your Creator. This is in service because He is in need of nothing that you have or feel. So to please Him is to serve that which He created. Pleasing Him is the source to experience lasting happiness.

OBTAINING COMFORT IN THE SYSTEM

We are saying that when you use your human potential to obtain comfort within the system of "white supremacy" you strengthen its power over the oppressed.

Our information is presented as a suggestion to give you a better understanding of power. For, plain and simply, when you work to earn money or anything else, you are working to obtain the POWER of said thing. Knowledge of this fact is power. The better understanding of the fact will give you the equivalent wisdom to overcome financial challenges. But what may be most important, the power can be used to overcome social challenges that are built into white supremacy doctrine. The challenges are white hatred of Black people, white fear of Black people, Black fear of white people, police brutality, racial profiling, welfare/poverty of the mass majority of Blacks as a race, & etc.

The social challenges cannot be overcome by working in the system. Social challenges can only be overcome with power that is generated in the unification of humans. Humans are social beings. There is certain power in their unification.

None of the social barriers is because of the lack of power of Black individuals. ***All of the above is for lack of the proper use of the power of Black individuals.*** Knowledge is power. Remember all humans have power. The sufficient unity of human power to do good is equal to any barrier that is controlled by other humans that use power to do bad.

When you actually realize that someone else is benefiting from your work more than you and your kind are – don't quit your job. The only thing required at that time is to PLAN TO QUIT YOUR JOB. Unless you are in a really horrible situation, never quit unless it is on your own terms: this is the proper use of that knowledge.

THE USE OF BLACK POWER IN WHITE SUPREMACY

The improper use of Black power within the confines of white supremacy benefits white people more than it does self and kind. The proper use of Black power in the system will help Black people to defeat the system, rather than work forever within the confines.

More understanding about the proper use of power will work against this fact. Seldom will understanding of proper knowledge of white people necessitate giving up living in white supremacy. However when one reaches the "tipping point," you will want to limit any contact with white people. Your understanding will be that white people have all of their own human rights and power. This is ok. What is NOT ok is they also have most of the human rights and power they took from Black people. This is not in the natural order. The best use of any power is to correct situations where we find things are not in their natural order.

When the Black individual understands the knowledge of this, he or she will find it necessary to use the wisdom from the understanding to struggle against white supremacy. You first struggle against white supremacy because it is so uncomfortable living within it. More understanding will unveil the fact that it is out of order in the ebb and flow in the natural order of the Creation.

We repeat, nothing said here should lead anyone to think that being successful in the system is bad. *Every thing said here should lead all of us to be mindful of not doing evil to attain success.* Moreover, we should be satisfied and happy because the success better prepares us to help others. Or in the case of Black people, help the race to liberate itself from oppression. When one has this knowledge, he possesses the power to defeat, or work against something that is not in the natural order. Once you have the knowledge, study, study and study it for understanding: for it is from the understanding that you will acquire the wisdom to, not only avoid evil, but develop the means to work to defeat it. This work pleases Allah, pleasing Allah is happiness in deed.

There are many great things that a wise human can do to take care of duties and responsibilities – out of "the system." Greater understanding will get the wisdom to do so. There was a time when I openly invited anyone who was stuck with a mind to "do for self" to call me. The invitation is not closed but I have been consciously giving up my material things for about 4 years. Since I acquired much over the years, I have given, or shared a lot, but there is still much I have to offer if the recipient can use it to fuel his or her own system or program. Contact the publisher of this book for more information

Chapter Three
BRIEF OVERVIEW OF THE ENCOUNTER OF BLACK AND WHITE PEOPLE

Since time we first encountered white people, we have been subjected to them in one way or the other. In the beginning Africans treated them as one should treat a stranger. They were treated as we treated other humans. When we found out they were a different kind of human it was too late. They had already applied their deceit on the unsuspecting people. Centuries later we find they were *made* humans. Not created as we are. They were made to do just what they have done: Challenge the goodness that was instilled within us. Their methodology is to challenge everything they find on or off the planet. They do so with the thought that they can make it better: so instead of striving to harmonize with what is already created [nature], they attack, beat it down where possible and rebuild/make it to satisfy their ideal of –

democracy, freedom, socialism, or whatever – all based on the false notion of White Supremacy.

White supremacist mixed a merciless brutality with deceit to suppress everything possible about indigenous people all over the world. Once a certain degree of suppression was applied, it was easy to subject us to oppression, and other forms of slavery. Since that time Black people have been in a struggle to "reclaim what was lost." Defeating white supremacy is what must be done to reclaim what was lost. In fact, overcoming white supremacy is the over arching purpose for Black people.

It is true that millions of Black people don't have a good understanding of the oppression we are in. In fact, millions do have a good definition of what freedom, justice and equality is, but the deceit of white people "mis-educated" them: they think that the way things are is the way things are supposed to be. They think that white people controlling the wealth of the world and Black people trying to be equal to them is the only sensible way to live. These mis-educated individuals have bought into the white supremacy ideal that the ways of white people is the standard for the world.

White supremacy is so immense and so pervasive that many simply accept the life they live in white supremacy as the whole game of life. It is not that they think it is right for white people to enjoy the great wealth created by the oppression of Black people; it is that they have accepted a life trying to be 'equal' to white people as just a part of the entire package of life.

Somehow or another, their knowledge centers have never fathomed what it is really like to be free of white supremacy. It helps when you tell them that we want to be as free as we were before we met the first white man or woman. When they are able to realize a large degree of what was stolen from Black people, one is able to show them ways to resist and attempt to reclaim our freedom, or parts, like Reparations. But more times than not, when you see a Black individual with a good job in the system, he has decided that this is 'it!' He doesn't know and he doesn't want to know! The sooner we realize we are in the presence of such a fool, the better we are able to resist white supremacy.

Don't dissipate your power on a certified fool. Jesus told us not to "Don't cast your pearls to swine." In other words do not waste your wisdom on something as useless as a swine or fool. Of course, the proper use of power means using it where it is going to do the most good. That is why PROPER use comes right after ACQUISITION of Power in the title of this book. So don't call a fool a fool because he will try to engage you in foolish conversation.

He or she will try to convince you they are not fools. But when you have strong suspicion you are in the presence of one, just get away from his or her presence as soon as possible. Whether they are a fool or not will soon unveil itself. Many time the certification that they are, in fact a fool will unveil itself by the way they'll try to prolong a foolish conversation, or any conversation after you make it known that you are ready to move away from them.

THE PRIME REASON FOR STRUGGLE

The challenge of white supremacy is the prime reason Black people struggle to acquire power. White oppression is the main impediment to the realization of their human potential. Unfortunately, the brutality of white people has been, and is such, that our survival needs foreshadows the nobility of the human potential of both Black and white people. The foreshadow in white people is natural to their own making. The foreshadow in Black people manifest in Blacks who mimic them – straight hair (perming) and bleaching of the beautiful Black skin color is the most ready evidence of the mimicking.

When you study the knowledge that you already have of white people, and their reasons for being so brutal and heartless, the wisdom derived will unveil the only effective way to overcome their oppression completely and reclaim our freedom.

First of all, when you began to really study the knowledge, you'll find that white people are not what you think they are. It is quite difficult to define exactly what we thought they were before we got proper knowledge of them. But whatever it was, we then had to make major adjustments in our thinking.

OUR FOCUS ON KNOWLEDGE OF SELF
IS THE BEST WAY TO GET PROPER
KNOWLEDGE OF WHITE PEOPLE.

Like many other important things in life, realization about who white people are, came after we got better knowledge of our own selves. Since obtaining correct knowledge of our own self is the best way to really get to know who we both are, in this book, we are going to forsake really focusing on white people and focus instead on self. After all, that is exactly what they do to understand life: they study us and our past civilization and accomplishments. Their archeological diggings in ancient Kemet & etc. was not to find anything worthwhile to benefit Black people. They are looking for ways to understand and enhance their own kind.

So let it suffice our needs to at least have a working understanding of exactly who they are, by saying they would not be in the world, if Allah did not allow them to come into being. And since He does not allow anything to come into being without a purpose for the good and welfare of the world, white people have a real purpose – white supremacy and all. When we study the knowledge we have of them, it is obvious their purpose revolves around challenging the good things in the world. Our "working knowledge" of them tells us that their mission is to deceive, or induce us to forsake goodness and accept the evil.

Meanwhile, our mission is to forsake evil and accept goodness. This is just the opposite of the mission of white people. This is the working knowledge we need of them to arrive at Proper Knowledge of ourselves. If the reader is able to accept this as the "working knowledge" of them, we will now go deeper into processes necessary to understand our own Proper knowledge. Less we forget, we want the deeper understanding so we can derive the deeper wisdom that will guide us to completely overcome white supremacy. We have one over arching dictum: ***The acceptance of Good and the rejecting of evil.***

COMPLETELY OVERCOMING
WHITE SUPREMACY

With the above said, let us look at some ways we can achieve our mission. There is a great reward for just being conscious of trying to accept good and reject evil. When you are successful at doing so, you are on the Path to manifesting the divinity that is the Essence of your being. The objective is that your words, acts and deeds reflect the Essence of your Being. Hopefully you understand, reflecting your Essence is using Divine Power. If this is not clear, please re-read the above before reading on.

HARMONIZING THE SPIRITUAL AND THE PHYSICAL BODIES

Keep in mind that we want to acquire and properly use power.

If we didn't already have power we would not be alive. We are constantly using our power to activate our bodies. The Spiritual and the Physical. But it is the physical one we are most immediately conscious of: The beating of the heart, the breathing of the lungs, and other brain functions, like walking, talking, running, & etc. are functions of the physical body. Study of this knowledge tells us that the physical body has a corresponding series of spiritual BODIES.

The fact that we have multiple spiritual bodies is something that confused the Caucasian man to distraction. When he found us in Africa giving due homage to various spirits, he mistakenly thought we were worshipping multiple gods. All Africans were doing was acknowledging the various attributes that are naturally occurring in the phenomena, creative life processes. The entire process is Governed only by The One God to Whom all Praises are due. It is an acknowledge fact that Allah has a multitude of Attributes. We are created in His Image. Our attributes are readily identified as spirits. But less we confuse our readers, we will stay close to referring only to the multitude of our spirits as one.

We will focus only on the Physical and the Spirit. They are necessary and enhance the functions of each other.

While it is relatively easy to understand the functions of the physical body, it takes a greater effort to understand the functions of the spiritual body. The Spiritual Body is like air, it is always there because we always need air.

A deeper understanding of the knowledge about air, unveils the fact that it is not the air we breathe into our lungs that is necessary. But there is a 'Special Something' in the air that the physical body needs. The Special something uses the air to provide what is necessary to keep the physical body alive.

That "Special Something" is the Essence of our Spiritual Being. The Spiritual Being is US. We are a Spiritual Being because we are the Essence of The Creator of which we are Created. Our

Creator, Allah, God, Jehovah or whatever Good Name He is called, is never apart from us.

So it is with the Spiritual Body. It is always with our physical body, because the spiritual is just as essential to its manifestation as is the physical entities of which it is constituted: though like air, it is never seen; and also like air, it is not the Spiritual Body, but what IT is, is the Essence of our Spirit that is necessary for our Being. It is deep!

Everything is power driven. At the least this is what we call it – POWER! We are going deeper – hold on.

UNDERSTANDING THE SPIRITUAL BODY

To understand the Physical Body, we study the known aspects of which it is constituted. Understanding the aspects gives us the wisdom to use the power of the body.

To understand the spiritual body, we study the knowledge that we have of the Creator, Allah, God, Jehovah, or whatever good name, as we said above, that He is called. The understanding gives us the wisdom to use the powers of the spiritual body.

The challenge is, in systems of white supremacy, the True Identity of The Creator is false, and much else about Him is distorted.

But regardless of the falsity and distortions, the same process is used to acquire wisdom to use the knowledge (which is power). When we understand the knowledge to be false, distorted and weak, Understanding will give us the wisdom about why we appear to be powerless and weak. It is because we have improper, or limited knowledge about The Creator.

With more understanding of the facts you already have, you'll find that the Improper knowledge was by design and purpose. And that it is within your ability to acquire Proper knowledge about our All Powerful Creator.

Once you understand that the knowledge you have of the Creator is improper, you will need to find the answer to the question "why is my knowledge of the Creator improper?"

The answer is, in white supremacy, it is necessary for the rulers of White Supremacy to give you improper knowledge of the Creator. But once you understand proper knowledge of the Creator is not within white supremacy, you will then look outside of the systems of white supremacy for correct/proper knowledge. If you accept the understanding, then wisdom will guide your search to find the Proper information about The Creator.

"Seek and ye shall find.
Knock and the door will be opened"

Wisdom will also guide you into avenues where you will find proper knowledge of Self. When you study the Proper knowledge of The Creator, you will find that neither the spiritual body, nor the physical body is the real you. But understanding will give you the wisdom to use the power of both to be successful in life. That is it! Don't look any deeper. Just study for more understanding. You may well find it plainer other places in life. But in simpler words I doubt you'll find than the above. Read on, there is more.

YOU AND YOUR MIND ARE IMMORTAL

You are mind and immortal. The Creator created us as we are. He created the spiritual to work as one with Him. We made the physical to work as one with our being. We cannot live without our Spiritual Body. But we can live without your Physical Body. The Creator can live without us, but we cannot live without The Creator.

The seen world is manifested in duality, as is every other thing, as far as we know, in existence, EXCEPT FOR THE CREATOR WHO MANIFEST SELF AS A DIVINE BEING. He is the only One that is Singular. He created every thing else in duality. Why he created things as He did is the Business of Allah. It is one of the enduring mysteries of life. This is very interesting to say the least. But knowing we have a spiritual as well as a physical body, and neither is the real us, is the key to the realization of our human as well as our spiritual potential. When you study your knowledge of this you will derive certain understanding. You will understand that your human potential is limited; but your spiritual potential is unlimited.

Once you have the knowledge that this is so, you must study what you know. You will only understand in degrees. And will receive corresponding degrees of wisdom about your spiritual self; the wisdom will direct and guide the "words, acts and deeds" of your physical body. At this point you come face to face with the challenges that you must overcome to achieve your human goals; as you overcome the challenges, your character is being built which will represent the goal.

Your study of the spirit is a very enjoyable experience. The more you understand The Spirit, the more you can get out of the Physical experience in life. The challenge here is to always do things from your spiritual nature. That is why we strive to embrace right and reject wrong in each decision that we make. That is actually your spiritual nature. However, your physical nature is born of emotion, sensation and spontaneity.

In order to always do things from your spiritual nature, you must overcome the nature of your physical self. When you understand and accept this, wisdom from the understanding will cause you to engage in spiritual work, or exercises, prayers, meditations, or what have you that is spiritual, to control the physical self. This molds and shapes your physical character to the nature of your spiritual character.

When the two are in balance, harmony and rhythm you will reflect your optimum power. The challenges in life will never stop manifesting themselves in your life. But you will be confronting and overcoming them with righteous power.

When you study challenges, you study and plan to overcome them from your spiritual nature, the understanding will give you the wisdom to know that when we balance the physical body with the spiritual we are at our optimum power to do, and achieve success to overcome challenges in our lives. It is a perpetual process in the *"Acquisition and Proper use of Power."*

No doubt, many will already KNOW what I Am saying above. That is good. What is not good is that we who know do not yet have enough understanding to cure the ills of the societies we live in. Specifically, we do not yet have enough understanding of what we KNOW to free Black people from oppression. So that is why we struggle (to understand what we know), that is why we fight (to use the wisdom from our understanding to overcome whatever the challenge that may be in our lives at any particular time).

WHY IGNORANCE IS DEATH

After Sister Reda Faard Khalifah* gave us the statement that "knowledge is power and ignorance is death," Her next sentence was "we must read!!!!!"

When you are reading, you are studying written knowledge. As you study knowledge you are acquiring understanding of the knowledge. From the understanding you acquire wisdom about using the power that is in the knowledge. Wisdom that derives from understanding in balancing the physical and the spiritual bodies optimizes your power, unveiling the means to overcome the challenges to, i.e. your human potential. As Black human beings, why we struggle and why we fight is to actualize the power to defeat the forces that circumvent our human potential, individually and as a Captive Nation, or National Community.

Now we understand why IGNORANCE is death. Yes it is death when you have no knowledge (POWER). Of course the "ignorant" does possess some power, otherwise he or she would not be on planet Earth. But since they are ignorant their power is seriously diminished. As we end this segment, let me share a little tale it told at Muhammad's Temple in Richmond, and one of our banquet. [*it seems that one day the Village idiot was such a nuisance in the community that the wise men and women ran an investigation on the idiot.*

The investigation took them back, way, way back to the advent of the idiot's origin on the earth.

It turns out that at the time that the idiot't maker was giving out brains, he was not paying attention and running his mouth and thought the maker said pain: so he said "give me the minimum."]

This is as far as we will go into this study at this time. But before we leave, I will remind us that our purpose is to share ways to acquire power. Then share ways to Properly use power. So please pay attention!

THE GENERATING OF POWER:
ACTIVELY DOING THINGS TO GET POWER

On the pages that follow, we will discuss the ways to wisely generate and use power. This is necessary because there are many who have come to see that power can be generated by concentration on the Physical or the Spirit (or in the balancing of the two). But after generating the power, it is still insufficient to achieve their goals. In other words they may have massive physical power; or great Spiritual power; and a good balance of the two, but still are not achieving their goals: they are not satisfied; they are not happy. This segment will help with that need.

In the cases above, the need is more understanding of Knowledge about what you propose to do to be successful. The increase of understanding gives one an increase of wisdom to use the knowledge/power. So they must apply the wisdom they have from this degree of understanding. It may well be enough, but if it is a large challenge, they still may not have enough power to reach their goals. In this case they will be given wise choices: the choice to get more knowledge/power before acting to overcome the challenge. Or going ahead with insufficient power and suffer the consequences.

Or #2, study to get more wisdom about the knowledge before they begin to act on the use of the power they already possess.

Not having a sufficient amounts of power, but going ahead anyway, they invariably make mistakes, commit errors or indulge in excesses. Sometimes this results in the loss of their lives. It may even be planned, knowing their lives will be lost. But, whatever the cost, it is your choice to use the power you already have at the present time, or acquire more power before you act. Let us now apply that process to the National Community of Black People in North America: The Black Nation.

THE ULTIMATE CHALLENGE OF BLACK PEOPLE

Let's see if we can apply the above process of acquiring power to the liberation struggle of Black people. We will use the experience of Black people for two basic reasons: 1) Resisting White supremacy is the paramount challenge in the lives of Black humans, and 2) When you are not knowledgeable or conscious of this fact, then we suffer, individually and as a people: so using Black people as an example will help to raise our consciousness.

The ultimate struggle of Black people is to overcome the evil challenge of white supremacy. It is this evil that suppresses Black people as individuals, as well as collectively as a race. White supremacy contravenes our human potential. This is why we fight. We are struggling to acquire power to fight the contravention of our human potential.

We need power to use in the liberation struggle of African people. The challenge to our liberation is the barrier of white oppression. The "struggle" is the acts we do to overcome the challenges. Black people who understand the challenge are wisely using their power to fight against it: they are not trying to reconcile their lives to, or within the confines of the "system" that is built and operated on the doctrine of white supremacy.

Black people who understand the challenge conduct their lives as human beings in or out of the system. As conscious human beings, they will not accept the contravention of their potential. Wisdom will guide their struggle against the challenge.

Understanding gives one or many the wisdom to know it is better to live in as much resistance to the system as possible, wisdom about how to be successful, remain relevant, and not "sell out" is a must. And if and when the contradictions become too dire with success "in the system," since you have used wisdom, no doubt wisdom has caused you to do things in case of this eventuality. Wisdom will have caused you to save money and acquire resources so that you will be ready to leave the system at any time. The minimum should, definitely be, to PLAN to leave the system.

Many well meaning Black people thinks their prime challenge in life is to successfully overcome white oppression and live comfortably within a white supremacy system. They are wrong.

The prime challenge is to live free of oppression. And this cannot be done unless you destroy white supremacy. In fact, any success that you have in a white supremacy system gives it strength. Meanwhile, the last thing you should want to do is strengthen a people, and a system that brutalized, and continues to brutalize self and kind.

Of course, there is an apparent contradiction in what I am saying. But the contradiction is covered above when we told you that success in "the system" is satisfying only if it puts you in a better position to serve Allah. We serve Allah when we are in service to what He created. Many of us have heard the expression, "to whom much is given, much is expected."

If the aim is only to overcome the challenge and be successful in the oppressive system, you will never be free, indeed. "Free in deed" means freedom to decide your own destiny. In the case of Black people, this is only possible if you collect the debt that is owed. In a word, the debt is called Reparations.

The debt owed is critical because you cannot overcome man made challenges by other humans if you are starting from 'scratch' and they are using high technology that was developed while you were their manual labor force.

Whereas it is very important to use the resources at your disposal to be successful, it is equally important to never think of this success as the end game of your life. The end game, in this use of the phase, is success without having reclaimed what is rightfully yours. It is rightfully yours because it was stolen from you.

The Reclamation of what was taken from you should be included in the definitions you use when speaking of success in life. Overcoming oppression to become successful in "the system," is but one of several aspects of your ultimate success. Success is easy to achieve, if you are willing to accept only parts of what is rightly yours. This is success in white supremacy. But it is not full freedom; or full success. The other parts of what is rightfully yours is your full human rights: this is "Freedom indeed!"

Parts of freedom may look and feel good, but it is not freedom. What was stolen from you must be returned. This is critical. This is critical because the Reclamation of what is rightly yours is a must, if you have overcome oppression. And it is not possible unless you have recovered all of your human rights. In fact overcoming oppression is only one aspect of the challenge. At best, defeating your enemies to regain your physical possessions is also only half of the challenge that must be overcome to be free. It may look like freedom. But does it feel like freedom. The missing part determines how it feels to be free.

FREEING THE SPIRITUAL SELF

The other half of freedom is freeing your spiritual self. No one can give you either of the halves needed to be free. You must earn them yourself. When someone 'gives' you what you might mistakenly call freedom, though the physical chains may be taken away, there is one aspect that they can never give you. This is the noble character that you acquire when you struggle to attain freedom yourself.

We told you above that many think development of character is the common purpose of all humans. And the struggle to realize, and actualize various parts of our human potential is why we struggle and why we fight. We call character development a residual benefit of the struggle to overcome challenges. But as we see, it may well be the whole "ball of wax." The whole thing!

Other words for "the whole thing", is Self Realization of Oneness with our Divine Creator. After Self Realization comes Self Actualization of the Attributes of the Divinity that is incorporated in each person. The thought is that the overcoming of challenges is an opportunity to build your character.

It is not my intention to write anything that is difficult to understand. In fact, I am willing to over teach the knowing, rather than to under teach things that any reader is not familiar with. An example is the above reference to "Attributes of the Creator." Attributes are various character traits of The Creator. Muslims say that The Creator is "Most Merciful, Most Gracious, Most Bountiful, Most Beautiful", & etc. These are Character traits of an All Powerful Creator. When we struggle to overcome challenges to the freedom, justice and equality which is imbued within us, our "character traits" become more like The Creator: strong and powerful! This too is acquiring power. And when we use that power, it is used akin to the character traits we have: The Power of God!

ULTIMATE SUCCESS

The ultimate success for Black people will be liberation from all shapes and forms of slavery. These are human rights. They include the payment of Reparations. Reparations will be used to repair the damages that were caused during the commission of the crimes that forced Afrikans into subjection – in the first instance.

As we offer some suggestions about how we can acquire power to use to overcome oppression, I hope we all keep it in perspective, as per the above.

Let us now move on to chapter four:
SUCCESSFULLY OVERCOMING SUVIVAL REQUIREMENTS WHILE STAYING FOCUSED ON THE LIBERATION OF AFRIKAN PEOPLE

Chapter Four

SUCCESSFULLY OVERCOMING SUVIVAL REQUIREMENTS WHILE STAYING FOCUSED ON THE LIBERATION OF AFRIKAN PEOPLE

Overcoming oppression presents real life challenges for Black people. Overcoming them correctly are also challenges that will be overcome before African Liberation Day. You can overcome some of the challenges in oppression and still make it to African Liberation Day. But there are some challenges that IF YOU DON'T OVERCOME you'll not make it to African Liberation Day. The number one of these challenges is the reclamation of that which was stolen by the oppressors. And while we will never be able to reclaim the particular value of some things, there is a Just Compensation that can be applied to what was lost. In fact, Just Compensation is the name of a Universal Law that governs the violation of the Human Rights of a nation, or identifiable community of people. When Just compensation is applied it forces the criminal to pay the attendant cost to begin healing processes necessary to restore the victim to the wholeness that the individuals in the nation enjoyed before their Human Rights were violated. Healing is necessary because in the commission of the "Crime Against Humanity," the criminal caused some injuries.

The healing of the injuries is to "repair the damage." From the word Repair came the word to identify exactly what the victims demand of the guilty party, or parties. That word is called REPARATIONS when the demand is made peacefully to get the criminal to admit his guilt and pay according to the penalty that The Just Law of Compensation says must be exacted. Or extracted from the wealth and other goods that the criminal built with his stolen property.

EXPROPRIATION IS THE ALTERNATIVE TO THE PAYMENT OF REPARATIONS

The only other process that can adequately compensation for a crime against humanity is when the victims or individuals take matter into their own hands to extract their compensation from the criminal. Righteous force is used and the word that describes the action is called EXPROPRIATION. Both Reparations and Expropriation has it's pros and cons; its pluses and minuses. And both require the proper use of power by the victim. Also, whether one or the other is used is determined by the response of the criminal to the demand of the victim that he begin the healing of their injuries.

In later chapters of this book we discuss the pros and cons in some detail. In the discussion, we also give examples of ways and means that individual Black people have applied power to the in the "struggle" to reclaim what was lost during our capture, our chattel enslavement, second-class citizenship and other forms of oppression under the domination of the evil systems that are based on White Supremacy. In short, we say that when you use your power, which is knowledge of your situation, when you use it properly, you use it in your own best interest. When you are in an oppressed situation, you are forced, compelled, coersed or miseducated into using your power in the best interest of your oppressor: We must stop this, which is why we struggle and why we fight.

MORE ABOUT AFRIKAN LIBERATION DAY

In discussing the glorious day in our future call African Liberation Day, we want to be extremely clear about what will be going on on that great day. And what had transpired during the processes that brought us there. Surviving to reach African Liberation Day is not required to have lived a successful life. This is because if you strive to overcome correctly, you are doing so on Principle. Standing on Principles helps to satisfy the purpose for living. That is the building of character. As we are wont to say, 'there is a right way to do anything.' The more of the "right way" that you perceive, see, accept and enact, the more sound will be the success that you obtain in life. Moreover, good strong character is instilled in your being in the same manner, to the same degree that you strive to achieve your goals as righteous as possible.

You need power to overcome any challenge. And you must have a degree of understanding that the knowledge that you already have is power. This means that you already have some power. The crux of the dilemma surrounds how to use the power to overcome the challenge before you.

You must understand the knowledge that you have about the challenge. The wisdom from the understanding will allow you to determine how to survive while struggling to overcome the challenge to your freedom. Remember, power is needed to do this. Remember also, your character is being shaped as you overcome the challenges; and never forget that knowledge is power.

THERE IS ALWAYS ENOUGH POWER TO OVERCOME CHALLENGES

You will always have enough power to overcome ANY challenge. Your understanding of the challenge will unveil the options that are available to do the job.

If wisdom from the understanding of the challenge is that your power is not strong enough to successfully go one way or the other - using strength or physical force. Don't pick a fight over any of the challenges.

You are more likely to pick a fight if what is challenging you was stolen directly from you – like a car, house, computer or etc. But the ultimate theft from you was the freedom, justice and equality that causes of the varying degrees of Post Traumatic Slavery Disorder [PTSD] that haunt every African individual. The traumatic event that caused PTSD in Black individuals – slavery, and other forms of oppression – stripped everything from you; everything except our unconquerable spirit. Yes, we may tend to fight to reclaim all the above and thereby wipeout PTSD. But you are advised to be wise in doing so.

One sense of your mind will say you are perfectly within your rights to knock down the challenge, kill anyone who may be benefiting from the use of your stolen properties, and reclaim what was stolen - with interest. Whether you are powerful enough to be successful or not, it is your right to make the attempt to reclaim your possessions in this manner. Right Now! But if wisdom prevails, you may or may not act immediately.

If wisdom doesn't prevail, this means you only have a little understanding of the challenge and you are going to be smashed! If wisdom does prevail, it means that you have gotten a good degree of understanding of the challenge. You know that the challenge is too large to be successful using the power at your command. In this case, the prevailing sense of wisdom will tell you to look at the other options.

The other options will tell you that you must first survive. You want to survive without doing anything that will diminish any of the power that you already possess. This immediately offers up another challenge before you can attack to reclaim your rightful possessions. This challenge is to acquire the additional power from what you do have to survive to make a successful attack. When in a Liberation Struggle the power you need is in alliance with other humans. These humans have needs. Start a business to supply the needs if possible.

If the challenge is to obtain food, clothing or shelter for you and some other humans or entities that you may be responsible to, you must take the option that will render you best qualified to provide for them. If you are living in a white supremacy system, the rendering should be tempered by ways necessary to do the job that will leave you in better position to resist, smash and destroy white supremacy.

With the given that you already have power gained from your knowledge of the challenge, understanding of it will render the wisdom that will tell you that you still may not have enough power to defeat the challenge.

Unless you are in a really horrible situation, or do not have the power to liberate the entire race, don't put the power you have at total risk. Rather use the power that you have to acquire other things needed to secure the liberation of Black people. This is very important.

Never over estimate your power. Never under estimate your enemy! Wisdom will mitigate against premature use of power. And remember we said that wisdom comes from the understanding of your challenge. So if you don't have enough power, or power strong enough, continue to work/use the power that you have to acquire additional power. But above all else, you must continue to study. Study, understand and use the wisdom from the understanding is the method that will allow you to acquire additional power. Wisdom derived will also guide your proper use of it. Your proper use of it will cause you to render great service to the humans you are determinedly committed to liberate.

UNIVERSALITY

For readers who dwell on, or have a healthy awareness of the Universality of The Creation, we acknowledge that we know the power needed to overcome anything is already in our own hands.

That is, the power we need is already ours on the spiritual realm. We know this. But presently we live in the Physical realm. Since we live in the physical realm, or on the physical plane (of existence), the work we must do as manifested material entities is on this physical plane.

It is good to know that the power to do and achieve necessary things is already within you. But having the knowledge is one thing, executing, or operating on the basis of the knowledge is another. If one already knows that the power within can be used to overcome anything in the outer world, that is a great fact to know. But most humans do not have as much command of their spiritual body as they do of the physical body. Put another way, probably a more correct way: your spiritual body does not have total control of your Physical Body. Yes we know this; and knowledge is power. For example, your physical body often craves for material things that are not best for you: sometimes we satisfy the cravings, other times we do not. [when we study the knowledge we have of the cravings, they too become opportunities to imbue our characters with something wonderful and powerful. Understanding the cravings will give you the wisdom as to how best to overcome the challenge of the craving for the best benefit of our character].

We will come back to the knowledge and execution of what we know, time after time. But we will move on now with some discussion about acquiring power and using it properly. Using it properly is using it in your own best interest. Or, for those who still insist on emphasizing the fact that we already have the power, we say 'understanding power' and using it properly. Of course when you understand power to a certain degree, using it properly is fundamental. This is because when the understanding is reached it will give you the wisdom to use it properly. The wisdom will be based on your degree of understanding: if your understanding is great, your wise [wisdom] use of power will be great. If you understand a little, your wise [wisdom] use of power will be little.

There are many ways to determine whether or not you have enough understanding. But the most obvious way this can be determined is to examine the physical needs to take care of your personal duties and responsibilities in life. If you find it hard to take care of your duties and responsibilities in life, it may well mean that you need a deeper understanding about what you are doing to take care of them. Wisdom derived from the understanding will guide your efforts to acquire more physical power. Then you must strive tot use it properly. Let's look at some ways that we can use physical power in our own best interest.

STRUGGLING FOR & PROPERLY USING POWER ON THE PHYSICAL PLANE
Knowing Planes of Existence Are Illusions

For readers who may be only slightly, or greatly confused about the different planes of existence, I advise you to read a good metaphysical book. In my own book on the subject, <u>"Melanin, Conscious Attunement & The God in I,"</u> we share information about the planes of existence, as well as divisions of the mind. I recommend that you read it.

It is necessary to have a "working understanding" of, at least, the divisions of the mind, if you are going to obtain a certain degree of understanding of power and its proper use. We will not detract from our point about the acquisition of and use of power and go into it now, except to say:

When we refer to the division of the mind, the term 'division' is purely for the sake of the mental capacity of humans on the physical plane. Divisions are Conscious, Sub-subconscious and Super-conscious.

In actuality, all divisions of the mind are simultaneously present at the time and place

that we need them. Apparent divisions of the mind are illusions in the same way as is the Master Illusion. When you get into the study of Metaphysics, TIME is called the master illusion. An illusion is something that only appears to be, but it is not in fact. Time is..... that's it. In other words whether we divide it into years, months, days, hours, minutes or whatever, it will remain as it was created to be from the beginning. Everything within what we call Time is ever changing – young to old, birth and death, spring, summer and fall, etc. but Time remains as it was created.

    The physical body is necessary for the spiritual body's Expression on the Physical Plane. In fact vice versa is also true: If the spiritual body didn't need the Physical Body it would not exist. With the understanding that there is no division of the planes in actuality, Let us take a brief look at the planes of existence. The look will be mainly in the terms and expressions that humans understand.

THE PLANES CLEARLY EXPLAINED

    On the Physical Plane, we struggle for the power to overcome physical challenges. The key to it all is in the word understanding. It is in this word where we obtain wisdom to act physically as well as to act spiritually. We must have the power of both. When you lose a certain degree of spiritual or physical power, both the physical & spiritual bodies weakens and the physical body will eventually die. But before it dies, the spiritual body will have begun leaving it long before it does.

The physical body was made by the spiritual self. It is useful only on the physical plane; and only then if your "spirit" is in it.

When the physical body was made, it was constituted (made) of certain properties. Some of the properties are essential to its use by the Spiritual Body. Some of the properties are: **the breath, the bodys' systems, such as the heart, lungs, circulatory, vascular, nervous and etc.** Some of the properties are more vital for its well being than others. For example, if the lungs defunct, the breath would leave the body. The body would die immediately. Other properties are not as essential for its continuation of life.

The eyes are not essential to continue to live. But when any properties of the body are damaged beyond repair, that particular organ will lose its ability to function. If it happens to be one of the vital organs for life, the entire body will fail to function and will die. It dies because it has lost its usefulness to the Spiritual body as well as the physical body. If it continues to have a use for either, it will stay alive. But sometimes staying alive is not preferable.

We have all seen physical specimens that were so damaged physically that we may think "they would be better off dead!"

We have also seen persons with such a paucity of spirituality that they had such a disregard for other humans – cold, uncaring murderers etc. – that we thought "the world would be better off if they were dead."

The above can be summed up by saying when you lose your physical power, you lose the vehicle that the spiritual self uses to achieve its mission on this plane of existence. We need power to maintain our physical bodies.

As were the explanation for the entity that functions on the Physical Plane: so it is on the other plans of existence. We don't see them but we know they existence. We know they exist because of unexplainable phenomena that happens on the Plane that our materials manifest on.

For the sake of our discussion and exposition on the inexplicable, we will say we came from the UNSEEN, and that is where we are destined to return when the physical body dies. All of the Planes of Existence are in the unseen to the properties of the Physical body. As stated earlier, though we don't see them, they are ever present and are as constant as the Master

Illusion called Time. And can also be used to facilitate the functions of the Physical Body. Spiritual power can be increased by practicing; or exercising, or getting a deeper understanding of what you already know.

THE ACQUISITION OF POWER AND PROPER METHODS TO GET AND USE IT

In any event, once power is acquired, the proper use of it is a must. Using it is when you apply the wisdom you have gotten from the understanding of your knowledge about a particular person, place or thing. *"knowledge is power, ignorance is death."*

With the above said, and hopefully understood, lets look at some ways to acquire power.

As stated, metaphysicians and universalist say, we already have all the power we need to achieve whatever we conceive. It takes some of us many years to come to KNOW this; and it is a subject that we will study for the rest of our lives. Undoubtedly the statement is true. Since it is, it begs the question as to why aren't everyone successful in using it to achieve their objectives? Or if they are successful, why did it take so long for them to get there?

The entire thesis of this book is that **"understanding knowledge begets the wisdom**

of the knowledge to achieve objectives in life."
If the knowledge is flawed, your understanding of it will be flawed to the same degree. Therefore, the wisdom begotten will also be flawed and used likewise – in a flawed manner!

So, if your knowledge is little, your understanding of it will also be little and your wisdom will tell you to use it in a little way. If you want to use it in a large way, get understanding about a large amount of knowledge.

Now let us make it more personal.

THE FIRST THING TO OBTAIN IS PROPER KNOWLEDGE OF SELF AND KIND

Proper knowledge is correct knowledge and is essential to being of good human character. In fact just the understanding of this fact will raise the elevation of an individuals evolvement by several degrees. ***Proper knowledge is essential to be of good human character.***

When we study proper knowledge of self we get proper understanding about *who* we are; where we came from; and a sense of what our purpose is for being in a physical body. The understanding gives us the wisdom that knowledge is power. We can use the power to be successful in overcoming challenges in life. Since all success in life is subjective, the understanding of knowledge of your self will give you the wisdom to see, touch and feel what you are subject to. More importantly. The understanding will give you the Wisdom to change either of these (see, touch and feel) that are not beneficial to you.

For example, if you are a Black human you are subject to the doctrine of white supremacy. If you KNOW this your success will adversely reflect one way. If you don't know that as a Black human you are adversely subject to white supremacy your success will reflect another way. And if you know your success is adversely subject to white supremacy, wisdom will tell you that the challenge is to destroy white supremacy, not to be successful within the confines of it.

Hopefully, the above suggestion as to how you can acquire correct basic power was not missed. We'll continue by suggesting the proper use of the power you have achieved. Naturally suggestions for the proper use of knowledge will also review, and instruct on acquiring power.

Once you know Knowledge of self is power, you'll want to use your power to be successful in life. The things you must do to be successful should be seen as challenges to your desire. You will use your power to overcome the challenges. If you are Black in the United States of America, you will discover that the human potential (the essence and basic source for the power) to be successful is adversely impacted by the oppression of Black people. So immediately, you must use some of your power to overcome this circumvention of your human potential by other humans. If you were 'free of oppression' all of your power would be available to develop your human potential. Any human with proper knowledge of self understands he or she would be better positioned in life if they could pursue the fruits of the experience by engaging in more pleasurable and rewarding activities. After all, does anyone really want to deal with "the ways of white people."

Another way to say this is, "who wants to deal with white people" when life is so wonderful without having to deal with what they do. And we know they do white supremacist kinds of things – demoniac kinds of things! Some cruel things they do are done consciously. Other things are unconscious behavior that was bred into their psyche. This is as sure as the fact that Black humans were mis-educated. And the mis-education about some vital knowledge of self, creator and devil, or adversary to our rise, was bred into our psyche.

Once we have knowledge of self, including the oppression part, the understanding of the knowledge may give you the wisdom to know that you need more power. You may need more power because of a number of different reasons.

But whatever you decide is your purpose will characterize your personal reasons for needing more power. Your personal reasons represent the challenges to your success - this is *why we struggle, this is why we fight* – to get power to overcome challenges in our lives. You now use the power that you already have to do things that will increase your power.

If you are a Black human, and you feel that your ultimate success is presently reflected in your life, we can safely say that you don't have "proper knowledge of self." At best, if you have proper knowledge of the liberation necessities of Black people, and you have the trappings of success in America, is that you have overcome challenges to acquire some things. But since you are Black, you are not yet free, regardless to what you own as a member of an oppressed race.

When you leave your house tomorrow, you are subject to be stopped and humiliated by the police. The police are empowered by "the system" to maintain the status quo. But wisdom has already told you (if you are not foolish enough to think you are free) that maintaining the status of free slave is not in the best interest of Black people. So the struggle continues for enough power to overcome everything that circumvents your potential as a human being.

[just a small, but profound point about getting stopped by the police: if you don't understand your status within the confines of white supremacy will never equate to Complete Freedom, any encounter with police will subject you to being brutalized and put to death. This is because if you act like, or try to act as a "free" man or woman, the police will disabuse you of that notion immediately – depending, of course on what kind of day he is having; or if he is just of a mind to "put this n----r in place."]. In other words, seldom can a Black man or Black woman forget – and not remember in time – how to conduct themselves around white people.

Final word here. The very best way to conduct yourself at all times is to be natural. Just be yourself. In other words be human. If you are sincere this will be sufficient in all cases. Even killer police will back off if you exhibit a good portion good human character. But you must deal with each situation as a human would: this means that if you are a human suffering oppression with your own kind, and you understand this, wisdom will guide you in your human disposition at all times.

ALL BLACKS ARE SUBJECT TO WHITE PEOPLE IN WHITE SUPREMACY SYSTEMS

Proper knowledge is true knowledge. White supremacist doctrine requires that whatever your life is about, as a Black individual, it is subject to the needs of white people. When your needs are subject to whites, then you suffer because individual human needs are different. If you are of the oppressed and your power is used to achieve or enhance the power of the white supremacist systems, it cannot be fully used in your own best interest. This is not a natural situation. The natural situation is that your power be used in the best interest of self and your own kind. Anything that may be left over is part of the common good for all humanity.

On the other hand if you don't see your success as limited to what you achieve within white supremacy you will want to change it. You will want to change it because of the nature of the challenges you had to overcome to get there: in a word, the main challenge, or culprit was and is called racism. Racism will let you know at any time, in any place that you are not yet free. So it is quite natural to want to change this situation.

Since you know white supremacist doctrine is the part of success you don't like, you may well want to change this situation. To change it properly, you need to acquire proper power. Proper power is correct knowledge about white supremacy. You then study the knowledge for the understanding of white supremacy. Proper understanding will give you the wisdom to see, touch and feel that white supremacy is evil. And depending on your degree of understanding, you will see that the only remedy for the evil is to destroy it.

This will bring you to the place where you want to use your power wisely. If you don't have enough power to do the job of destroying white supremacy, you must struggle to find a way to get enough power.

It all starts with proper knowledge of self. The proper knowledge will give you the awareness of your own power. You can use it to acquire the other power needed to do the job. Or to strengthen the power that you already have. You mustn't be tempted to act before you are ready. Temptation to NOT use the power in your own best interest will come in many ways. The temptation will cause you to think that since you are comfortable, even though you don't have all of your human rights, you are free. And since you are comfortable you may not want to rock the boat. But if you don't rock the boat (use your power to correct what is wrong), you will not be free. And if you are not free, you will never realize your human individuality to its fullest potential. So it is critical for you to learn the proper use of power. In short, 'proper use' is having control over it so you can use it in your own best interest.

We will now discuss the proper and the improper uses of power.

Don't despair if you have difficulty understanding all of the nuances of what is being written. These words are purposely being written to be read many, many times for the rest of your life. They can be read for both pleasure and fun on the physical as well as on the spiritual plane. There is more: so read on.

The direction of the "Caves" where Nat Turner was re-captured 1831

Chapter Five

PROPER AND IMPROPER USE OF POWER

Once you have gotten true knowledge of self (the power), or have acquired power, you know from what we have stressed above, you must use it in your own best interest. I hope you also remember that only wisdom, or luck, can guide you to act in your own best interest. I know 'luck' is a new word that is just now being introduced into this book. We are not going to discuss it at this time. Perhaps later. What we are going to discuss are ways to use the other way to use power properly. That is by being guided by wisdom gained from understanding correct knowledge about *whatever*.

Wisdom alone will guide your proper use of power. And as we have also stressed, wisdom is gained from understanding what it is you may be trying to do, achieve or love. Your success will be limited to the degree of understanding you have about what you are trying to achieve. But the proper use of power is not always using it in what you are trying to achieve as an individual. It may be in your own best interest to use it in support of others, including your nation, community, organization or family members.

The main thing about proper use of power is that you be in control of how it is used. Which means you can entrust it to others to empower them to champion causes or overcome situations that they are talented to do, IF THEY WERE PROPERLY EMPOWERED.

IMPROPER USE OF POWER

The main precipitators to using power improperly are the ego, peer pressure, greed, fear and anger. Anyone of these can cause you to improperly use, or lose the power that you already have. But if you have understanding of knowledge, the understanding will give you the wisdom to use the power/knowledge correctly.

EGO

The ego is named first when power us used incorrectly. This is because it will likely be the first temptation to invite you to use your power improperly. You will want to "show off" your power. When you show off you may become an object of envy, or create enemies. These are negative connotations. It is not generally a good idea to use your power in ways that will generate negative connotations. You want to use your power in ways that bring positive connotations. Just be sure not to do anything that is not correct to please, in order to get the approval of anyone.

Peer pressure happens when someone invites you to use your power improperly because others are doing it - and you accept the invitation.

Greed causes an improper use of your power to obtain much more than you need.

Fear causes one to act improperly, when "there is nothing to fear." This does not mean it is not proper to fear racist police. Provocation by police should invoke the fear that if you don't let him or her get away with the provocation, you may lose your life. And become one of the terrible statistics in an oppressed system. One of the terrible statistics is that a 'crazy' disproportionate number of our Black men have an encounter with the criminal justice system in America. This statistic is borne mainly in the fact that the police feel it is in their best interest to give each Black male a police record. So at any opportunity, the Black man will be unjustly provoked and charged. The "fear" you should have of police is a strategic fear: it is predicated on the thought that if police abuse you real bad, and you want to "get him," you have little chance while he is armed and you are not. Strategic fear will let you survive to plan to get him when the odds are better to take care of him or her.

Anger can cause one to act improperly because it is emotion driven. Anything that is emotion driven is subject to chaos, out of order. The aim should be to be in order at all times.

Success, as it is defined within the confines of white supremacy is a temptation to use your power improperly. It is a temptation because the oppressor, or devil, as some of us feel he is, wants you to believe it is ok to have your human potential suppressed if you are comfortable in oppression. But this is unnatural. And anything that is unnatural is wrong and out of order because it impedes humans from becoming all they can be. It hurts your fellow humans.

The apparent difficulty of overcoming white supremacy is another temptation. But when you have proper knowledge of Freedom, anything less than defeating White Supremacy will be unacceptable.

And less the reader feel that I am suggesting that you live a life without the fun, love, happiness, joy, gladness, tranquility and peace that radiates to the human spirit, this is not so.

The sense of winning and being successful at anything in life is an incomparable feeling. As horrible as chattel slavery was, Black people must overcome it all without engaging in anything that will depress the spirit. We must overcome oppression in a strong, righteous and courageous manner. When you strive to overcome oppression in a strong, righteous and courageous manner, your spirit is uplifted.

I tell people often that it is critical that you enjoy the process in everything that you do. If you delay your enjoyment until you reach your goal, you will miss out on some really great, fulfilling moments. Enjoy the process as you keep your ultimate victory in focus. The 'process' is the compilation of things that you must do to win at any endeavor, including the Liberation Struggle of African people. And remember, during processes of life your character is being shaped and molded into that of a wonderful, human being – if you are careful to do things the right way. The right way is to reject wrong and embrace right in all of your words, acts and deeds.

THE PROPER USE OF POWER

Since the power within is a power that is a part of your being, it is yours to use in the best interest of self. Or in the best interest of others. The choice is yours. It is a human right. If you have determined that one of the things that *is* in your own best interest is the destruction of white supremacy, this is what you will use your power to achieve; this is a just way to use your power. This is a proper way to use your power. But though it is a just use of power, the destruction of white supremacy must be acted on wisely. Assuming you have a good understanding of white supremacy, wisdom will guide your attempt to destroy it. This is the proper way to use your power. Use wisdom.

Wisdom is easy to obtain. As we repeat constantly in my work, it comes as a by-product of understanding the object. In this case, the object, or aim is to be completely free. The destruction of white supremacy is a challenge to overcome the physical part of the oppression. Get understanding about what it means to be completely free. When you do, you will receive wisdom as to how to achieve what you conceive as freedom.

The first thing that I personally found when trying to conceive of and define complete freedom was that I was living in a society where my people were suffering oppression. Studying further, I found that the oppression was partly because of the brutal nature of our enemies; coupled with our ignorance of true knowledge about self, The Creator, and the enemy that was purposely mis-educating my nation.

I now had the causes for my lack of freedom, but freedom was still a very hard concept to define. After reflection and writing on this dilemma, I concluded that it is easier to know when you are not enjoying Complete Freedom, then to define exactly what it is. So I focused on things that you must have, but did not presently possess in my life as an individual in particular; or in the National Black Community, generally.

It turns out that some of the things that we do not have are our human rights; and the most identifiable ones are Freedom (self determination), Justice (not given same treatment under the law) and Equality (not paid on same basis). You cannot have one if you do not have all of them. I then found that in order to enjoy freedom, justice or equality, you must remove some barriers that prevent you from enjoying them, or any particular one. I then crystallized one of the main reasons why I did not enjoy these three human rights. That reason was the fact that some one, or some race of people had found it profitable for them to steal them to my race.

But then to my great pleasure, I found that since the very beginning of our oppression, some Black people had been fighting to reclaim the lost Freedom, Justice and Equality. And they were still in the struggle, or had died and left good records of what worked and what did not work.

I was of a mind to be free so I found out as much about how to fight for the return of our freedom, justice and equality as I could. In other words, I set out to UNDERSTAND the fight. I came to understand that the fight is called The Liberation Struggle of African people. If you study "the struggle" you will find what I found.

After obtaining some understanding about the Liberation Struggle, wisdom may tell you, as it told me, there will come a point, or time that it becomes necessary to confront the enemy. When will that time come? At what point do you apply all of your force and power to confront and defeat the enemy?

Here it is again, get a better understanding of why you may be feeling that you want to confront the killers who protect white supremacy immediately. What is the urgency?

If after getting a certain degree of understanding what your urgency is, and you still feel you must confront the killers, let wisdom guide you in your confrontation. No doubt, wisdom will cause you to prepare before you attack. During the preparation, you must consolidate your power. And make your plans according to the nature of the power: these are the wise things to do before the confrontation with a vicious, merciless enemy.

I am describing the proper use of power; specifically, the urgency to confront the enemy. For there is no doubt that when you know who the enemy is, and the cruel, evil things he did to you and your people, there will arise an urgency to confront him. We are advising that wisdom guide your actions in the process. That wisdom will come from understanding of the urgency and power that you propose to confront the killers, or protectors of white supremacy.

In short, if power is properly used, your action will be driven by wisdom. For as unlikely as it is that you can act in any way as an individual to destroy white supremacy, some times individuals who achieve great feats act against all odds and are successful.

Anyone who doubts this fact should look at the lives and actions of some individuals in history: Nat Turner is the all time model in this regard for Black people (more about Nat below). My main point is any use of power that is driven by wisdom is properly used. But as brought out above, if your power indicates that you do not have sufficient power to be successful in a confrontation with white supremacy, wisdom may cause you to put off the confrontation until you get more power.

But I also said, the choice will still be yours to proceed or not. Less we forget, Nat Turner had great command about his chances for successfully defeating white supremacy back in 1831. Some think Nat Turner's organizing of a Black Liberation Army, and revolt, was not successful. But there are probably more people who think he **was** successful in carrying out his purpose....Just keep in mind about the relative positions that we are in 2009, as opposed to 1831.

Read on, there is more.

PROPER USE OF POWER
WHILE LIVING WITHIN OPPRESSION

As a Black human, you are required to use an inordinate amount of your power on a daily basis to overcome white racism. But this is necessary if you are going to act in the best interest of self and Black people. This is because, as we have already stated, white systems to govern are based on white supremacy. And white supremacy is not only evil, it is completely out of order. The aim of all good, conscious humans is to contribute to the natural order or its maintenance. Racism is the verb that is the action word in a white supremacy system.

Since we live in nations that are all governed by white supremacist doctrine, our abilities in life should be used to defeat the evil systems that give the lie to the inferiority of Black humanity.

This is the main predicate of white supremacy. If you don't understand the last sentence, or disagree with it, it means you have not yet accepted nor understood the challenge of white supremacy. You may be confused about what real freedom is; and the kind of lives we'd be living if we were free. I suggest we all continually study the intrinsic nature of the systems that we find ourselves in today. Understand what is missing in our lives and the lives of our fellow beings. I am simply suggesting a way of living your life. There's no need to be uptight about it. Just live to enjoy your life and the things needed to live it in a beneficial way to liberate Black people will be found. But this only works if you are also living it as truthfully as possible. If you understand that overcoming racism and defeating White Supremacy is just a challenge to your life, you will not get uptight. You will just go about your business and order your life so that it stands in opposition to your challenge. You don't want to reconcile your life to live "side by side" with the evil doctrine. You want to defeat it.

If Black people live our lives in a natural way, white supremacy will die a natural death. Black people have work to do. The aim is not to have it made to live in white oppression. So-called having it "made" and being successful only means you are in a position to help enlighten others.

I will now move on to discuss ways and means to live enjoyable lives in resistance to white supremacy.

CHAPTER SIX

NO ONE ASPECT SHOULD HAVE THE POWER TO CONSUME OUR LIVES

Of course you must be careful to not let your life be consumed in the effort to destroy white supremacy. The ideal is to have a successful life whose meaning is part of the destruction of white supremacy. The first requirement to live in ways that destroy white supremacy is to never, ever think that the freedom all humans cherish can be obtained in a system that is built on white supremacist doctrine, thought and practice. When you get your mind to the point of knowing the ideal of freedom that our hallowed ancestors longed for is not possible within the confines of systems built by white people, it is still not required that you spend your words, acts and deeds consumed with destroying white supremacy.

It will help if you remind yourself continually the reasons why white supremacy is not in the natural order of the creation: white supremacy is a social system that intervenes in the potential of Black humans. It is not in the natural order of the creation; not only is it not in the Natural Order, it is a challenge to it. Not being in the Natural Order, it will eventually, naturally, self destruct.

White supremacy will not die a natural death, unless we live a natural life. White Supremacy feeds on the ignorance and oppression of the subjected people. And it uses brute force to keep the subject people ignorant. But brute force is not their preferred m. o. (modus operandi). They would much rather enforce white supremacy peacefully. By enforcing it peacefully, like mis-educating the populace, for example, the subject people use their power in the best interest of their enemies.

Of course, if you study what you already acknowledge to be true; if you study for understanding of what you know about white supremacy, then the wisdom from your understanding will suffice your needs to take direct action against this evil. With understanding wisdom prevails.

Since wisdom will be the case, you can still live a balanced, happy, peaceful and productive life while making a mighty contribution to the needs of Black people. As a Black human, the challenge of white supremacy must be overcome to live that balanced, happy, peaceful and productive life. This is why we refer to our lives in white social systems as our struggle. When we struggle against the challenges of white supremacy, it too will have the neutral result of developing and shaping our character – depending on our wisdom in struggling against it. The first order of business is to get correct information about white supremacy. This is not as easy as one would think. But once you do get correct information it will be similar to turning on a light to dispel the darkness.

WHITE SUPREMACY: USING POWER IN THE BEST INTEREST OF OTHERS

There is no greater necessity than the destruction of a power that forces you to live in the best interest of others – rather than self and kind. But you must be wise.

You may go into the mountains and conduct guerilla warfare against Caucasians, if you feel this is your calling. But in 2009 there may be a more effective way to beat white supremacy than living that life: instead, why not qualify for a good "system job" and apply the rage and determination that would be required to live in the mountains to that work environment? We are certainly not underestimating the challenge of working in a "system job." It may be even more challenging than living as a guerilla freedom fighter. But a dedicated, motivated individual can be infinitely more effective in "the system" than living in the mountains. But if you are unable to overcome the main challenges in "the system," you would be better off, and more effective in the mountains.

In either case, system job or guerilla fighter, with understanding and careful planning, all challenges can be overcome: our assessments for the two are based on our own understanding of both. Having lived my life at one time in preparation to be a system worker – this was during a time when there were few ways to overcome the main challenge of white supremacy, while working "in the system."

The main challenge in my time was estimated to be the preservation of my own Black consciousness. And second only to preservation of my own Black consciousness was serving in ways that brought others into such a mindset to 'buy black!" and be black, or Afro Centric in all of your words acts and deeds. Admittedly, my understanding and planning was not what it would be today. But such as it was, I understood the greatest danger working in "the system" was the impact such, i.e. the big money, would have on living in the best interest of Black people. So I quit before I could carry out the plan I'd concocted to "make my maximum contribution to the total uplift of African people."

The main plan was to keep working and save enough money to finance a business of my own. But when I felt the weight of the threat to my mindset in blackness I quit and never went back. Fortunately, the understanding I did have at the time caused me to see a niche in the Liberation Struggle to which I could apply the skills I'd acquired in "the system." That is the publishing, printing and distribution of relevant Black literature. But finding the niche did not come in the near term; the near term was utilized to concentrate almost exclusively on feeding my starved Spiritual Body.

After leaving the system, I accepted the teaching of The Honorable Elijah Muhammad. For awhile I attended the Mosque three days per week. I fasted and studied like a person enjoying a feast after not eating for two or three days. It was during this period when I also developed my skills as a journalist. I was engaging all of the above while planning to "go into the mountain" to enjoin the physical part of the Struggle; or more correctly, begin the revolution necessary to free Black people. But someplace along the way Wisdom from my understanding kicked in, causing me to settle in and reconcile my qualifications to effective service in the Liberation Struggle. I have written in detail about my work in the 1970's & 1980's, so in short, what I found is what a-would-be guerilla fighter will find today: It would be nearly impossible to get Black people to physically engage the requirements necessary to physically destroy white supremacy. As a result, I was, and am of a mind to increase the knowledge/power in the National Black Community – and maybe, just maybe if I am successful, I would also have time to help increase our understanding of how to properly use knowledge: hence this book!

I MAKE IT A POINT TO
NOT TELL ANYONE NOT TO
SERVE AS A PHYSICAL FIGHTER

Besides the obvious challenge of police agencies, if you become a guerilla fighter, Black people would likely be the ones who are most fearful of you. By and large they certainly would not join you in 2009. But if you are driven to fight physically, all I would say is, get as much understanding [wisdom] about what you propose to do as possible. Meanwhile, whether you fight physical or not, you will need power: Why not amass power, while re-educating Black people at the same time – re-educate and prepare Black people for your future actions.

That is right; and I mean it. So I am not saying NOT to take the physical fight to the enemy, however radical, or far fetched it may appear to be. What I am saying is that whatever it is, do it from the stand point of wisdom. Plan wisely before you act.

When your life is lived the proper way, it will be lived in contradiction to injustice. When you do live in contradiction to injustice, or live on principle, there is a great residual reward.

As you struggle for success the right way, it develops strong character. If you have incorporated the destruction of white supremacy into your success, your character will be strong in that regard.

As I hope we have made clear, whoever you are and wherever you are, you already have power. Strive to use your power in your own best interest. The next best thing to using power in your own best interest, is to plan to use it in the best interest of your black human kind.

It seems that in life we are always called upon to do one thing before we can do the other thing that we like to do the most. Few things can be done 'all at once.' If you are the kind of individual who believes in living a fun, fulfilling life, you will be very happy when you get more understanding about why obvious evil in the world, including white supremacy, is not destroyed 'all at once.'

Since it is not destroyed 'all at once' it gives us an opportunity to enjoy the process - interim between now and the ultimate destruction of everything in the world that is not in the Natural Order of the Creation. There are processes in all that we do. Understanding how to live within the 'processes" of life is the ultimate key to living a successful, fun filled, satisfying happy life.

USING BLACK POWER WITHIN WHITE SUPREMACY

In the use of your power in white supremacy you first want to stop supporting it with your own power. As stated earlier, to stop supporting white supremacy does NOT require that you give up the power you have acquired within it. The requirement is to START using your power in your own best interest. It may well mean to stop working with them, and for them, but working for your self and kind. If you can reconcile this and work with them, get an understanding why this is so. When you do, wisdom will guide your moves.

We also want to avoid confronting white supremacy directly until wisdom lets you know that it is possible to defeat it. Or you can predict that the consequences from the confrontation will be spectacular and positive [And you are willing to become a casualty]. Whatever the choice you make, it must be your own and predicated on wisdom. In fact, in the year 2009 it is not necessary to be a "casualty" in a spectacular and positive action against white supremacy. In Nat Turners time it was. But not today. First get over any notions that you can do anything that will have the same impact that Nat Turners action had on chattel slavery. Nothing we do can have the sheer impact that the campaign of this Black Liberation Army had in 1831. But we can do things to white people today that Nat Turner never could have done. But unless we plan as well as Nat Turner did, whatever we do will fall short of our potential to do damage to white supremacy. Today, if we study well and act wisely we can be part of the total destruction of white supremacy. We must focus on living naturally.

Since it is likely you were living in white supremacy long before you realized it, it is also likely that your life up to now will be worth more to the maintenance of white supremacy than it is to you and your own kind. One possible reason for a confrontation may be to stop this, or change it in ways so your life will be worth more to you and your kind than it is for anyone else on the planet.

Once you know a confrontation will be positive for your own interest, you must then get a good understanding about the confrontation that you contemplate. The wisdom gained from the understanding will guide you in the confrontation. We shall not specify any confrontations here. But if you do your "due diligence" your research will bring forth many Black ancestors as examples. But above all, you must not find yourself applying methodologies to white supremacy that did not work in the past. The only time you should apply past confrontations to 2009 forms of white supremacy, is if your study has found the reason it failed before. Fix the weakness in it and move forward and you will be successful.

Chapter Seven

EFFECTIVE USES OF POWER THAT IS NOT CONFRONTATIONAL TO THE ENEMY

Your aim should be to live ways of life that the use of power benefits yourself and kind more than it does your enemy/oppressor.

In all likelihood, it will not be wise to immediately give up working in "the system," even when you know doing so is actually in the best interest of white supremacy. You should be happy to know quitting is not required. What is required is to be a healthy human, of good character who is ready to face up to certain facts about your life; make no excuses for it because it may really be a good life with many great possessions and achievements. Accept them, you have earned them. With that said: **What is required is that you began immediately to *plan* to stop using your power in the best interest of whites, or others. This may well mean that you will continue to work to earn the big money. But you will make plans that ensure that your children do not "follow in your footsteps."**

After deciding to change your life from benefiting white supremacy more than self and kind, you should decide first to change certain things about your life. More likely than not, you can change some things immediately that are not healthy for you, immediate family and Black people. Doing anything that is in the best interest of your enemy is not healthy. Earning the cash in "the system" must be used to assist your struggle against white supremacy. This is in service to Black people. The financial needs in the Black community are evident on every facet within the community. Nobody in the so-called Hood makes enough money. So if you are making some, find ways to bring that money home: "Buy Black" wherever possible.

And whatever you do or don't do, stop living according to, or above your means. In fact, your means, and your great possessions and achievements may allow you to drastically change your life. Drastic change is seldom required, but in the understanding of proper knowledge, the wisdom derived will determine the degree of change you should make.

TAKING A CLOSER LOOK AT CHANGE

Let's take a closer look at change; change that you will be required to make when you get understanding of proper knowledge of self. When proper knowledge of self indicates that your life is worth more to the oppressor than it does for self and kind, it is time for a change. There'll be signs in your life to look for that will indicate that it is time to change.

These words are written in the year 2009. Since we spend our lives working in environs of white supremacy, we must not wish this life on our children. Further on in this book, we have a chapter that advise parents of today TO STOP PREPARING THEIR CHILDREN TO WORK IN "THE SYSTEM. For the most part, we may already be working in the system. So our earnings should be spent and saved to change this fact. To be clear, the change we speak of is changing from working directly in the system to working for self, or kind. Or living your life in ways that will free your children from having to work directly for white people.

SIGNS, FEELINGS AND REALIZATION
OF A NEED FOR CHANGE IN YOUR LIFE

When you get near to the place in life where you realize your words, act and deeds are executed more in the best interest of others than for your own self and kind; you may already be successful in life. But you will begin to feel that something is wrong. What causes the feelings could be any number of things; You may notice that, though you are successful, all of your colleagues are white; all your bosses are white.

When you go home, you may notice that by the time the public transportation you are riding to your home, everyone on the train or bus is white. The Black passengers got off before your stop. When you get to the community where you live, most all of your neighbors are white. A Black person who lives in white environs pays more than just "too much for his home." We should never under estimate the impact that living in white societies have on our character.

    At some point in your life you will realize that life is not meant for you to take the slights, or overt insults that you may have thought just came with the job; or to live in a "better neighborhood," or whatever else you find distasteful in society. Whatever it is that wakes you up to the fact that there is more to life than seeing white people in charge, these are indications that change is needed. It is here that you will realize that white people will be in charge of every vital aspect for the rest of your life. This means they are favored in everything (you're likely to have known this all along). Or maybe the feeling that there is something fundamentally wrong did not dawn on you because you were too busy knocking down barriers to be successful. But now that you are successful, you know there is more to life than living in places where white people make it very clear that you are not wanted.

    If your feelings are acted on at the beginning, this emotion will decide your next move. This may cause you to confront white people for every insult or dirty look. This is not the preferred way to go. The best way to go is to let wisdom dictate your next move. Get wisdom, for if you don't, your emotions cannot bring what is missing in your life. In fact, if you spend your time fighting every injustice that you find in a white supremacist society, there will be little peace for you and your character will be shaped accordingly.

You certainly must act on the feeling that something is wrong. Just the thought that white people will be in charge of vital things in your life, for the rest of your life, should put you in a bad mood! After the "bad mood" you will likely be determined to do something to change.

First disabuse yourself of any notions that white people are in charge of everything because they earned the right to be there. If you have any inkling that white people deserve to be in superior positions to Black people, this is a sign that you do not have enough knowledge about Black history. If you do have enough knowledge you don't have enough understanding; enough understanding will give you the wisdom that white wealth was made possible, for the most part, because they stole Black people wealth. Wisdom will also tell you that we must attain various stages of planning to reclaim that stolen wealth before we will ever be free. We are discussing the signs to look for as well as what to do when you see or feel the signs.

Change you must, but act wisely. You can find the wisdom by getting a better understanding of both your feelings and your surroundings. REMEMBER: it is from the understanding of knowledge that you will get the wisdom to act. There are plenty of books in print, written by Black people, about what things have been like living in white environs. There will be plenty of wisdom you can gleam from reading these books. Most tell how the author got out or through white supremacy to be successful.

The books include some that were written when Black people were chattel property for white people. These books tell what they did to change their status, or circumstance. And there are also books written by Black people who decided to do something while living as a second-class citizen in modern, white supremacist America. There are many great books to choose from. The authors of the books tell how he or she acted to change their conditions in white environs. As I stated, be guided by the actions of others in the past; you may even try to duplicate their acts if the result of their actions got a result that you are seeking. At this point I must tell the reader, that however successful the individuals and race have been up to the end of the year 2009, we have not yet gotten our Reparations.

But it has never been for lack of demanding that the oppressors return what they stole from black people. So as you make your plan to change your life, be sure to include supporting black people and movement to get our Reparations.

The need to get our Reparations is for two paramount reasons: 1) The theft and abuse to steal the possessions of Black people, by white people cause a myriad of injuries. The injuries are summed up today in the deep, deep research that incorporates them all into a disease [DIS – EASE] called Post Traumatic Slavery Disease (PTSD). We further expound on PTSD in later chapters. But in short, it turns out that every Black people, at the least in the U.S.A. has some level of degree of PTSD.

#2) The other paramount reason we need out Reparations it will "begin the healing process" to cure the injuries that was caused when our wealth and other possessions were stolen [land, wives, children, language, names & etc.]. The least of the injuries that need healing is NOT the diminution of our characters – caused by the stealing of correct information about Self and Kind.

We strongly suggest that you it is not possible to be free without the payment of Reparations. But just having correct information about Reparations in your plan adds to the success you will enjoy when you free yourself of the notion that white people will be in charge of vital things about you and your Kind for the rest of your life.

ADVICE TO SUCCESSFUL SYSTEM BROTHERS AND SISTERS WHEN THE NEED FOR CHANGE IS EVIDENCED

Let us continue our discussion about the character of the so-called, or successful brother or sister who is working in "the system." However successful one is, there will come a time; the feeling will come over you about the need for change. Or it may come in the form of a sign. If you miss the sign or ignore the feeling, your character will be shaped accordingly.

If the sign for change is in the form of overt racism, regardless to what your success portends on the job. You will be humiliated but are powerless to do anything about it. If you blow your top (get angry and show it), it will change your image to white folks who are not comfortable being around an "angry Blackman. If you do nothing you must internalize the insult, which compounds the PTSD (degree of Post Traumatic Slavery Disorder, which all Black people have to a certain degree). My point is that when the sign induce the feeling that even with your level of success, something is wrong. That will be a time to change your condition or situation from what it is to what it should be. In this case, respect for your accomplishments, not some blatant racism, whether from an underling or high executive.

The healthy, or righteous way to deal with it is to get angry in a controlled way and let the perpetrator know you don't appreciate it one bit. If you handle it correctly, the "underling" will be shamed and recoil (keep in mind that racist are cowards at heart). If the racism is from a top executive, he will not fire you at once if you handle the situation correctly.

You may well get over it as a hero to your fellow Blacks and white colleagues. But nevertheless, it is a sign that it is time for you to change and move on. So in this case (handling it correctly) you will *use your Power* (successful position) to begin a process that will lead to a CHANGE from your present circumstance. Your success indicate that you do have serious, good power. But the chances are overwhelming that you are not using that power in your own best interest. So get more understanding of this fact about your great power. The understanding will give you the wisdom to develop a successful process that will precipitate your change. Don't try to do anything "all at once." I emphasize, once again the need for proper use of your power to institute a deliberate process for change.

Let us now discuss the feelings and signs that indicate it is time for a change when you

have little success, in or out of the system to show for your life experiences.

SIGNS AND FEELINGS ABOUT THE NEED FOR CHANGE WHEN YOU HAVE LITTLE SUCCESS TO SHOW FOR YOUR LIFE

For the Black human who comes to the realization that a need for change is prevalent, and he is not yet 'successful,' he too must study to find the wisdom to act and change his condition. The opportunity is also present to act and build success that is meaningful to the liberation elevation of Black people. In fact, few Black people are living to their full potential as humans. So when the need for change does come over the less successful brother, he or she will be more likely to change. However, you can precipitate that need to change in ways that will have a dramatic affect on your present circumstance. Or you will use the power you have to change your circumstance more deliberately. Either way is fraught with danger for the Blackman or woman.

THE REVOLUTIONARY APPROACH
THE APPROPRIATION OF THINGS TO MEET YOUR DUTIES AND RESPONSIBILITIES

Most of the feelings and signs for change for the less successful Black individuals will manifest in life as a lack of money to take care of "duties and responsibilities." The way to use your power to precipitate dramatic change in your present circumstance will manifest as a physical act to reclaim what was stolen from you during the slavery process in the United States of America. In short, you will plan and act to expropriate the money and material things that you need – stick up a bank, or some other institution that has the funds that will make a dramatic impact on your present circumstances. This is the revolutionary approach; this is the way that Assata Shakur and Zayd Shakur used their power to impact their situation.

The other way to use your power to precipitate change is not, I repeat, NOT the way of the revolutionary. It is important that you don't convince yourself that anything short of planning to expropriate your needs to meet your duties and responsibilities, is revolutionary. Saying this is not to make any judgment about which way is best and more appropriate. In order to make a judgment or give an estimate of the worth of any action, I would need to know the particular individuals fitra (disposition) at the time. So the other way is to use your power to make a move within "the system." Get a better, higher paying job. Don't settle for low pay, or remain in a job that doesn't offer possibilities to get to the top of your profession. Or depending on your degree of consciousness, the job may not leave any room for you to perform it, for the reasons you are there in the first place, and have time left to make any contribution to the liberation struggle of African people.

As stated elsewhere in this book, *"all Black people should commit and see it as a duty and responsibility to do something directly for their own kind."*

So whatever the case of your circumstance whether you are not making enough money or not, you must make time to engage your duty to give back to the race (self and kind), if you have any command of your power, and you will if you have any inkling about the need to help your own kind, you can use that power to get a better job. Earn more power so you can do more.

Preparation and planning to change job will begin, as always, by studying the knowledge that you already have of your present job and situation. You study for more UNDERSTANDING. The increase in understanding will get you the WISDOM to move, to act, to change, to get a better job. Or to increase your chances to be successful if you are compelled to do something more dramatic – like expropriate your needs. I can't emphasize enough the need to study and get more understanding about what you already know. This is a vital part of your planning.

When you reach any of the above notions, this is the beginning phase of your awakening. Do not make any rash decisions; keep your job and keep studying, maintain your modest possessions and plan. White supremacy did not become this pervasive all at once. And it will not leave us all at once.

Where ever you happen to be, or whatever you feel to do, it is simply your life. You must live it as fruitful as possible. Fruitful in the case of living in ways more meaningful to the uplift of Black people, means to first put your own self in proper shape. It means proper shape mentally as well as physically. This requires studying the proper materials. As well as, eating proper foods and treating your spirit with proper literature/teaching.

You must seek out the required information. It is out there to be found. The information you need in the beginning will be easy to find. All you need do is wake up to the fact that something is not right in your life and in the lives of people who look like you: Black people. You'll soon realize the basic understanding that something is amiss in your life. It may have been missing all the while. But you were so busy trying to be successful in the system that you did not see. You can change your vocation in the system, and your feelings about it immediately. Once you do, hopefully you will be of the disposition to do something about it. But you must study. Studying is indispensable. It is a must. Studying the right knowledge will beget you the wisdom to change successfully.

THE ESSENCE OF LIFE

The 'essence' of life is referred to in various ways. Life purpose is one of the usual phases. At some times in our lives we all wonder: *what is the meaning of life?* Why are we here; and why are white people in charge of everything? Deeper understanding will let you know that this life is just a minute slice of the Cosmos.

The cosmos is referring to everything within the universe. And everything within the universe has an essential purpose. The purposes are not always self evident. But our life purposes are always parts of us but we must study self and the universe to be awakened to the acknowledge and accept it.

The proper knowledge of self is almost a sure way to discover your life purpose. Like other things in life, when you study proper knowledge, there are many things that you get besides the understanding of that particular knowledge. For example, you may find there are several ways to achieve your purpose; and the residual benefits in one path or the other will benefit self as well as others.

A degree of Wisdom is necessary to achieve all success. And you will get a healthy, abundance of it while studying the true knowledge of self. You must give yourself a chance. The study of self is a very enjoyable experience. Just be prepared to fight to even get the proper knowledge to study. Most all of what you may have to do or study at any particular time is subject to white people.

No doubt this may sound strange, because all you know in depth is knowledge about the interest of white people. Once you get proper knowledge of yourself, you must work hard to ensure that your words, acts in deeds in life are spoken, acted out and done in your own best interest. White people stole and tried to distort or destroy the true knowledge of Black people. They did so to establish a society causes Black people to use their power in the best interest of maintaining white supremacy [rule].

Everything you do may appear easier if you just go along with the great life you think you have within the confines of white supremacy systems. But when you study proper knowledge of life for understanding, the wisdom derived will tell you that your interest and the interest of white people are not necessarily the same.

Once this is realized, you must study the reason why this is so. Your understanding from this study will tell you the reason why. First of all, you will find that what you do to obtain the comfort or success in white supremacy is ultimately in the best interest of white people. Your actions as well as the actions of your co-workers (black or white) may well be in your individual interest. But study will unveil the fact that both interest are also in the best interest of white people; and more likely than not, it will be detrimental to the interest of black people.

Then you must study this fact so you can understand why, what you are doing is not in the best interest of black people. This understanding will give you the wisdom to effectively plan to stop doing things in the best interest of white people. The operative word here is PLAN. You must plan because since what you ARE doing is not in your own interest, NOT doing it may well be in your own best interest. After you get the requisite understanding [for the wisdom in understanding] you will plan to change what you are doing so it will be in the best interest of Black people. Or you will eventually stop doing it.

As we said earlier, it all comes together when you are awakened to the fact that something is wrong in your life. You may be comfortable, but are ill at ease for whatever reason, in whatever place you may find yourself. When you examine why you are feeling as you do, the 'why' represents the knowledge that you must study to understand your feelings. After you get the understanding, it will give you the wisdom to study self. Understanding Self will open up all that you need to live a happy and productive life. Let's take a look at Self and ways to acquire the proper knowledge thereof.

HOW TO OBTAIN PROPER KNOWLEDGE OF SELF & KIND

There is the physical knowledge of self. And there is the spiritual knowledge of self. The physical knowledge revolves around the history of your physical body. The spiritual knowledge of self revolves round the history of your spiritual body. When you study either you'll gain a degree of understanding of the other.

Your search for proper knowledge of the physical body is found by using the tools of the spiritual body. This will be at a time and place where it is easy to see the physical and the spiritual working together. For example, a knowledge that tells about the history of your physical birth. At the same time, when you were born, you were born from some place other than physical. That place is a spiritual unseen place. Furthermore to get any degree of understanding you must use your mind; the mind is a property of your spiritual body.

If the knowledge of the spiritual body is in a book, you still must use a physical entity to read the book (your eyes), but the understanding of your reading comes from an entity that is an entity of your Spiritual Body. This is your mind, an unseen entity. But you can't read the book unless you use it.

The last paragraph is extremely important: Please read it again.

THE SAME THING SAID ANOTHER WAY

Let's see if I can say the above another way: you read the book with your brain, which is a property of your Physical Body. But understanding comes when you use a property of your spiritual body. The spiritual property is called the Mind. The Mind is the place where your understanding of the knowledge about what you read will happen.

This kind of discussion may not be all that easy to understand, but once you begin your study, you'll find that it get increasingly easier and very enjoyable.

If you don't already know, you'll find there isn't anything more interesting in life than seeking knowledge of self. Of course, seeking knowledge of The Creator is more interesting, but seeking knowledge of self is actually the only way to really find proper knowledge of The Creator.

This is only a brief passage about the process that we use to acquire knowledge. Another part of the process will be about your purpose and the wisdom to act to fulfill the purpose. The understanding of knowledge equals wisdom.

When you understand true knowledge about yourself, the purpose for your life will be unveiled. Your purpose will be connected to the holistic well spring of the Creation. The better you understand the knowledge, the clearer will be your purpose. And the more you understand your purpose the more the 'mysteries' about life will be unveiled.

MEANS TO FULFILL YOUR PURPOSE

At any particular time your purpose may be better understood than the means available to you to achieve or fulfill it. This fact may throw you for a 'loop' when your purpose is first realized. The loop may cause you to forsake everything else in pursuit of your purpose.

Things folk in the past have done when thrown for the 'loop' may be helpful. For many, doing things as they were doing them, especially working a job, instead of working on, educating, or expressing your purpose may become a distraction.

Many of the things they now feel are distractions may have been extremely important to making their lives work at another time. Things like 'going to work' may be the activities that they do to earn the money to take care of their food, clothing and shelter. Or to take care of other responsibilities to self and others in the life they are living up to that point. However, once one gets any inkling of their true purpose, the thrill of working out your purpose can become so compelling that you will forsake everything else in pursuit of it. And this will be nice work if you can get it; or engage yourself full time in pursuit of your purpose. But if it is your true purpose unveiling to you, you will be compelled to fulfill it one way or the other. As the "Spirit" said to Black revolutionary Champion Nat Turner, as he planned to strike out in pursuit of his own purpose in 1831, *"be it smooth or rough you must surely bare it."*

There is a great education for all people in the study of the life of Nat Turner. However, there is a special education for Black people in the study of the life of Nat Turner. He pursued his life purpose in a wise manner. In fact he was successful in fulfilling his purpose. We will not get into a discussion about my feeling about Nat Turner's successful attempt to free Black people from slavery in 1831 – not at this time. Since he wound up losing his life in fulfilling his purpose I would have to give all the evidence that cause me to say he was successful, and that would take me from my purpose for giving his story as an example of one who pursues his purpose regardless of cost, odds or anything else. For like I said, once our true purpose unveils itself we are compelled to pursue it. My purpose for introducing Nat Turner at this time is because he was successful in fulfilling his. I want to share the paramount reason why he was successful so we can discuss that reason with the readers of these words.

As we stated above, when your true purpose begins to unveil itself you will be compelled to pursue it. Nothing that is done in pursuit of your true purpose is dumb! Except, maybe doing something beyond a plan before hand.

You may Forsake work, desire to talk endlessly about your purpose or any other ways that you act to fulfill your true purpose. No sincere pursuits of your true purpose are dumb. But on the other hand when you forsake everything else in your life in pursuit of them, whether this is a wise course of action is a different question.

There is no question that Nat Turners pursuit of his life purpose was a wise pursuit. Nat Turners pursuit was wise because of what he did when his true purpose began to unveil itself to him. He did not forsake everything else so he could pursue his purpose. He planned before he acted!

When Nat Turner "ran away" from the slave plantation in 1825 he took a decision to forsake everything in his life at the plantation. But apparently Nat Turners decision to return to the slave plantation was a decision to reclaim things he'd left when he ran away. The question has always been, 'why did he return' to the ridicule of the other slaves – and a possible flogging by the slave master? In his own words he says that while away "the Spirit appeared and said that *"i'd been too much in pursuit of the things of this world."* Instead, *'I should first seek the kingdom of the Creator and all things will be added to me."*

This says that while he was away Nat Turner found a greater purpose than the one that caused him to forsake the slave plantation. To fulfill this greater purpose required that he return to the plantation. And this brings us to the point where we discuss what we all should do when we find our true purposes in life.

Nat Turner says in his own words that he went into some intensive planning. He said that he spent all of the time he was not doing the will of his 'master' fasting, praying and awaiting the instructions/means to act to fulfill the purpose.

So instead of forsaking his Black people, suffering in chattel slavery, including his wife, Cherry and their children, he stayed around. He planned for the day when he could act to fulfill his true purpose. And while in intense planning, he made himself useful to the Black Community. He was the equivalent of today's "Community Organizers" of Community Activists.

Like the individuals I described above, **"For the individual whose purpose begins to unveil, you can act immediately if that is what you are feeling."** But it would be a wiser choice to "pray on it" for awhile. While praying to the Creator, which is a spiritual act, your physical body is not idle. There is much work to do. This is true even if the purpose is your true purpose. Like Nat Turners', there is always the chance that a greater purpose will unveil itself while you are doing the wise thing by planning to fulfill the purpose you are perceiving.

I've known many brothers and sisters who give up their "system jobs" so they can spend all of their time pursuing other things – including what many will call their true purpose in life. Meanwhile, if they have done little planning, it is quite likely that the money needed to pay for food, clothing and shelter will not be in their possession. Here, I am speaking from personal experience.

When I quit my 'system job' I didn't have any money saved; and my plans to earn money to take care of food, clothing and shelter was shaky to say the least! I made it, but not without some dire moments – and some terrible inconveniences for many people who were close to me. But mine was a case of forsaking the creature comforts in "the system" to pursue my true purpose. In fact, like Nat Turner, my purpose was far from being clearly defined when I left my job. But fortunately for me, the week after I left my job I hit the number in the Bronx, New York for $3000.00! This was not necessarily a sign, as per Nat Turners visions/signs, but it made my decision a little easier. No doubt, I will share more about my decision later about the quitting of my system job. But for now I'll just say that I have no doubt whatsoever that where I am today is because of the plans I made while still on the plantation. But the plans were developed during plans that were made, as I did some intense, valuable study of the knowledge that had already been compiled by present day historians, ancestors and keeping abreast of current events as they were occurring in the early 1970's. The understanding I got from the knowledge gave me the wisdom to discern and utilize the lessons of my service.

    The decisions I made, the lessons I have learned, the visions I had for United Brothers

Communications Systems have carried me over the entire span of my career. But marked changes had to be made in the visions and my plans, but the essential ideals are the same as they were at the beginning. I have used my skills as a master printer to produce and distribute literature written by, for or about Afrikan people – "with as little dependency on the enemy as possible."

So, in short, anyone of a mind to make a change, or transformation in their lives, should plan before they precipitate the change. And even after carefully planning before you act, be prepared to make additional changes to the plan as you go along. And be careful to not spend valuable time in planning too long before you act. I know many who fell into that trap who are still working in the system. They wanted to wait until everything was perfect before they acted. But this will never happen: Things will never be perfect, however long you plan, watch and wait. Like other things in life, and life itself: Striving to attain perfection is what life processes are all about.

You will never attain to a large goal in a straight line. The crooks and changes in direction as you drive a car to a goal have their equivalents in life as things that you don't get right the first time: you do them over, or simply make changes, and go for it again.

Finally, I have been heard to say: *"I believe that at least one half of everything we do is correcting prior decisions that we made at a prior time in life."*

SUMMING UP

In summing up, I'll say for those who decide to forsake everything and live only to fulfill your purpose, be more conscious of what your decision will mean to those around you. If you have children, you should be conscious of the fact that when you forsake your child, you are taking something from him or her that can never be replaced. If possible, don't leave unless you have thought of the consequences of being out of your child's life. Or being in his life as an object of scorn. The "scorn" need not necessarily be there. If you have children, no decision should be made without consideration of how he or she will be kept and provided for, by you, in your life.

Most time when you make a decision to forsake system creature comforts, your standard of living is also "forsaken!" Until you get your methodology together. Until you get your methodology together your money will likely be a lot less than it was while you were working in the system. The playmates of your children; your in-laws, friends and family members will not understand why you would give up so much to live with so little. These, for the most part will be folk who have not yet found their own life purpose. Or if they did find it they have not forsaken the things, in the system, necessary to pursue it.

Very few people will like the decision that one takes to pursue their life purpose. Some of the people who'll not like your decision will be the ones who will take up some of the duties that you may forsake to your child. So your child is going to find out sooner or later that someone else is paying for you. Worse, he will likely hear things about you that put a negative image of you in his mind.

Being conscious of ramifications for your decision will and should not deter you from acting to fulfill your true purpose. But being conscious should be a part of the plans for your move. Hopefully you will have planned your pursuit. If you have, what you tell people who will assume some of your responsibilities will be "spin offs" from your planning. The more planning you do, the more knowledge you will acquire about your purpose. The spin off from your plans will be your justification for making your move.

Just remember that "knowledge is power." So the more proper knowledge that you get the more powerful you become. It is then just a matter of ensuring that you use the power in your own best interest. It is in your best interest to pursue your purpose. It is also in your best interest to do something about your duties and responsibilities that you may have to forsake, at least for awhile.

Understanding the Knowledge about what you are doing will also be a tremendous help here. Become very articulate about what your plans are and their meaning to the liberation struggle of African people. You may not have the money to pay for the upkeep of your child support, but if you have a thorough knowledge about your life purpose it will be easy to connect it to the duties that you must forsake for a while. You must understand that it is in your best interest, in all that you do to pursue your life purpose. Explain what you are doing in ways that leave the person who is "paying for you" with feeling that he is helping you to do something great on behalf of Black people. For it is quite likely that he or she would like to help in some kind of way, but for whatever their reasons, did not. Have as little contact with them as possible.

Remember there is always a good way to do what is in your own best interest. Understanding of this will free you from the burden of ego entrapments. Your best interest can be found from the wisdom you derive from the understanding!

And this is what The Book is about: Understanding knowledge to obtain the Wisdom to act in your own best interest. Your best interest will not always be to act for self first. But the Wisdom will help you to discern when to help others, instead of self as the first order of your business, in what ever you do in life.

We will now take a brief look at the proper use of the power that you obtain from all knowledge; including knowledge about your life purpose.

As for your children, remember, Nat Turner while he was a chattel property still found ways to contribute to the support of his wife and children. You too can find a way. Plan and look for it.

END PART ONE

CHAPTER EIGHT

THINGS IN LIFE THAT CIRCUMVENT YOUR HUMAN POTENTIAL
-The Proper Usage of Power-

The acquisition of, and proper use of power is necessary to overcome the challenges that circumvent our human potentials. Proper knowledge of self makes you aware of your human potential. There are many benefits for the individual that studies information that gives a proper knowledge of self; finding out what your human potential is, is one of the benefits.

Your human potential is closely related to your purpose for living on planet earth. So anything that prevents you from using your human potential to achieve success in life must be overcome. You need power to overcome any challenge to be successful in life. As I said above, we are all born with a certain amount of power, but as you evolve in life you'll need more and stronger power. This is because the challenges in life get stronger. This is not coincidental. It appears that the greater the challenge that you overcome, the stronger you become as a human. And if you have not neglected your spiritual self, the stronger your character will become in overcoming the challenge.

The human species uses multiple ways to acquire power. Some acquire power from other humans who write books. You must read the books to get the power [remember, knowledge is power]. Many never think about the fact that when we read books we are acquiring power. There is power in the knowledge. The critical thing about power after you get it is having the wisdom to use it properly.

Understanding of the knowledge will give you the wisdom to use the knowledge. You can have the [book] knowledge without getting understanding. In this case the power derived will be limited. Maybe simply limited to the possibility of using the book as a weapon to strike your enemy. Or the power will be limited to specific items of information in the book, enjoyable things like romance or crime narratives. Whatever the power is used for, it is power nevertheless. And absolutely no one has the right to usurp your power for use in their own best interest. That is what you aim to do. Make decisions that are based on what is in your own best interest. Your own best interest may rest in letting someone else use your best interest. But this will be your decision. Of course, there are many reasons to allow someone to use your power in their own best interest. We will get to them later. For now we will give two graphic examples of cases when you will let someone else use your power in their best interest. But this too may well be in your best interest, though they feel it is in theirs. .

1 When you love someone you happily give up what you love to give your best to your beloved.

2. When you are under the oppression of another and you either give up what is in your own best interest or pay the consequences. In the chattel enslavement of Black people in the United States of America this meant being severely beaten up, killed or having a loved one sold for money out of your household.

Of course there are many variations in numbers one and two above. In Love the variations range between love and hate. In Oppression, the many variation range from chattel slavery to freedom. Just keep in mind that it is your conscious use of power that maximizes its effect. In other words be aware of why, when and reason when you use power.

MORE WAYS TO ACQUIRE POWER AND USE IT PROPERLY

Taking direct teaching and instruction from others, is another way you can acquire knowledge (keep in mind that Knowledge is Power). Once you have the knowledge, you don't have to do anything with it. But the power is yours to use in whatever way that you choose. Since the knowledge is about something, or 'some thing,' you can apply the knowledge to that thing that you have knowledge about. The limits will be two fold: 1) the nature of the power 2) the understanding that you have of the nature of the 'thing.' It is quite likely that the power will reflect the nature of the individual who is doing the teaching. If the teacher is a businessman or woman, the seeker will gain business power.

Some humans use their power to build businesses. Then others may buy the power by hiring themselves out to them. The owner of the business receives what they need to operate their business. The worker gets for his labor to the company, power in the form of money. You then decide on the proper ways to use the power to overcome challenges in your life.

The first challenges normal people use the power to overcome is the use of the power to acquire food, clothing and shelter. This is the proper use of the power for some. Others will have different priorities they will use their power on. There is no limit to numbers or ways to use power. But they all pale to the use of power to remove white supremacy oppression. Prepare now for a discussion about ways to use power to overcome white supremacy.

CRIMINAL USE OF POWER TO STEAL HUMAN POTENTIAL IS OPPRESSION

When one is subjected to criminal acts to steal or impact negatively on their human potential, they, as individuals are the victims of a crime. When a government is complicit in the acts to steal, or impact negatively on the human potential of a different nation, or identifiable group of people, the people are said to be oppressed. The oppression of humans is a crime against humanity. White supremacy oppression is the most devastating crime in the history of the earth. As such, it is so pervasive and brutal that the only way to be rid of it is through a comprehensive approach. In fact, to me, the only way to really get the job done is to develop a life style that counters white supremacy. Read on, I hope your reading of this book will help you to neutralize white supremacy.

However pervasive white supremacy is, it is a challenge that must be overcome. The proper use of power to overcome it can be determined by understanding the challenge to your human potential: You must study to understand how the challenge/white supremacy was established; how it is maintained and how it is enforced. This can only happen when you are educated to use the power that you already have; use it in your own best interest.

If you are "Mis-educated" you will, not only *not* be using your power in your own best interest, but you will be using the power you presently possess in the best interest of your oppressor. *That is the worse possible use of power.*

It is the worse possible use of power because it helps to perpetuate the crime that is being committed against you. In fact, you become an accessory in a crime against yourself as well as humanity. This is un-natural behavior. And it can only be used successfully when the oppressor, the white supremacist uses deceit to trick you out of the natural ways and wherefores of the Creation.

But when you acquire and accept proper knowledge; and study you will gain an of understanding of white supremacy. With degrees of understanding of the challenge before you; you will find the wisdom to apply to the crime and overcome white supremacy. Other ways to say overcome white supremacy is to say defeat it, smash it, bash it to smithereens, beat it, destroy it, etc.

Then when your degree of understanding attains to a certain degree, the wisdom thereof, will render you capable of living your life in jux-a-position to the "un-natural behavior" that mis-education in white supremacy has rendered to you. You may not yet be living naturally according to the Master Plan within which you were created; but you will be on the Right Path. On the Right Path is where you will find the tasks and challenges that must be overcome to be successful, by degrees, in a successful life.

LOOKING AT TASKS & CHALLENGES

Let's look at some of the tasks and challenges in a particular way: let's see them as opportunities to obtain the necessary degrees to live naturally in jux-a-position to White Supremacy. Living in jux-a-position to White Supremacy is not directly destroying it. Fortunately, this is not the task before you. The

Creator gave you the only task necessary; that is to strive to live naturally as you were created to live. When you do...well...let's see how to say this: I'll say it by repeating what The Honorable Elijah Muhammad told us to do with the "clean and dirty glass."

Or put another way, living naturally is like turning white light off in a pitch Black room. The light goes away. The day that you realize that you can eliminate white supremacy by simply living naturally as you were created to be, is a happy day. But this is where white supremacy becomes very acute and uncomfortable in your life. You will want to live naturally, but you'll find that the white man and woman, have put so much garbage on top of the natural way, that it is difficult to find the right way. He has made the wrong way fair seeming. And to compound this fact is his physical brutalization.

If he did not have the means to suppress you, he could never get you to bend to his will. But he was brutal in putting you in this condition; and he is just as brutal to keep you in the condition. But there is a correct role to play in our resistance to his system. The correct way is also the natural way. He used criminality to put us where we are. It will not be necessary to use criminal means to get out of this condition. But it will require defending self in whatever way brutality is visited to hold us in subjection. It is beyond this discussion, right now, to say how we will defend and overcome his physical dominance. But let us take a closer look at the criminal methods use to get and hold us in subject: perhaps the study will give us the wisdom to defeat him in this way also.

ACQUIRING POWER
BY USING CRIMINAL MEANS

The ways that white people struggled with the so-called American Indians; as well as the ways and means white people struggled to chattel enslave Black people is well known. Of course when we study improper knowledge, we will only know their sides about the level of physical resistance waged by African people and the so-called Indians to white pathology. The main things that we need to know, and accept, here, is white supremacist crimes against both peoples was to steal their power.

When the spiritual nature of African and so-called Indian people is known, the first question is why were white people so brutal. Like any other question, to get the answers you must get a proper understanding about the knowledge that you have of the 'thing' in question. When we study the 'spiritual nature' of Black and Indian people, we understand our nature is to share what we have that is good.

And the knowledge we have about our early encounters with white people is that we did share what we had that was good with them. They didn't even have to ask for it, let alone steal it. But they did. Wisdom from this understanding tell us to be careful with whom you share good things that you may possess. This is especially so when sharing with anyone out of your race. It is not that other races are not in need of what you share. Or will do exactly what white people did to exploit, brutalize and steal from us before. It is that our people are in such terrible need of anything we have extra today. It is not difficult at all to find extremely needy Black people in the United States of America.

REASONS WHITE PEOPLE SO BRUTAL

When we study proper knowledge about white people we understand the reasons why they brutalized and abused a people who meant them no harm. They did so to force the people to use the power that was inherent in them individually, and as a race, in the interest of white people. The understanding of this fact will render you the wisdom to change it.

This, as will any knowledge that you study about white people will give you some ideas about how to live in a white supremacist system/white oppression. Most of the ideas will be short of the proper way to deal with the devious nature of the criminal. But unless you suppress what is coming to your senses, the understanding will serve you well because it will cause you to look deeper into the nature of white people. When you look deeper into any of their nature, you will find correct knowledge about the nature of this pathological human.

This is extremely important because the first knowledge you have about him will be only the knowledge that he wants you to have about himself. Any part of his [story] that he tells will be improper knowledge, incorrect knowledge or incomplete knowledge. Understanding of ONLY his knowledge of himself will only render you the wisdom to fear displeasing him. [but as you know, or will find out shortly, **"There is nothing to fear!"** – but until you have understanding of this fact, you can lose your life if you don't act as a fearful person acts around white people in general; but especially around some particular white people – like brutal police].

Apparently white criminal acts against people who are kind to them is to steal their possessions and wealth. The criminal brutalization is also to force the people to use the power that is not stolen for the good and welfare of white people. As stated, we all have power. Otherwise you could not continue to live on earth. You would not be any good to a thief if you didn't have power to, "pick cotton," for instance.

In using power for the good and welfare of white people, you are not using it in the best interest of self and kind. Remember, the primary purpose for this book is my sharing with the reader my understanding of how to acquire power; and how to use it properly. Let us look deeper into white pathology so we can acquire a deeper understanding/wisdom of their behavior.

WHAT IS THE ORIGIN OF WHITE PEOPLE?

We will not speculate on the mystery of how white people originated on the earth. But without speculating, we know white people did not originate at the time that the earth was created. So they were NOT created. Since they were not created, they do not have the sense of kinship, one to another, as it appears created beings and things have.

Since they were not created at the beginning, at best they are MADE from what was created. In other words they are copies, duplicates, and other things in the English language that says they are not original. They were made by the originals. But we can only make things from the creation in similitude to the ways we were created. It is much like making an artificial body organ, like the heart, arm or leg. The artificial limbs may function well but they are incomplete.

Later we will go deeper into how they supplement what's missing by filling in the blanks with falsehoods, or just simply leaving it out. All you, the reader need to know right now is instead of obtaining what they need from fellow humans peacefully they made/make war on them. War is a criminal act to steal what they needed.

The only thing required after getting proper knowledge of white supremacy is to understand it and act accordingly. This is not an easy thing to do because they make it quite painful when you find out the truth of them and act accordingly [we concluded long, long ago, it is not prudent to let them know what you have found out until you can defend it]. When the Honorable Elijah Muhammad called them "blue eyed devils" for 40 years, they could not touch him because he'd mastered so much else about them and their behavior. Apparently, they were like an open page to Mr. Muhammad. But then, of course Mr. Muhammad was taught directly by "God in Person, Master Fard Muhammad." According to Elijah Muhammad, it was the God Himself that gave him The Message.

Many, many thanks to Mr. Muhammad we have a considerable amount of knowledge about their behavior; their history. When we identify our problems with them, we then study the problem so we can get an understanding of the challenge that must be overcome to get back our power. White people possess all of their power. And they have almost of all of ours. This must change. This will change with the acceptance of reality.

Let me see if I can share some more information about them and why we must reacquire our power. We will now take a closer look at them: HOLD YOUR NOSE!

We take a closer look at white people by, addressing ourselves to the source of their brutality.

One of the main books Caucasians use for guidance in the acquisition and maintenance of power is called The Prince. If Black people make the mistake of using this book in their struggle to overcome our challenge, we may get some idea of why our use of the power we already have is not used in our own best interest: *we may well be using power that maintains oppression rather than fighting to destroy it.* With that said, I do recommend that all black people living in white supremacy read The Prince. Read it as you do the Christian Bible. In fact I have heard this book referred to as their real bible. Since you are reading this book, I am sure you know there is much untruth and outright lies in the Christian bible. And so it is in The Prince.

THE PRINCE
BY NICCOLO MACHIAVELLI

Black people's subjugation to white people, and others with their mindset, is maintained by brutal oppression. This is one of the methods of control that was taught in a book by Niccolo Machiavelli.

Machiavelli was an Italian "court jester" in the 17th century. He wrote a book called The Prince. The book advises his boss, the king, about how to acquire new territories. He then advises him to maintain his power over them with the use of brute force. He advised that rule over new territory must be as brutal as necessary to maintain the control. White people in the United States of America used this methodology to control Black people.

Machiavelli also wrote that the King should establish colonies to govern the people. A colony is a place that only uses enough of what it produces to maintain itself. The raw materials and common good that is generated by the populace is taken out of the colony and given to the central government. This methodology has worked very well for white people.

It has also worked reasonably well for anyone, black or white, who abide by the laws that were established to maintain the rules in such a system. Methods used are brutality and deceit. Machiavelli says that both methods must be used without mercy.

The problems (challenges) arise when the subject people in the colony can no longer be deceived, or brutalized into thinking that the oppressive system offers all that is required to be free to realize their human potential. In a word, when you cannot use what you produce for self and your own kind, in any system, you are not Free. When there is a system that systematically suppresses natural rights of the people to maintain their rule ship, the system is an oppressive system [Machiavelli's book, "The Prince" was introduced into our discussion to give some historic background to the origin of and progression of oppression and white supremacy. We shall now use for example, as well as for practical use how this teaching was applied and is used to continue the oppression of Black people].

NATURAL ROLES
IN OPPRESSIVE SYSTEMS

In every oppressive system there are natural roles for the oppressed people. And there are natural roles for the oppressing people. These roles are natural consequences of societies that profits one segment of its population over other segments. The oppressed people must struggle/fight to get from under the oppression. The oppressor fights them to maintain its control over them. In its purest terms, the fights are about the human rights of self and kind. The human rights of self and kind are to be used in the best interest of self and kind. It is the natural right for anyone to use their own inherent power in the interest of self and kind. It is never right for anyone to use power to steal from fellow humans and use this in the best interest of self or their own kind. This is not the question in an oppressive society.

The question is the recovery of the power that was stolen from the oppressed. It was stolen when the oppressor greedily used his power to get control over the people. So when the oppressed people understand proper knowledge [proper knowledge is defined as correct knowledge] about the oppressive system in which he or she lives, his understanding will tell him in a very clear way that he is living in an unnatural system. It is unnatural because he does not have power over his own natural rights,

When he studies the knowledge he has about his lack of power, he'll come to see that the oppressor has control over his own power as well as the power he stole from the oppressed. The power that the oppressor has of the oppressed must be returned. But it will not be returned unless the oppressed struggle/fight to force the oppressor to give it up.

Power is needed to fight to defeat the oppressor. After he is defeated he is forced to give up what he stole. And pay Reparations to heal the wounds that were caused in the commission of the crimes that he committed to steal them. The oppressed must defeat the oppressor to get back his rights and his possessions. Not only will the oppressor be required to give up his human rights and possessions, he must pay compensation to the oppressed. Just compensation is what restitution is called when what was stolen was done by an individual or an entity in a nation, like a corporation, that is within the society.

When the stealing is done with the approval of and backing of the laws of government, against the whole community, or a different nation of people, the restitution is called Reparations.

REPARATIONS OR COMPENSATION
THERE IS A DIFFERENCE

When the central government supports the abuse of a nation, a distinct community or race of people, they are liable for the repair and restitution of that people. This is where the words Reparations, Compensation, Restitution, and etc. originated.

In the commission of the crime against African people, there were injuries. Reparations are due from the U. S. government because the government enforced laws that protected the criminal act of it's citizens. Reparations are due to the nation of people who were violated. In other words reparations are paid by the government to the other government or nation.

Compensation and restitution is basically the same. But is paid by individual citizens or other entities within the criminal government. The restitution restores the property of the victim; Compensation is payment beyond the restitution.

Reparations is a demand that is made on the guilty. But it is a demand that will not be ceded until the victim has the power to back up the demand. Then we must use the power in ways that will get the desired result.

THE SPIRITUAL AND PHYSICAL STRUGGLE AGAINST OPPRESSION

Black people individually and as a race are in a perpetual struggle for power to maintain selfhood in our struggle against oppression. We are powerful, but for the most part our power is used to survive within the confines of oppression. The power is used within the systems of the oppression that maintains the subjection of Blacks to white people. In fact Black people should be using their survival power to struggle against white domination and subjugation. And for the most part most will tell you that is exactly what they are doing. But let's take a look at our use of power that we generate .

Some black people say they are using their power to "beat him at his own game." This is impossible and will not do the job even if it wasn't, the Oppressors game is to oppress and brutalize us in order to maintain "the system." If you play that game, at best you will be the one who is presiding over the systems that oppress. The most you can be is an efficient tool in white supremacy systems. This is not freedom. Being an efficient tool in white oppression is not the best use of our power.

But when we get a better understanding of knowledge about our condition, this will give us the wisdom to see and act like it is impossible to use the rules of his game to gain our freedom. Once we understand this as fact, we will have "turned the corner in our quest for freedom, justice and equality. We are not saying break all of his rules. Some of the rules are good rules; they only require the proper application to the condition in which we find ourselves. But there are other rules that you must break. This means you must go outside of the rules and laws that govern white supremacy societies.

Meanwhile, anyone who plays outside of the rules is subject to be brutalized back into submission. That is, if they are caught. But a subject people will continue to strive for freedom, regardless of the intimidation and brutality. If the desired result continues to escape the people, the people must get more understanding of the nature of the challenge. One of the first facts that you learn when you get the proper knowledge of the challenge, is that using his rules will never get the job done.

In fact, what you are doing when you accept the system as your way to freedom, you are using the text from the writing of Niccolo Machiavelli. His text teaches that the "means justify the means." This is not so, but millions of Black people are trying to realize their human potential by following the rules of the mindset of the oppressor. As a minimum you must not have the same intention as he does when you use his rules and laws. Of course greed is the over arching motivation of the white supremacist. So your intention for striving for success within white supremacy must not be motivated by greed. We have told you above that the greedy person in one who uses more than he needs – at the expense of others who don't have as much as they need.

SECOND MAIN WEAPON IS DECEPTION

It is very clear when you study the knowledge of how, why and when Black use of power supports the oppression of self and their own kind – that they have been deceived. Many, when they find out this is so, try to overcome the ramifications of the deceit with physical power. But it cannot be overcome using only physical power. This fight must be a spiritual fight as well. It is extremely important to know as early as possible when you have been deceived. Evolving your spirituality increases your power to do so. Here again is the need to study proper knowledge of your situation.

When you study the known knowledge of how we became a subject people, you'll see that the natural spiritual medium was taken over immediately by the oppressor. They were taken over after brutalizing the people into submission. This was a physical defeat and brutalization. But somehow, the oppressors knew that they must also control the spiritual, as well as the physical expression of the people.

How Caucasians knew this is one of the mysteries in the creation. They practiced chattel enslavement of Black people, but knew it would reinforce their control by giving the Black people a spiritual expression that they control. They added something to the natural spiritual expressions of Black people.

To deceive Black people, we were forced to use a false religion to treat our spiritual selves. Once this was done, it was not difficult for the evil people to force Black people to exercise their spirituality in the interest of white people – not in the best interest of self and kind.

Moreover, white oppressors rewarded black leaders of the spiritual expressions. Black preachers down to this very day still practice, preach and spout the religion given to replace natural spiritual expressions of their own. So Black preachers and other leaders not only preach a false notion of religion for selfish reasons, they also do so to please white oppressors for selfish reasons.

The false religion/spiritual expression that was forced on Black people was Christianity. Saying this, to tell the truth about it, is not to insult this spiritual expression as it was practiced by Black people.

The working of the spiritual law is very exact. It is all based on faith, belief and other unseen entities that is actually the food for your spiritual body. The unseen entities include Sincere Intentions. We call the unseen entities food in the sense that material substances is called food when it is consumed to sustain the physical body as a seen entity. In this instance, Faith, belief, intentions and other unseen entities are called spiritual food for the consumption of the spiritual body. So even though Christianity was forced upon the people for a evil purpose, the intention in the practice of it, by Black people, still have a positive, residual effect. Intentions govern much more than we can ever know in all aspects of our lives.

BASIC, SEEN AND UNSEEN, KNOWN FACTS ABOUT THE HUMAN

There are some things that we know about humans. We have two bodies. One is spiritual and unseen. The other is physical and is seen. This is easily proven to the intelligent human. Using the unseen entity called thinking, you can't see it but you know thinking works. And though it is an unseen property of the body called thought, it does not work because of the spiritual body alone. It is working because it has a corresponding physical component called a brain. It takes both bodies to do anything in this life.

In the religion that was forced on Black people, (Christianity), for the most part, the spiritual expression was practiced with a Sincere Intention. At least, we can state this as fact about Christians until they found out the truth. But though sincere, it had limitations and failed because of the false notion that Christ Jesus is the Creator and God of the Universe.

So my intention in calling Christianity a false religion is based on the object of worship in Christianity. It is to say that the basis of Christianity, (Jesus Christ as God does not stand up to the principles and Universal Laws that govern the Creation). It doesn't take long for anyone who studies the teaching of Christ Jesus to know this. Even in the rewrittten, transliteration, and several translations the man called Jesus is quoted in places that says clearly that he is not The Creator, but Jesus is quoted as telling everyone to not worship him, but, "my Father Who is in Heaven ..." though this is clear, and many know it, they (Christian teachers, preachers and others) find it necessary for selfish reasons NOT to teach what they know Jesus said. They were forced to tell these lies as chattel slave preachers. Today there is no excuse to preach as they were forced to during slavery.

We give selfish intentions to white oppressors and Black preachers, but excuse so-called lay people when they are first introduced to the religion called Christianity. We cannot give a blanket excuse, so to speak, because when you study the bible, you are exposed to known facts about Jesus. They will not be excused later because they know what the words mean and what Jesus meant when he spoke them.

Yet if you do not study the words for yourself and believe what someone else tells you, you will gain some spiritual food to feed your spiritual body.

Though it is a fact that Christianity is based on the false premise as to who Jesus was, does not mean all of it isn't working for the individual who believe it works. The problem is it isn't working in the best interest of self and kind. It is working in the best interest of the person who forced it on you.

When you practice Christianity you cannot execute its physical dimension in the best interest of self and kind. If you executed the physical dimension of Christianity in the best interest of self and kind, you would use the power of this expression to break down the physical things that oppress us. But to be a Christian you must believe that Jesus Christ is returning and he will take care of the things that impede your physical freedom.

If you are a "born again Christian," you do not believe in revolution. You must believe in working within the system to get as much as you can within the laws that are designed for the selfish interest of the oppressor. Thinking thusly is in the best interest of the one who gave you this religion.

Here you are using your spiritual tool of thinking, not in your own best interest but in the best interest of the oppressor. This is not the best way to use this great, essential tool for humans.

We must feed our Spiritual Body just as we must feed our Physical Body. When you feed your physical body food that is depleted of much of its nutritional value, it will last you for a long time. But eventually the fact that it has diminished nutritional value will devalue it's potential to keep you in good health – functional at your optimum potential. We will not take the time to go into details about it, but even with physical food that is depleted of nutritional value, you can add things that will make it a beneficial food. You must get an understanding about the knowledge you have about eating such food. The understanding will give you wisdom about how to supplement it with missing nutrition. This will be in your best interest if you are eating it for its nutritional properties. If you are eating it for reasons other than its nutritional value; or you are ignorant of its lack of nutrition, you will benefit accordingly.

EATING NUTRITIONAL SPIRITUAL FOOD

When we feed our Spiritual Body food which comes from a source that is of Our Creator Father, it is like eating nutritional food. The teaching that comes from a Prophet will enhance the potential of your natural self. If you follow his instructions, it's like eating food that has nutritional value. But if you accept the lie about a known Prophet, that he is God, or the physical son of God, it's like eating food that has no nutritional value. You may still eat it and gain whatever your intentions have been for eating it. But it is like eating food of no nutritional value: you must add something to make it worthwhile.

I certainly do not want to belabor this point because I happen to believe that when the student is ready, the master will appear. The largest responsibility of the person who strives to live by the guidance of The Creator is to NOT shirk from telling Christians the Truth as they know it. But I know many good, largely advanced individuals who hesitate to tell friends and family the truth, as they know it. The hesitation is to spare them the anguish of trying to rationalize the emotional experience of Christianity with the science based knowledge that they, themselves are living in. I don't agree with holding back the truth and not bear witness to what I believe in as opportunities presents themselves. Of course, I will never pick a spiritual fight with anyone. But it will be a rare occasion when I do not match my spiritual expression with anyone who is expressing theirs in my presence.

We, especially, must cultivate, and find a way to share scientific truth with our elders. The cultivation is to tell them the truth without giving them the least bit of anguish. But we must share the truth with them. Truth as we know it. This is important for those of us who love our elders. Since they are advanced in age, we can surmise that they are closer to the time when the truth of the misunderstandings of spiritual matters will be manifested more clearly. When they hear the ways we have presented the truth to them, it may well cause a recognition in them that can spare some concern they would otherwise have when they return to the Unseen.

'WHY' WE DO NOT ALWAYS ACT
IN THE BEST INTEREST OF SELF

Many may ask "why" we don't always act in our own best interest. The first part of this, layered question, is to find the answer to why only a few individual beings always act in their own best interest. This is the spiritual component to the question. It addresses the question to Self. And the answer must be found here, within self, before you can deal effectively with the outside force that may bear on the reasons why we do not always do, share and be things in our own best interest.

Almost the entire spiritual answer to why we do not is because of ignorance! Ignorance about known truths. The ignorance breeds fear and the fear cowers us to act other then in our own best interest. Fear is second only to NOT having heard the truth in the first place. We shall share some discussion about the physical reasons why we don't always act in our own best interest. But let us first deal a little with the emotion of fear.

THERE REALLY IS NOTHING TO FEAR

There is Nothing to fear. Most of the time, when we face up to fear and resign ourselves to bear any consequence it portends, fear dissipates and dissolves back into the ether from where it came. This happens because when you resign yourself to bear the consequence of what you fear you must prepare, or brace yourself for the consequence. In bracing yourself, you must learn more about it than the 'scary part.' In learning more you get a better understanding of fear itself; this understanding gives you wisdom of how to dear with what you are fearing. That is all: 1) Learning more yields more understanding 2) more understanding yields more wisdom 3) wisdom gives wise alternatives to face up to what you are fearing 4) When you face up to it with wise options, you don't have to fear anymore because you have taken care of the object of your fear.

IGNORANCE ABOUT THE TRUTH
CAUSE US TO ACT IN OTHER THAN
OWN BEST INTEREST

Ignorance about known truth, of any matter, is slightly different because an outside force may well have some involvement in hiding the truth from you. But once you have heard the truth, and the excuse of not having heard it is removed, you are subject to what is reserved for those who hear but continue to live as though they didn't.

It is still another thing to hear the truth and continue to act in other than your own best interest because you didn't understand it. But this is a short lived excuse. It is short lived because our Creator Father created us from His own Image. Since this is the case that few of us dispute, the truth is an essential part of our being.

When it's heard clearly, Truth reaches the parts of our being that were implanted within us at the time we received our ears, our eyes, our noses, our feelings, our touch. The human is bound to respond through one or more of these senses when he or she hears the truth. That is, when truth is presented in the right situation, in the right volume. The 'right volume' is the degree to our understanding of the knowledge we may have about the truth of a particular thing.

If the degree is only to the emotional level, we respond emotionally. When it reaches us to another degree, which may be rational, we respond by asking for more information. My point is we will respond to some degree when and if we hear the Truth.

Remember, as we move on, that when you increase in knowledge you are increasing your potential to understand more degrees.

TRUTH ABOUT BLACK OPPRESSION IS WRAPPED UP IN OUR SPIRITUALITY

We can see truth wrapped up in the knowledge about HOW the oppressed was made to express their spiritual needs in the best interest of the oppressor. The 'HOW' must be understood, because when we understand the method, we'll see that in order to regain control over self, you must, wisely, either destroy the method that is used to control you or make it work for your own best interest.

The HOW is the physical dimension, or counterpart to the why. The how component is a seen entity. The why component is unseen. Let's discuss this a little.

THE CHURCH AS THE METHODOLOGY OF CONTROL

The church is the physical place where the spiritual expression is practiced. Put this aside for a moment.

Radio stations, televisions, newspapers and etc. are the physical manifestations of the socialization of the people. Socializations are systems that humans devise to interact amongst themselves. This is usually identified as the places for human political and cultural expressions. In white supremacy, the spiritual expression is nomally exclusive of these two expressions [cultural & political]. REMEMBER, these are addressing the HOW, which are seen components of socialization systems.

When we study how we were induced to act in the best interest of oppressors, we find decadent culture values, social values as well as corrupt politicians, operating corrupt political systems.

The truth of the matter is, for 'spiritual food," he forced Black people to use the church that he established to control the people. It is a well known fact that he would not let the captive people worship unless he was present. This was in the early days. After the indoctrination, it was no longer necessary to have a representative of white supremacy present at services. Dr. Carter G. Woodson described the behavior of a captive in white supremacy perfectly: *"when you control the thinking of a man, when he doesn't find a back door, he will make one."*

The above is a short description of HOW we were made to act in the best interest of white people. We also offered you an example of the behavior of such a person – at the least, the behavior of one who hasn't knowledge about our captivity to find the wisdom to counter the behavior. Now we shall look deeper into WHY we act in the best interest of others.

WHY WE ACT IN THE BEST INTEREST OF OTHERS

We will look now at some of the phenomenon as to WHY individuals, groups and races, especially the Black Race, collectively, do not always act in our own best interest.

To intelligently discuss why, we must have knowledge of when such behavior is practiced. When you understand correct knowledge about when, you will see that the work of the d (evil) is a perpetually reinforcing system of mechanisms to maintain the status quo. The status quo is to keep the power working exactly as it is. That is to have all things within it working for the self and kind of white people. This does not mean changes cannot be made in the status quo. But whatever the changes are, the practice of the changes will also work in the best interest of the oppressor.

In the examples we shall use to illustrate our point about why we don't do things in our own best interest, we will look at how the individual or people relate to the natural inclination to treat the spiritual body. Remember, in the very first line in this section, we told you that the answer to why is found within self. Within self is where the spiritual body is found. The oppressor forced a false religion on Black people to ensure the religious expression was practiced in his own best interest. Remember now, religion and other things that are related, is food that feeds our spiritual bodies. The false religion that put Prophet Jesus Christ as the object of worship feeds spiritual food that has diminished nutritional spiritual value.

Christianity did the job whites designed it to do. Christianity is still doing the job. Christianity requires that the believers wait for their ultimate rewards after they die. It is in the best interest of white people that you believe this. Our congregating and worshipping as we were forced to back in chattel slavery is in the very best interest of white people – from the power that is generated when people congregate to the fact that when oppressed folk believe they are going to be relieved of the oppression by the 'return of a savior' it pacifies the people while the oppressor is enjoying the fruits of their congregating [unity is massive power]. So we see that one way we are induced to do things in the best interest of the oppressor is in the legacy of the ways we treat our spiritual selves; and in the allegiance we have to social systems to indoctrinate us into political, cultural expressions that are in their best interest. But there are other means that are used.

BRUTALITY FORCED BLACK PEOPLE TO ACT IN THE BEST INEREST OF OTHERS

As we continue our discussion about the struggle for power, I remind us to never neglect the spirituality in any aspect of the struggle. Physical acts will be necessary before you become free. But to overcome oppression completely the spiritual expression must be a part of our struggle.

We have the basic ways that were used to force Black people to work in the best interest of white people. We have plenty of knowledge about these facts.

We also have knowledge about the facts that when neither control of spiritual, social, nor cultural expressions did not get the oppressor the desired result he visited unmerciful, relentless brutality never before experienced by humans against humanity.

We must continually study the knowledge we have. The study will get us the understanding. From the understanding we will derive the wisdom to act against and defeat white supremacy.

CHAPTER NINE

69 YEARS OF EXPERIENCE IN OPPRESSION LIVING IN RESISTANCE AS A DUTY

We are writing this book from the context of a Blackman who believes that resistance to oppression is the duty of all Black people. The challenge to fulfill this duty is not unlike all challenges that humans must overcome to live successfully in life. We get nothing significant without putting forth significant effort. When we understand the efforts that we put forth, we enjoy the process. *The righteousness and amount of our efforts will determine the significance of our success*.

THE BLACK STRUGGLE IS FOR POWER

The resistance Black people must put forth to live free of oppression is called struggle. You are most effective when you see and accept resistance to oppression as a duty. **The state of living in freedom has zero tolerance for oppression.** Zero means NONE. For Black people this means we must move from positions of trying to convince ourselves that comfort within the confines of oppression is freedom; to positions of striving to resist the confines of oppression in the noble character of human beings.

For no matter how much comfort you attain in the system, the pain and embarrassment of being subjected to racism is always just a moment away. There is absolutely no sane question about the rightness of the cause for Black Freedom. This leaves only one question for the sane mind: *should my efforts be to destroy the systems that oppress or to be successful within them?*

I shall address this question in the next few pages. I am aware that my words should bring scrutiny to my own life. I actually welcome the scrutiny. Not that my life is free of challenges or all description. However, the challenges, or imperfect nature of them will be flawed in the attempt to live as I write that we should be striving for: That is freedom, justice and equality – the main part, or essential part of which is Reparations and the development of our Spiritual Being.

IT IS TIME TO BEGIN TO PREPARE OUR CHILDREN TO WORK OUTSIDE OF THE SYSTEM

We are at the point in our struggle to be free that our children must be taught skills to work outside of the system, rather than getting educated to get a job in it. We must stop preparing them for any job that is perceived to be "in the system." They must be taught to "do for self" as part of the lifestyle they are expected to live.

This training for vocations outside of the establishment is not as astonishing as it may seem. It is obvious that the corporate world has use for very few black youth. I dare say too much of their human potential and energy is wasted applying for jobs, or training for vocations that will be dependent on people who don't like them for a "break."

It is time to teach our youth from the time they are babies to do for self. We need a generation of Black youth who are determined to live their lives without ever working in "the systems" of white supremacy.

BLACK YOUTH ALWAYS IN STAGES OF DISCOVERY ABOUT OPPRESSION

Black youth are always in one stage or another in discovery about the perniciousness of white oppression. This is actually true about life in general. The human being grows through various stages. At each stage, he learns about the responsibilities that are best for his development into his or her next level. In a society where individuals may not be suffering oppression, the community of people establishes certain ways to instruct the individual about what is expected of him when he attains to a certain level in life. This is the first job of parents: preparing their children for the progressions and levels of life.

These are the natural means that humans use to pass on culture to subsequent generations. But as we all know, or will if you study the history about the Black Experience in the United States of America, the ways of the mother and father was interdicted during chattel slavery. Parenting the knowledge about the history of Black people was not in the best interest of the white people. Today, the oppression of black people also serves to interdict effective means to pass on the things necessary to prepare Black youth for the progressions of life. It is still in the best interest of white people that we do not have the means to help our children overcome some terrible challenges, in advance of mistakes. As a result, some absolutely vital information is not taught to Black youth before they make mistakes, or settle on values that are not in their own best interest, or in the best interest of Black people.

In an oppressed society, knowledge about how pernicious, pervasive and permanent oppression is, does not keep pace with the other developments in Black youth. This is mainly because we do not give our youth a spiritual expression that is practiced in the best interest of self and kind. Whatever the thing that may trap them up in the dregs of white supremacy; or with wrongheaded notions about what success and happiness is, teaching them from the cradle to live free of a "system" job will get the desired result. We must teach our children how to attain to real success. I mean "money, good homes and friendships in all walks of life."

WAYS TO PREPARE OUR CHILDREN TO RESIST OPPRESSION AS A LIFE STYLE

The spiritual expression we teach our children must be practiced in the best interest of self and kind. The importance of what happened to cause Black people to be last in every society on earth must be taught from the very beginning in the life of Black youth. A value of what was lost in oppression must be taught to Black youth. And we must cultivate the thought and feelings in them that they must be part of a process to have that value returned to self and kind.

Values are unseen entities so the teaching must come through spiritual expressions that we practice ourselves; and pass on to our children. At certain ages, experience is the best teacher. But when the child is young, his mind must be molded and shaped with a correct history about our oppression; and given a successful mission to reclaim what was lost.

Too much of what should be regular training for Black youth is left to happenstance. In "happenstance" or learning from experience, one is more subject to error, mistake or indulge in excesses. It is time that we parents put "heavy hands" on our youth when they are still babies. We are not advocates for the training of robots. We are not all the same, not even father and son are the same, so learning critical thinking is extremely important; but critical thinking should be about subject matter that is helping to shape and mold him to be successful in 'doing for self'.

We don't want robots, but when the son or daughter is young and learning the rudiments of life – like reading, writing, dancing, singing, playing sports, he should also be given direct teaching about the Liberation Struggle of Black people. They must be taught that unless they live correctly, they will see no end to white domination over their lives.

We must teach them early in life that the life style they live must be in resistance to white oppression. Teach them early so they will not spend an inordinate amount of time thinking that living in white oppression is the only choice they have to be successful in life. If you teach them properly, they will equate their life style with happiness and with success doing for self, in business or working to empower Black people. They will develop duty bound and entitled to live free of white domination.

BLACK PARENTS MUST TEACH
A LIFESTYLE THEY THEMSELVES
MAY NOT BE LIVING

Since most Black parents have not taken on living and teaching resistance to white oppression as a duty, they have not told their children about the intention of white people. We must teach our youth that white people intend for Blacks in white oppression to be a lifetime sentence. In fact if resisting white oppression is not taught as a duty, the youth will waste too much time and energy figuring it out for themselves. By the time it is figured out, it will be too late for many. Not just in life, but in life styles. We must tell them at an early age about the nature of oppression. Tell them what an evil system white supremacy is; and they should never want to be happy in an oppressive system.

WHAT I AM DOING TODAY

Long before this day, 2009, I stopped attempting to wake up Black people of my own generation. Of course I hope they read my stuff and act accordingly, but my message is written to give Black youth a place to read the views of a Black nationalist Muslim about the human experience. This experience is a view from the mind of a Blackman who understands that our subservient role was designed within "the system." So you can't be a part of it without being subservient to it.

This subservience is not a part of the Natural Order. So the basic challenge for Black people is to get things back into the Natural Order. Since the "system" is out of order, or incorrect, it must be changed or corrected. It is not up to us to change the system. It *is* up to us to break free of the system. The breaking free will require some radical departure from the old ways of doing things. The main old way of doing things is getting a pay check from white people. There is nothing inherently wrong with getting a fair wage for your labor. But when your labor is given against your own best interest you are better off not to hire yourself out for any price. The youth must learn this early in their lives. If they learn this one lesson, all of the reasons why they do not fit into certain places in society will be better understood. The better understanding will get them the wisdom to make better use of their human potential. It will be a use that is not trying to get along with a people whose brutality against their human potential is well documented.

RESISTANCE AS A DUTY

I repeat, 'you should accept resistance to oppression as a duty.' This duty should be passed on to your children. And as a duty, one of the things you can do to fulfill this duty is to not work for white people. In order for a duty to be carried out, it must be accepted by the individual. When we see a duty as a necessity, it is easier to take care of.

The acceptance or resistance of white oppression can easily be buttressed by the fact that it is a necessity. This will be apparent if you accept the fact that you are duty-bound to solve personal problems. There is no civilized Black human who has not personally felt the inconvenience, the sting or the brutality of white oppression. Personal responsibility for food, clothing and shelter is a natural. We are duty bound to provide these things for our youth. We look forward to the day when resistance to white oppression is a duty in part with the above. For white oppression negatively impacts our ability to fulfill our duties and carry out our responsibilities as patents. Since we cannot reach our full potential as humans, it is hard to earn a decent living in white oppression. This is not true for many, but it is true for the mass majority.

OUR MAIN IMPEDIMENT AS HUMANS

Yes, the white suppression and oppression of Black people is the main impediment to our potential. Anyone, Black or White who do not know this, or is in denial about it, have two major problems. For when there is a problem in your life and you don't realize it, or are in denial about it, you are at a severe disadvantage in life.

Any knowledge about a problem in life must be studied for understanding. If you study for understanding you obtain a degree of wisdom about the problem. For every problem there is also a solution. When you apply a degree of wisdom to a problem, it will guide you by ways and means that are within your own capability to find the solution.

I will use the oppression of Black people as an example. I have 69 years of experience living within the confines of the problems presented by white oppression (white supremacy). Long ago I accepted resisting white supremacy as a duty. Designating this challenge as a duty prioritized it as a basic requirement to fulfill my purpose. At this point the duty also became a responsibility.

I could have used any number of examples of problems that humans face as challenges that must be overcome to reach its potential. But Black humans had their freedom stolen some 500 years ago: so we have faced every imaginable challenge in our efforts to reclaim it. Black individuals who do not understand oppression as their number one problem in life, do not have sufficient knowledge about freedom. Oppression is a "catchall" kind of word for the challenges that we must overcome to reclaim that freedom. Some of the challenges are seen and some are unseen.

We must struggle to overcome our individual as well as collective challenges within oppression. Another word for struggle is fight. In a language other than English, the word for struggle is Jihad. The struggle is against two forces that constantly challenges us human beings. We use our power to fight the forces. There is a slight but significant different meaning for "struggle" and "fight." There is also only a slight difference between the two forces that are constantly challenging us: Internal and External forces are so close that we may use them interchangeably at times. Which ever name is used, the challenge must be resisted in order to overcome them.

PHYSICAL FIGHT – SPIRITUAL STRUGGLE

The first of the forces we struggle to overcome is a internal struggle to know self. As it is in nature, our self is in duality. One self is seen and is called your physical body. The other self is unseen and is called your spiritual body. As per "struggle" and "fight," there is also little to no difference between the two. But the difference is significant.

One is seen the other is unseen. Your physical body must be used to resist a seen challenge. Your spiritual body must be used to resist an unseen challenge. As we have said, and will make even more explicit, it is all one struggle and fight. The Physical body works at the will of the spiritual body. That is when the physical body obeys its spirit, which is the guiding force within the body.

We understand that "In the Beginning," there was only Spirit, or a Primal Entity that we call Divine Spirit. The Divine Spirit was "Created out of Triple Darkness." It is a Divine Spirit that created everything else, including the self that is within the body of all humans.

The Spirit within human bodies is the primal source for the 'making' of the physical body. The processes and power needed to "make a man," and woman is wrapped up in the Divine Mysteries of what is commonly called life.

However, studying what we know of the Divine Mystery yields certain degrees of wisdom: this wisdom tells us that "since The Source of Our Creation in the beginning, when everything else was created, including our self, have its origin from the Only Entity that was there at the time [The Primal Spirit, Force, Creator, Allah, God, or whatever we come to call the Source of our Creation]," the Original entities from the Divine Event have a Portion of the Creative Spirit as a part of our being self. As such, we have the potential to replicate, or make things, in similitude to how we were created.

So given the above discussion, that I have recorded it in the *Spiritual Manual of the Mystic Order of U. B. U. S.*, the degree of understanding we have is that our self being (which is original) "made a man" and woman consisting of portions out of all substance that was created. To the understanding of the knowledge that I have, wisdom tells me our earth, or physical bodies are the makers of our spiritual self: so it is us that the human body struggles to obey. Whether or not we have proper knowledge of self, we normally suppose our struggle is with The Primal Source [Allah, God] – this is true only in the sense that our self being struggles to please our Primal Source. We want to obey Divine Guidance because when we do, we receive help to attain and realize our potential: that potential within our self being expresses itself through the words, acts and deeds of our human body.

THE DIVINE UNFOLDING MYSTERY OF LIFE (DUMOL)

This discussion is possible because of our study of the Divine Unfolding Mystery of Life. The degrees of understanding we have of the DUMOL is a wonderful experience. Each degree of understanding gives us the wisdom to master tasks to advance, by degrees, to the achievement of our ultimate goal. That goal is called Self Realization.

We may share our Spiritual Manual if we can successfully impart and share what we intend in this book. So please read on.

Though we may have varying degrees of difficulty in our life right now, read on anyway. One day, the difficulty that I, myself, am in, right now, may become known. So the difficulties in life – the challenges – continues so long as you have life. We study what we know of life, especially the difficulties, but other things too. For when we are not studying, understanding and enjoying the processes of life we are not living to the level that is possible in any circumstance. This level will be reflected in our dispositions, in our characters.

With understanding also comes wisdom to find the peace in all endeavors. For all endeavors will surely have challenges that must be overcome to achieve them. With a certain degree of understanding, the challenges become wonderful opportunities to overcome tasks and become master of another part of the DUMOL.

Life is a beautiful experience, yet, all lack of comfort within it must be dealt with in real time: so we struggle for freedom, justice and equality as a matter of course. The purpose of which is to reclaim our Human Rights to use the substance that "our Father" created at the beginning.

The human bodies that we made have certain rights. We have certain Human Rights that are necessary in our striving to reach our potential. As its maker, we guide it and provide for it the things it needs to be successful in life. Anything, or anyone that circumvent the potential of the human, is out of the order within which we made the body in the first place.

Just as our good, obedient behavior pleases our Divine Creator; and we are rewarded with the force and blessed power to overcome and understand more of the DUMOL, this force and power is also expressed, reflected and brought into manifestation through our Physical Body.

CHAPTER TEN

THE NATURAL DESIRE TO KNOW WHO YOU ARE AND YOUR PURPOSE

There is a natural desire to know who you are, where you came from and your purpose for being alive. You cannot have clear answers to these questions unless you have proper knowledge of self. This is the natural order of the creation. It appears that you must know one thing before you can know the something else.

If there is no interference with the natural order of your own creation, knowledge to find answers to the questions can easily be found. Remember, we stated above that when you approach a challenge as a problem, you should study it for understanding. The problem represents the knowledge that you must have in order to overcome the challenge.

Having the knowledge is necessary, but it does not end there. Simply having the right knowledge is good. And it is essential. But if you don't understand the knowledge you will not solve the problem.

Just knowing it is a problem is going to give us a degree of understanding of it. That degree will give you the wisdom to relate to the problem. If the problem/knowledge is of white oppression your wisdom may tell you that you don't have sufficient power to physically overcome it. If you fight it with this degree of power your physical body will be crushed.

As you study white oppression you will understand it more, the wisdom gained from the additional understanding will guide you in your struggle to get sufficient power to overcome white oppression. This is necessary to solve the problem. There are many things that can determine how much understanding of the knowledge that you have of a particular thing (like white oppression). The essential thing needed to overcome it completely is that your knowledge be correct knowledge. And when you get sufficient understanding of the correct knowledge, you will receive sufficient wisdom to overcome white oppression.

HOW MUCH UNDERSTANDING
OF KNOWLEDGE DO YOU HAVE

The Creator of the Universe did not create chaos and capriciousness. He created everything in Divine Order. And everything that was created has a purpose. Another way to say the above is, "everything is in Divine Order." And everything was created with a purpose within the Order. Divine Order is also called the natural order. One of the primary ways to understand if something is correct or not, is to determine whether or not it is Natural. If it is natural, it is in the Divine some place.

The Honorable Elijah Muhammad was quoted as having said: *"If it is natural it is Islam; if it is Islam it is natural."*

The Natural Order is unchanging. It is like the truth. There is only one Truth about any particular thing, in any particular instance. Because you don't know, this doesn't change the fact that it is true. You just don't have all of it. Hopefully your perception of it will let you know that it is not natural. Of course you could be mistaken. And the perception that you do have is wrong. If your perception is not wrong and something seems out of order, an investigation is called for. And if your perception is wrong, but something seems to be out of order, an investigation is called for. My main point is that everything has a purpose. And when you don't see the purpose, it can be found if you investigate it properly. We all have a purpose for being birthed into this life. One of the keys to success is to find that purpose.

EVERYTHING HAS A PURPOSE

Unseen truth may be like our purpose in life. You may have it but do not recognize it. But not knowing your life purpose does not mean you don't have one. And like knowledge of the truth, if you look for your purpose in the right place you will find it. In fact it is called *Your True Purpose.* Your True Purpose is always with you but it is not found in your hands. It is found within your self.

Like I said if you look in the right place you will find your own true purpose. The right place is within your spiritual Self. If you don't know yourself you'll not find it. If you don't have correct knowledge of self, you may well act incorrectly.

It is possible to find, or be told correct knowledge about Self and still not understand self or purpose. This happens when you hear the truth but do not accept it as truth. This doesn't necessarily mean that something is wrong with your "hearing." It could simply mean you have not had sufficient information to make a judgment.

In an oppressive system – like the United States of America, many vital things for good physical and mental health are just the opposite of good. We all know the story of bleached white flower and sugar. This is a physical interference with the natural truth about sugar and flour. The most healthy nutrition in sugar and flour may be the colored ingredients [and we should all know that there is little or no nutritional value is food colorings). The good things about the product itself are the things white people bleach out to make it white. This is a physical example of interfering with something that is natural.

For a spiritual example we don't have to look very far in our lives. Many of us have overcome this example, but many of us are still not "fool proof."

The example is the fact that in an oppressive society, you may find yourself trusting your enemies but distrusting your friends. Our enemies are able to deceive us spiritually in the same way they take the good properties away from sugar. But in this case they will put something in the enemy that is attractive and appealing to your senses. He or she may look much better than the friend. Never mind, your friend will have done many intangible things that made he or she your friend. When you are attractive to someone it is easier to deceive them.

Like I said, your understanding of knowledge of a thing determines the degree of wisdom you'll have to relate to the object. You must study it. It is NOT different when you want to find out things about self. If you want to know your purpose, study what knowledge you already have about self.

When you study correct knowledge of self, you will find you were created for a purpose. Since you still may not understand your purpose, what you know about self will be either incorrect or you will not be accepting the truth of the matter of who you are. If you feel you were created for a purpose that you don't understand, when you "seek you shall find."

You must consult with the True Creator. Since He created you, surely He knows all about you, your purpose and what you must do to fulfill the purpose. The imperative here is that it is truly The Creator that you consult.

THE TRUE CREATOR

If you don't know it, your situation is exactly like your purpose and the truth. Not knowing who The True Creator is will not change Him in the least. He is Unchanging; the truth is Unchanging; and your true Purpose is also unchanging.

If you are looking for help in the wrong places you will never find the Creator. If you are looking for your Purpose in the wrong place you will never find your purpose. If you are looking for your True Self in the wrong place, guess what? You will not find out who you are.

Since everything was created in Divine Order, why do you not naturally know Who The True Creator is? Why don't you know your True Self or your True Purpose? You would know if your self image had not been interfered with.

In further answer to the question about where The Creator is, He is always with you. You don't see Him but he surely sees us. It is a tremendous help to us in our work when we are reminded, or remember this fact: in every situation and condition wherein we find ourselves. The God is always there. The Creator is much like your limbs. You are not always conscious that you have two thumbs. But when you have need of your largest, most versatile finger it will be there.

So in answer to your question, which is really my own, wisdom from my understanding of what I know is that a portion of my Creator is Within me. This knowledge is based on the fact that I was created from His Essence.

I also study the knowledge that I have of His Essence. When I use the wisdom from my understanding of The Creator, wisdom tells me that my character is such I can make things in similitude to the created universe.

This is great, but I'll keep studying and carrying out my duties and responsibilities. My understanding is such that I am convinced that doing so is very pleasing to Allah. And when He is pleased, it is at this point that miracles happen!

THE SUPPRESSION OF OUR TRUE SELF

The suppression of our true self by an outside force caused us to forget The Creator and knowledge of our True Self. Why the outside force was allowed to suppress the body and cause us to have a distorted perception of reality is one of the mysteries of life. The best estimate I have concluded about why this is so is to give us a challenge to overcome to develop our character to be like The Characteristics of our Creator. Another name for characteristics, as used here is the Attributes of The God.*

I will venture to say that nobody knows for certain why the outside force (soon I will begin to call that outside force by its proper name, just as I am beginning to refer to the Internal Force by a proper name*) was allowed to deceive the world – giving its inhabitants a false perception of it. But first we want to continue our quest to share with the reader a view of how the person manifesting self in an earth body comes to see that true knowledge of self, Creator and devil is found within. But before we leave this, let us be very clear. The devil has no power to change our true self.

He can only deceive us into thinking that his false or partial truth is all there is. When the deception doesn't work, he uses fear and he will brutalize us into doing his bidding. Later on you will see "there is nothing to fear." As it is with the tools of the devil, fear is only apparent. It only stands when courage is absent.

As we end this portion I want you to repeat six (6) times in an increasingly sincere tone of voice that *"there is nothing to fear!" There is nothing to fear! There is nothing to fear! There is nothing to fear! There is nothing to fear! There is nothing to fear!*

If you really say the words with *feeling;* (you may want to repeat it daily for awhile – in front of a mirror). This creates a kind of shield against all false notions that come around you. I have already shared in many different words that two forces are constantly challenging you.

But I wouldn't actually try to consciously use the 'shield' until you have read my suggestion as to how it may best be used. But if you must use it immediately, please study carefully the thing that you want to use it against. Get all of the knowledge you can about it - understand it. Once you understand it, then use the wisdom from the understanding to deploy your shield. That's all.

THERE IS NOTHING TO FEAR

Knowing "there is nothing to fear" is a great thing to know. You must study this knowledge for understanding. In a fast paced world you may be someone that thinks they don't have time to study. But remember if you don't study for understanding your wisdom will only be what you get from the knowledge. Understanding will increase your wisdom. If you don't have time to get more wisdom you'll only be able to overcome the challenge to the degree that you do.

TRUE SELF AS WELL AS
THE CREATOR IS FOUND WITHIN

If it appears I am repeating myself, you may be right in one sense. But in the other sense, you may see that I may be using the same words to make slight or greater points.

When you do realize that your True Self as well as the Creator is found within, you must accept the fact then study it for understanding. When we say "study it," we are not talking about study something that you have to look for outside of your own self. We are saying study what you already know about God, and your own self. These things are not nearly as complicated as it may appear. Studying what you already know will no doubt lead you to seeking information that will be found outside yourself. That is ok. When you study, you are simply trying to get a better understanding about the Creator and self.

From the understanding of your True Purpose other good things will be unveiled to you. The good things include wisdom to achieve your purpose. You will gain the wisdom about how to deal effectively with outside forces. Before you study you may have the false idea that what you see is all there is to life. The false perception may also have led you to thinking that what is manifested is all there is to life. The purpose of the devils work is based upon this false perception.

You have been advised that all things are created in Divine Order. The false notions of the devil will prevent you from seeing it. But there are many ways to find the truth. It all begins with the study of what you already know. When you get an understanding, it does not matter how much or how little, ways and means to find more will be unveiled. Let's discuss some of the ways that will be unveiled.

WAYS TO FIND GREATER TRUTHS

We must find and accept correct knowledge about self and The Creator. For Black people, this used to be **problem number two** within white oppression. After you begin to study you will come to see the knowledge we had about ourselves was incorrect; so that which we did know about ourselves, our Creator and our kind was also incorrect. Moreover, you'll also find the correct knowledge about self and kind was stolen.

The crime to steal the correct knowledge was committed by white people. They stole it as part of their methodology to oppress/enslave Black people. White people suppressed the vital information about Black self, kind and The Creator. The suppression allowed them to oppress Black people. I say lack of knowledge of self used to be problem number two, because fortunately, "we once were lost but now we are found." This leads to problem number one, we may get to it in detail, but now suffice it to state that **Problem number one** is getting Black people to accept the what was found. But for now, we will complete our discussion about the processes that are attendant to problem number two: INCORRECT KNOWLEDGE.

When knowledge about a problem is incorrect, any answer based on the knowledge will be incorrect. If knowledge about self is incorrect, anything you think you know about self and your Creator will be incorrect. You cannot get correct answers to the questions of who you are, where you are from or your purpose when the knowledge you are basing it on has been tampered with by The Oppressor. If the knowledge you have is incorrect, of course you will have incorrect answers to the questions.

Incorrect knowledge cascades. And will negatively impact on the wisdom to do anything about a particular problem. Since the wisdom that you use will come from your understanding of incorrect or incomplete knowledge. At best, your understanding will only confuse you: so when you act, you will act in a confused manner.

At worse your understanding will be so confused that you will do nothing. And this is exactly what many Black people do. Nothing. And when they do nothing it is a slam dunk for the oppressor. But when the people have understanding of correct knowledge, the wisdom they use to act will wipe out the problem. With wisdom applied to the understanding of correct knowledge about white oppression, white oppression, as well as the defender of white oppression will be smashed.

USING CORRECT KNOWLEDGE
TO OVERCOME LIFE CHALLENGES

Just a little more about internal, or spiritual ways to overcome outside challenges. When correct knowledge is known to you, you must then study to get a good understanding of it. It is not enough to just know about self and The True Creator. You must study to understand Self, the oppressor and The Creator. Wisdom from understanding correct knowledge is undefeated in the world.

IT IS NATURAL TO WANT TO KNOW WHO YOU ARE

As we said, the desire to know who you are is natural and fundamental. This is a spiritual quest. You must go into your mind to really get knowledge of self. Someone else may tell you where you are from, what race you are and many other things about you. But even if they are well meaning and really know you, at best they can only tell you correct knowledge. You still must study the well "meaning knowledge" yourself.

So your job is not over when you find proper knowledge of self, but it is the place where you must start; it is at the place where you get an understanding of the 'work' *that job requires.*

When you study proper knowledge of self, you will soon find the need to know who your Creator is. In your search for The Creator, you will see an energy that is challenging your efforts to know your Creator and Self. This is the energy of the devil. Power is necessary to defeat the devil. Knowing you are being challenged is also knowledge that you need. Remember,

"Knowledge is Power."

Understanding knowledge gives you the wisdom to use the power.

Power is necessary to overcome challenges to our acting in the best interest of self and kind. When you act in the best interest of self and kind, you will be acting to fulfill at least part of the purpose for which you were created. But someone must tell you the Truth about internal and exterior forces. Or you can find out the hard way. The hard way is "the school of hard knocks." The school of hard knocks is when you learn by making mistakes rather than learning from what someone tells you. Or learn from the mistakes of other people.

LEARNED MEN AND WOMEN GUIDE OTHERS TO AVOID ERRORS AND MISTAKES - RESTRAIN FROM EXCESSES

In essence all learned men and women of the Creator teach correct knowledge. They are mere human beings, but some way, some how they have tapped the Creative energy of the unseen. What they practice to 'tap' the Unseen to receive "revelations," it appears, is received with a duty and responsibility to share it with their fellow beings. And one way or the other this is what they do. As opposed to "the school of hard knocks," the easy way is to learn from learned masters. Or learn from anyone who already has a degree of what you are trying to learn.

Learned men and women live out their lives on earth as mere humans, but sharing the revelations they receive is a duty and responsibility. Many set up human made orders (organized instructions called rituals) on earth to share ways and means that other humans who accept and practice what they teach will follow to connect to the True Creator

I don't know how to introduce an example of one of these Great Teachers, or prophets without turning some of my readers off. The devils perception of The Honorable Elijah Muhammad is such that in the mere mention of his name, devils image of the man comes to mind. [I will pause at this point and advise the reader of what follows. If you don't want to read any of "the black Muslim stuff" you can go directly to the next section

I understand that some of my readers do not prefer that I use Mr. Muhammad as an example to illustrate my next points. I understand. And I hope you understand that it is necessary for me to tell the truth about the Learned Master who had the most influence on my ways to find knowledge of self, The Creator and the devil]

ELIJAH MUHAMMMAD, BLACK MUSLIMS AND THE NATION OF ISLAM

Mr. Muhammad was one of the great teachers we described above. His basic teaching gave us Proper knowledge of self and a Proper name for the Creator (Allah). He gave us the true knowledge of ourselves (we are original beings that are created of the substance of our Creator). And Mr. Muhammad gave us the true knowledge of the force that had deceived us. We were deceived by the devil.

Like learned men and prophets before him, Mr. Muhammad not only gave us the proper knowledge of The Creator and a good name to call Him; he also imparted a certain teaching that is designed to connect you to the Source of The Creation. This is the order that I said "Learned men and women establish to guide and "yoke" you to the Source of the creation. He based his order (organization) on a dictum of five little words, "do for self and kind." The order he established, or re-constituted is called the Nation of Islam.

Also like others before him, Mr. Muhammad's job was finished after he delivered the message. When you hear him or about him it is your job to study The Message that he delivered. He told us about the benefits that are promised if you "hold to forgiveness, command what is right, but turn away from the ignorant." (Holy Qur'an) He said you would have "money, good homes and friendship in all walks of life if you follow his teaching." The things his message promised are things that motivated millions of humans to use the Message of Elijah Muhammad to find True Knowledge of self. Within the Message is also instruction about how to use the Knowledge to achieve success in life. The instructions are based on the understanding of the Knowledge. This understanding is where he received the wisdom to guide others.

Self and Kind and everything else in existence was created by Allah. It is important that you know by now that Allah, the word God in Arabic, Jehovah and other good names in other languages are names for the Creator of all. That is if they are referring to the Creator of everything.

CORRECT KNOWLEDGE: NOTHING CREATED WITHOUT MEANING AND PURPOSE

Nothing was created without a purpose. Since Allah is The Creator and He is Divine. When we are acting in the best interest of self and kind we are acting divinely. Everything is created in a particular order. The order is Divine and it is governed by a Universal Law. We use the Law to overcome challenges to act divinely. When you know there is a law that governs a particular thing, you can study the law and this will help you to understand what is in order and what is not in order. This is what the scientist does: he or she takes what is known about the law and they study it. From the study comes understanding. From the understanding comes wisdom. The wisdom is used to make rules to govern society. This is the correct way to establish a particular social order. The social order could be a nation. It could be a family. Or it could be the individual.

     We shall not go into the dissection of social orders at this time. That is except to point out that the white supremacist social order called the United States of America was established in violation of some particular Universal Laws from the beginning. The most important of the violations was the inclusion of Black humans as chattel property. The basic work of those who serve in the liberation struggle of Black people is to correct the violation and bring Black people back into the divine order of the creation.

Chapter Eleven

THE STRUGGLE IS TO OVERCOME CHALLENGES

The struggle is to overcome disorder, get in and stay in Divine Order. This is true in regard to race and the individual. In this section we may refer to both interchangeably, but mostly the discussion will talk directly to the individual human. Just don't be confused because the application of Universal Law is in divine law that works to whatever degree in creation that it is used. Just remember, knowledge should be studied and understood for its correctness.

If you have incorrect knowledge about The Creator, you will have incorrect knowledge about the Divine Order of the Creation. So it stands to reason, it is impossible to get into Divine order if you try to use incorrect knowledge to get there. This is what the white supremacist Founding Fathers did to establish the United States of America. That is they purposely used incorrect knowledge to make rules (U. S. laws to govern the country). The rules are a vain attempt to support the injustice that was there from the beginning. However, now that Black people, and all people, have knowledge of this fact, we work to correct it. Remember that "Knowledge is Power."

Having the knowledge does not mean you are in Divine order. But understanding of the knowledge will give you the wisdom to apply the knowledge/power to overcome challenges to get there. And how to stay there; or get back in order when you go out of order while living within the confines of white supremacy society.

When we understand Correct knowledge it unveils the fact that the best way to get into Divine Order is to accept good and reject evil. The study of correct knowledge will also help with decisions in this regard. The wisdom derived will help you to stay there while living out your purpose on earth.

We are created beings so we were created in Divine Order. When you study Correct Knowledge, you will not only understand why you are not, but the wisdom will be yours to get back into Divine Order. This is using the knowledge/power.

When you do anything in Divine Order you are most pleasing to the Creator. And there is a great benefit we derive when we please our Creator. The benefits are called Blessings. We cannot possibly count all of our Blessings. But our greatest Blessing is the Mercy of Allah when we "make a mistake, go into error or commit excesses in our affairs."

When we do these things we are also NOT in Divine Order. Only by the mercy of Allah are we given another chance to get into Divine Order.

DIVINE ORDER IS A STATE OF PEACE: PSYCHIC POWER IS WITHIN THE PEACE

To many the greatest Blessing is the state of Peace that you experience when you ARE in Divine Order. There is a particular kind of power that is available for use against our challenges in life when we are in Divine Order. That power is called psychic Power.

Psychic Power is Power of the spirit. If your spirit is correct it is in divine order. With your spirit in divine order you are actually connected to the power of the entire creation. For this means that everything that your spirit does is in harmony with the other entities in creation.

When you are in divine order, you are in the order that you were created in. If you could stay there you would never lose. With Allah on your side you will never lose. He is on your side when you act as He would, speak as He would and think, etc. as He would each time that we execute our will. When you execute your will [power], you are putting it to work. The stronger your will the stronger your power. We want badly to substitute the word DESIRE in place of the word will. But there is a slight difference in the two words.

But let me see, let me understand more of my own knowledge about both words. It doesn't take long since I already have a great deal of understanding about both [please don't miss this example I am sharing]:

DESIRE is what precipitates the individual WILL in this life. Will is the part of your spirit that you consciously use to contact the unseen.

The manifestation for what you desire will be dependent on the power of your will to convince your spirit that this is what you really want. DESIRE is the aspect that you use to convince, so to speak, your spirit. So "be careful of what you desire, you may get it."

HOW TO CONSCIOUSLY INCREASE YOUR WILL POWER

There are some things that you can do consciously to increase your will power. Here again, I will refer you to my book called *"Melanin, Conscious Attunement and The God In I."* I am not going to offer any of the explicit exercises that book shares to increase your will power here. And this is not to induce you to get the book. Rather, I want you to reflect on the knowledge that you already have about Will Power, Desire and the Unseen. There are some exercises in the book that will help you to increase your Will Power.

When you have the three of them in Harmony the demonstration of what you want in life will be according to how much you believe. Remember, the usefulness of what you desire in life will be dependent on it's harmony to the Divine Order.

You may get what you desire but what use will it be; how long will it last; and how beneficial is it to your fellow humans. Is it instructive or destructive to the Natural Order. Prayer, Meditation and other things that are done to connect to the unseen will increase your will power and your ability to use the power instructively. Prayer and Meditation will help you to accept what is right and reject wrong – as you are using the power.

We leave this discussion to share some thoughts about raising our children,

Chapter Twelve

RAISING CHILDREN THE NATURAL WAY SHOULD BE TAUGHT IN THEIR YOUTH

I hope you understand why it is difficult in an oppressed society to see the natural order of things. Your degree of understanding will determine the wisdom of not only how you conduct your own life while living in oppression; but it will also determine what you teach your own children while living in oppression.

Your children should be told that there is a right way to do everything. The right way is the natural way and this is the way you should strive, or intend to do things in the beginning of any endeavor.

As the child grows, he or she will be told about things that are going on outside of themselves. Many of us now feel that it may be at this juncture that our children are either awakened to the truth; or the notion that what he sees is the way things are supposed to be.

The determining factor will be how the parents are living their own lives. To the extent they are living in the Divine Order, the child will see this as the way to go.

However, if you are living like you understand the natural order has been interfered with, or covered up (more appropriate term) this will also be expression of the child. He will soon see that you are living in contradiction to the prevailing order. They will grow up with the understanding this is the way to live. Of course the 'contradiction' to the prevailing order (the white supremacist order) will be a challenge for them at some point, as it was to us, but it is best to have the opportunity to answer the questions about both than for the child to grow thinking that the norm is the white supremacist order. Do not try to avoid the questions that your child is bound to ask. Be happy if he give you a chance to answer his questions. The pervasiveness of white supremacy will always be there. It is for this reason (exposure to white supremacy living in America) trying to live as you live without question will last only for a period of time for a child.

While the child is trying to duplicate your life is the time that you can point out why you are not living like everybody else. Hopefully by now he is so enamored by your way that those who are living out of order will not be that much of a temptation to him. If you don't have any success in your life to show, it compounds the problem.

Another thing that will cause him to question and then eventually forsake your way, at least for awhile is seeing few others who are living as you live. There are many things you can tell him, or her to balance the pervasiveness of white supremacy society.

You can tell him that in order for the oppressor to establish an oppressive society, he DOES have some vital things about the natural way, but he will misuse them. We must tell this to our children. And when an example of the misuse is available, we must show it to our children.

Tell them about the need to establish a righteous society; and such a society is necessary to reclaim the things that were stolen and hidden from you. Let the child know on no uncertain terms that what has been taken must be returned.

In the growth stages of our youth, the things that are in order, parents and others around the child must share the facts. If you are living in an oppressed society, like the United States of America, you must share the fact that vital things in life are not in the natural order of how they would be if they were.

In an oppressed society, you must tell your youth which things are in their natural order and which are not. That is if you know yourself. If you don't know you can learn if you study. You can start with easy to understand things for your children; things that you can easily explain. Tell him the reason why white people are in charge of all public things in the American government – school, hospitals, and etc.

If you are a Black human in America the examples and object lessons about what is NOT in order are seemingly endless. Let's see if we can take a closer look at some.

We will start with the family when baby is born. We find lots of things out of natural order surrounding the baby. Each baby is conceived though the agency of a man and a woman. They are baby's mommy and daddy. This is natural. But too often daddy is not the case when baby is born. This is out of order. It is not in the Natural Order of the Creation for a baby to be born and the father is not present. Of course this information is for the man and woman. So if you are either parent, you can work to ensure that this unnatural fact is not there when your baby is born. But if you are a woman, and this is the situation when your baby is born, you'll not have to worry about this until years later. But the question is bound to come, when it does come be prepared to tell baby the truth, as much thereof as they can handle, at particular ages of their growth. If father is no where to be found, just tell baby that he went away.

If you are the father, you must double your effort to ensure that the mother of your child never have to tell him this – you should be in the life of your child at all cost.

Let us take a closer look at when baby is born.

IN THE NATURAL ORDER DADDY IS PRESENT AT BABYS BIRTH

After baby is born, he or she is taken from the hospital to a home that has been planned for his arrival into the world. As we observe the natural habits of birds, the nest will have been constructed by both parents. The nest will be baby birds first home. But too often for Black humans, daddy hasn't had any involvement in the securing and maintaining of baby's first home. This is out of order.

The baby came through both parents. But mommy will naturally be the first teacher and primary care giver for the baby. This is in Order.

Baby's Daddy should naturally earn the things needed to secure, clothe, feed and shelter the baby and his mother. This is in Order.

There are many other things that are easy to teach about baby's early education that are out of order or woefully inadequate. This being the case, it is easily observed. It is also documented for those who need such.

It is advisable for the well being of the baby that only tell it things that are in order to him or her in the beginning. Most of this is the abundant love that mommy unconditionally have for baby. In the United States of America, for the most part, mommy is a single parent. Or Daddy's capacity in all aspects of parenthood is woefully inadequate or he is simply not there. This is out of Order.

Mommy will sacrifice things needed for self to provide for baby. This is natural and is in order. What is NOT in order is the lack of things needed that she simply does not have. This is not in order. If she is doing her part, the part that is causing the inadequacy is the absence of the father. Hopefully the father is at least maintaining a presence in baby's life. If he is, it is his responsibility to tell baby why he is not doing things needed for care of the baby. If this is not in the home, then Mommy must tell baby, but only at a certain age.

WHEN FATHER IS HOME AND THINGS STILL ARE NOT ENOUGH

As baby grows through stage after stage you can tell baby HOW things should be. You also tell him why things aren't as they should be. Then tell him or her what you are doing to make them right. If you are doing NOTHING, explain why you are not doing anything to correct it.

In an oppressed society, the stress must be on "how things are supposed to be." As opposed to the way things are. This is true for all humans living in "the system." I can get extremely racial at times. But most things in the beginning that a child needs to know about the natural order are non-racial. That is if you are teaching him or her about the way things are supposed to be.

The teaching moments about things racial come when he questions you about why things aren't how they are supposed to be for you and your kind. Then you tell them. You tell them the truth or suffer the consequences.

At this point I must point out again that I am a Black Man with 70 years of experience of living in an oppressed society. Once I was exposed to certain truths about the brutal nature of oppression I naturally wanted to know what I could do to lift the oppression from Black people.

I say this to let the reader know that I have studied the knowledge I have about oppression for about 40 of the sixty nine years. The sum totaled information that I am sharing in this book is the understanding I have of the knowledge; and the resulting wisdom that I got from the understanding. I am more spiritual in my outlook than physical. But the wisdom from my understanding causes me to try to harmonize the two forces.

You aim for balance and it will be there if you have studied and have a great deal of understanding about oppression as I have. But since there is such an imbalance between the oppressed and the oppressor in United States of American society, I can work the side of the balancing scale from the side of the oppressed and stay a long, very long way from the balance from where you want to begin to build a just society. And justice is what we all want.

Black people have the collective responsibility to do the work that is necessary to bring balance to the Black nation: but politically, economically, spiritually and all other social aspects find The Black Nation in North America imbalanced. This is the way it is. So we must accept the way it is, then identify the things that are causing the imbalance and go to work to take care of them – do the work necessary to bring them back into balance. This book is designed and written to help identify the necessary work and offer definite ways and means to bring balance back to the Black Nation. Power is needed to do the job.

WE ARE CREATED OF SPIRIT AND MATTER

We are created of Spirit and our body is made of matter. We will see later that they are one and the same – part and partial of the one being. But for the sake of clarity we will only refer to them by their distinguished characteristics: the spiritual body is unseen. The physical body is seen. Our spiritual body is unseen because it was created with properties that are unseen. These are spiritual properties that the Self uses to struggle against challenges unseen that impact the body. The power of the spiritual body is increased when its properties are exercised.

For example, when you exercise a property of the spiritual body called thought, it will become more powerful. One of the great things about increasing your spiritual powers is that, when you do, they can be used more consciously by the physical body in the world.

We also have a body that is made of matter. This body is called our material body. The material body can be seen. The properties of the seen body are used by Self to fight challenges that we see. The power is increased when the properties are exercised. For example, the property of the material body called muscle will get larger and stronger if it is exercised. And of course you are using spiritual powers to increase the building of the muscles. You can't see the muscles increase in size, but knowledge about what exercise does gives you the understanding that it will do job. Wisdom from the understanding aids you in determining what to do to exercise certain muscles and for how long.

Spiritual power is also called Psychic Power. Or power of the Spirit. Whatever it is called, it is the name for the power of the spirit body of human beings. We increase our psychic power when we engage the unseen forces. The unseen forces are used by the powers of your mind. The tool used by your mind is one of the properties called Thought. As I said, the Blessings that we receive from our Creator are unbounded, or uncountable. The ability to think is indispensable for using the spirit as well as the physical body. "Nothing is done without a thought."

PROPERTIES OF THE FORCES

Unseen forces can be good or not so good. The Blessings are ours when we use our power to do good deeds. Our physical Body is the part of Self that is constantly being challenged for good or bad. Your mind is made of properties you can use to overcome the challenges. The challenges are overcome when you consciously use them to do good deeds. Good deeds are properties that are generated by thought.

You are a Powerful human being when you know there is a Divine Order. Understanding this, you'll know there is a right way to do anything. The wisdom derived will cause you to think in a particular way. This is what you aim for in each decision that you make – acting, speaking or thinking the right way. Thinking the right way is the essential property of your mind.

I think you already know if you are still reading this book, there are two basic ways that the mind thinks. It thinks consciously and it things subconsciously. I have also written extensively about the divisions of the mind in my Melanin, Conscious Attunement book. Briefly, the subconscious mind is the action part of your mind. It receives things to act on from your conscious thinking.

I have also made the point, probably to distraction for many, that you can get your body to do absolutely nothing without a thought first. The thought that puts your physical body into action can be one of your own thoughts or the thought from the mind of someone else. Your subconscious mind can be trained, consciously, to screen out thoughts that you do not want acted on. Thought and action is part of a process that cannot be avoided if you want to be successful in life.

We talked about will power earlier. It is important because with the ever presence of any number of thoughts the subconscious mind has to decide instantly which to act on and which to store. Yes, it has been called a store house for good reason. It stores every thought that ever comes into your conscious mind. Fascinating I know, and it all can be scientifically understood. Your own desire is the determinant for which thought is acted on. So as I state in the Melanin, conscious Attunement book, "control you mind by thinking good positive conscious thoughts."

Today let yourself go
let the veil fall
see the Glory of Allah within us all*

EXTERNAL FORCE AND HOW WE DEAL WITH AND BALANCE THEM

Our second constant struggle is against external forces. The external forces confront our efforts to be successful in a material sense in life. To overcome external challenges we use physical power. Physical power is the power of your physical body. That is, it is the power of your muscles, and other properties of your physical body. We need Physical Power to overcome the challenges when physical force is used to hamper or contravene our potential as human beings.

Remember we said the forces are one and the same? As such you have the ability to use either to support efforts to overcome challenges, whether they are spiritual or physical. It may be confusing if I constantly remind the reader that the only reality is your Spiritual being. But the Spiritual being was created by The Divine Creator; and the Spiritual being made the physical body out of what was created. So the discussion will be in language that is commonly understood. It is commonly thought that when one says "I" or "me" they are talking about the Physical body. We can say they are wrong to think that way. But what I would like to add to such thinking is the fact that the physical body does the bidding of the body that made it. This is the Spiritual Body. The God, The Creator, Divine Spirit, Allah, etc. CREATED the Spiritual Body/being and everything else. The spiritual being that was created MADE the physical body. These facts are probably too intricate for many reading this book: so our language will, for the most part use commonly used terms to denote what we are discussing. But if you, the reader, do understand, don't put the understanding aside, but use the wisdom from the understanding to act on that fact. Or if you are already advanced in the so-called "spiritual language," you still may want to read this book for enjoyment. I know it is a pleasure for me to read the perspective about things I already know and have a degree of understanding about. Of course, if you have things to do; things to enact the wisdom you have already derived from understanding such knowledge, you'll not have the time to read about things that you already understand well enough to already be in action about.

However, I think how I am saying things, from the perspective that I am, will be of benefit for all who read what I am writing. Moreover, the oppression on black people is so pervasive and so late in the 'day' (2009) it is self evident we have not yet put the correct plan in motion. The correct plan will be a plan that is in harmony, rhythm and order with the Divine plan that governs the creation. We will now move on with some discussion about the common denominator of it all.

Chapter Thirteen

THOUGHT IS THE COMMON DENOMINATOR FOR HUMANS

Thought is the common denominator, whether you understand or accept the last paragraph or not. It must be deployed whether you have a physical or mental challenge to fight. This was brought out in the prior section. But we are going to constantly use the information about the powers of your mind: so you may want to review all of the previous information before you proceed. But if you have a good understanding or simply a "working understanding" of such knowledge, use the wisdom derived from that understanding then proceed.

Thought is the common denominator for humans because you can do nothing that is not preceded by a thought. The thought will be from you own mind, or from the mind of someone else. At this point, I feel I should review thought processes, but I am not of a mind to rewrite something that I have already written quite extensively about. So I will excerpt a portion from my book called, Melanin, *Conscious Attunement and the God In I.*

Worshipping sticks, stones or other material objects has limited benefits to one who believes it to be so. By thinking a thing has power, you exercise the power of Divinity within your own being. This is the power of thought. We know that thought has a certain power: "thinking makes it so." When you think something has power, this is actually what give it power – the power of your thought. We must accept thinking as the most direct way by which we can activate the Divinity within us.

PHYSICAL POWER – POSITIVE AND NEGATIVE FORCES –

We are stressing negative force as a challenge because we are discussing fighting against other entities that use them to contravene our human potential. But both negative and positive force can be used, and *are* used for good or bad effect.

Whether the struggle is internal or external, we are born with abundant amounts of the powers needed to overcome whatever challenges we face. Physical as well as Spiritual powers can be used negatively or positively to achieve the desired result. It is critical that one understands the consequence for either way it is used.

When they are purposely used negatively to achieve personal gain and the user knows it will cause harm to a fellow human, the user could be called a devil – depending on the history of the user and severity of the harm. Such a user, if not a devil is his representative.

Remember we said that the common name for the powers of the spirit is called Psychic Power. But for the sake of our discussion psychic power will be called Spiritual power. Psychic power is a particular kind of spiritual power. Saying "spiritual power" incorporates all power of the specific spiritual powers together. We may separate, and identify some particular or specialized use of these – maybe in this book.

All humans possess physical as well spiritual power. This is the reason we used the word *increase* when identifying what is needed to overcome challenges. We are born with both spiritual and physical powers. The Wonderful Thing is that both powers can be increased. To increase physical power you do physical exercises. To increase spiritual power you do spiritual exercises. Identify the muscle or energy center that supply the area of the bodies [spiritual and physical] and develop ways to exercise them. This is the great value of a good teacher. When you have a good teacher, he or she will give you exercises that will do the job that is unique to you and your evolvement.

Another Wonderful Thing is that both powers must be used together before you can use any of the properties necessary to engage them. For example, to use physical power you must think. Thinking is an unseen act but you must use a property of the physical body called the brain [brain power] to think.

When the powers are balanced, your Self, or Personhood is at its optimum – or most powerful. So when you act from balance, you are acting from your strongest point of power. In other words when the Physical and Spiritual Powers are balanced both are as powerful as they can be at that particular time. This is optimum power. But contrary to the belief of many, balance is not the result that we aim for, and I will tell you why after making my next point. And while making the point.

When the powers are not balanced, you may be trying to do something physical that your spirit does not agree with. Or you may be trying to do something spiritually that your physical body is not capable of doing, or in agreement with. But if you use them in harmony to each other, all will be well and you will accomplish what you will. When they are in harmony, they will be in 'agreement' with each other and all will be well. But they will NOT be balanced, and I will tell you why.

HARMONY AND BALANCE ARE TWO DIFFERENT STATES OF BEING.

When the spirit and the physical bodies are balanced, they are equal. When they are in harmony, they may not they be balanced, but they are in agreement with each other. In fact harmony is where music and beauty comes from. The different musical notes on the scale are in harmony to each other – creating one melodious sound. In beauty the colors are blended together to create one harmonious picture, where the parts of the picture compliment each other. The beauty gained through the harmony between the contrast of the colors. They may be balanced in the sense that you have equal kinds of flowers. But harmony is created by the contrast of different flowers.

THE TRUE VALUE OF BALANCE

We don't intend for the above to indicate in any way a discrediting of balance. Whenever possible, we should act to achieve balance in all that we do. This is not possible, but should be our aim. Since balance is when we are at the optimum of power, it is from balance that you should want to act. Act, then go back to balance.

Once you reach the balancing of the physical and spirit, your optimum power, you will want to use that great power to achieve something. ***Free Black people!***

To me, this is the most noble of all physical acts in the use of balanced power. The oppression of Black people is a physical state within a doctrine of white supremacy. The oppression of white supremacist doctrine is enforced by laws that have physical consequences. To break free of the oppression the laws must be abolished, disobeyed or cease to be the man-made law which governs your sociological being. Ideally, if you want to abolish, or destroy oppression, you will act physical by striking out to kill the oppressor and abolish his unjust rules. This may well be what will be required. So let's take a closer look at what it will take to have any chance to succeed. Keep in mind this is the traditional way to free a people from abject slavery and oppression.

But if you don't have enough physical power to achieve the desired result, your act will not be in a harmonious way. You still may want to enact your plan, but the consequences for not having enough physical power to achieve the result must be paid.

Remember, we have already spoken about the fact that any time that you use power there will be consequences. So getting understanding will beget wisdom you can use to deal with the consequences for having tried to free Black people with an imbalanced act. Black people have tried untold thousands of time to do it this way. And I dare say there has never been one physical act carried out against our oppressors that did not have a good benefit for the progression to Freedom Day.

I am not saying don't physically attack our enemies. I am not saying that. Each individual will have to decide on his or her own methodology. So I am also not saying DON'T exact a physical action against oppression. What I am saying, whatever you decide to use your powers is that it be done in your own best interest; and then ONLY AFTER YOU HAVE understood to the utmost degree what your act portends to self, family and race. The understanding will give you the wisdom to Plan, Plan, Plan and Plan. For without a doubt, if you are of this disposition you are a very valuable human, with much you can give to deliver our people. It is quite likely you will be more valuable to help awaken others – especially before you carry out any act that may mean giving up your life for some ill defined goal.

DISAGREEMENTS BETWEEN OUR SPIRIT AND PHYSICAL BEING: CONSEQUENCES

If your spirit doesn't agree with what you are using power to do, you may achieve it but the spirit of the thing will not be as spiritually healthy. Same if you are trying to do something physical that your body is incapable of doing. You will do it spiritually, but it will not be right physically because you may not be strong enough to do the job.

Whenever you decide to do anything, try to do the thing so that your spirit agrees with what you are doing. And be careful about trying to do things that your physical body is incapable of, for the way you may be trying to use the body.

Most times where the spirit and the physical are not in agreement, is when either is being used in ways it is not capable of achieving what you are trying to do. This causes disharmony, rather than harmony. The "disharmony" is the negative and the harmony is the positive. I hope you still see the possibility where either could still be used effectively to achieve a good result. Whatever we do from balanced positions, afterwards we should try to get back to a balanced state.

WHY BALANCE IS NOT THE END GAME

There is nothing wrong with balance. And if that is what you want, get the balance and use it as balance is used. I mean it is good to enjoy being balanced for awhile. To be clear about what we mean by balance, for the sake of this discussion, we are talking about balancing your spirit with your material body.

If you are using physical force that is not balanced, or in harmony with your spiritual power, the spiritual part of self suffers. If you are using spiritual force that is not balanced, or in harmony with your physical power, you suffer.

But when the physical and the spiritual are balanced all is well. When the physical and the spiritual are in Harmony you are in a state of peace!

Now you may be wondering why you are not in a state of peace when they are just simply balanced? Why must they also be in Harmony before you attain to the desired state of peace?

When they are in balance that is great. But when they are balanced, theoretically, neither is being used. The moment that you begin to use your spiritual or physical power the balance is thrown off. If this is not clear, just think about it for a moment before you proceed.

* * *

When your spiritual and physical bodies are in balance, you are powerful. And you may be at peace. But you will not have peace for long because in this life we are here to achieve good purposes. Your spirit is not going to be at peace unless you are working to overcome the challenges necessary to achieve your purpose. We have already discussed purposes and how to obtain them. When you are using the powers in harmony with your physical body to achieve the purpose, "it feels good all over." This good feeling is the harmony created when the moves you make are in agreement with each other.

Peace is your state of mind when the Internal and External powers are in Harmony. This peace is slightly different than the peace you have when things are balanced but are not being used. They are in harmony when either is used to do good deeds. If either is used to do bad deeds the other will not be in harmony with it. In life there a dictum that will do us all well: That is the acceptance of good and the rejection of evil.

If you are using physical force that is not balanced, or not in harmony with your spiritual power, the spiritual part of self suffers. If you are using spiritual force that is not balanced, or not in harmony with your physical power, you suffer.

But when the physical and the spiritual are balanced all is well. When the physical and the spiritual are in Harmony you are in a state of peace!

Now you may be wondering why you are not in a state of peace when they are just simply balanced? Why must they also be in Harmony before you attain to the desired state of peace?

When they are in balance that is great. But when they are balanced, theoretically, neither is being used. The moment that you begin to use your spiritual or physical power the balance is thrown off. If this is not clear, just think about it for a moment before you proceed.

* * *

When your spiritual and physical bodies are in balance, you are powerful. And you may be at peace. But you will not have peace for long because in this life we are here to achieve good purposes. Your spirit is not going to be at peace unless you are working to overcome the challenges necessary to achieve your purpose. We have already discussed purposes and how to obtain them. When you are using the powers in harmony with your physical body to achieve the purpose, "it feels good all over." This good feeling is the harmony created when the moves you make are in agreement with each other. Peace is your state of mind when the Internal and External powers are in Harmony. This peace is slightly different than the peace you have when things are balanced but are not being used. They are in harmony when either is used to do good deeds. If either is used to do bad deeds the other will not be in harmony with it. In life there a dictum that will do us all well: That is *the acceptance of good and the rejection of evil.*

The last part of the above was repeated accidentally. I decided to leave it here for its repetitive value.

Chapter Fourteen

THE FIRST LAW OF NATURE:
YOUR FIRST STRUGGLE

The first fight is always to overcome forces from within your own self. Good and the not-so-good, or evil, is built into the human being. In short, the struggle is to "accept the good and reject the evil."

Self preservation is the first law of nature. We need power to achieve what is best to preserve self. We also need power to help our fellow man. Unfortunately, many are confused about what is best for self. *And the ways and means that are allowed to do for self without infringing on our fellow men and women.*

Some think that doing for *others* at the expense of self is what you are supposed to do. Others think that doing for *self* at the expense of others is what you are supposed to do. Still others think that doing neither is what you should do. Then there is the question about how much you should do for self when others are in need. Or how much you should do for others when self is in need. Or, God forbid, thinking that you are not to do anything because The Creator will take care of everyone's need.

CLEARING UP SOME OF THE QUESTIONS

We are going to share ways to clear up some of the questions above. Some individuals know what is best for self, but have problems overcoming challenges to identify and do what is best. It should never be a problem to know what is best for self and kind. When it is, the problem should be in deciding when and whether you should neglect self and do for others. When you have a problem knowing what is best for you it is because you have not settled on a life purpose.

The problem of whether and when may be because of an outside motivation (where you are forced to act against your own best interest). Or you may just decide that you'd like to have what is best for you done on behalf of someone else. In either case, ultimately, you have decided to do what is best for yourself: Your own Self Interest.

But it is a problem when you are forced not to act in your own best interest - no one likes to be forced to do anything against their will. When the *something* is done on behalf of someone else in need could also be a problem because you may need the 'something' yourself.

If you are forced NOT to do what is best for self because someone causes you to fear what may happen to you if you do, that is a criminal act against you. It may still be best for you to do the bidding of the criminal. Of course there will be consequences for the one who forces you not to do for self. And there will be consequences for you also.

We will discuss this eventuality later. But what the criminal person is doing is using a negative means to achieve an end result for the moment. The victim is following a rule of self preservation. His intention in doing what is not in his best interest is to avoid the consequences that the criminal threat uses that cause him to not act in his own best interest.

Some think that the end justify the means. This is not so. It is ok to look out for self by obeying the first law of nature (self preservation). But you must do so without infringing on the rights of your fellow men or women. This is a serious challenge that we all must devote much effort to defeat. It is a challenge we can only overcome correctly when the psychic and physical powers are used in harmony. In the case above where force is used to stop a person from doing what is best for self, self preservation is still the rule of thumb. But peace and harmony will only be achieved if your intention is to act contrary to your self interest until a future time when you will rectify the injustice. The future justice may not necessarily be to avenge the crime, but the intention must be to bring justice to the situation.

How does one know when he is doing it correctly? Wisdom. You must study what you already know about the challenge or problem and look for the right way to overcome it.

In the case of a crime against your personhood, you study the severity of the crime; you study the intention of the criminal; and you study the strength of the criminal. But most importantly, you study your own strength. The idea in all that you do is to be successful doing it. We must be careful that our success does not come at the expense of others. Just keep in mind your own preservation in your decisions about what to do with or to a criminal that force you not to use your own power in your own best interest.

WRITING TO EMPOWER OTHERS

I am writing this book to empower the individual: so the first thought is to give suggestions that place the onus to act to achieve success on the individual. As righteous striving individuals, we understand it is not wise to use criminal means to be successful. This is because, as we will show later, "what goes around does, indeed come around." Normally it is criminal when you infringe on the rights of others to achieve your own success. And that infringement must be rectified at some future time. It will be rectified peacefully, by yourself, if you atone and make amends. Or by the victim of your infringement when he or she acquires the means to apply justice to your criminal/infrnged act against them. Justice is based on balancing severity of the infringement, or crime.

There are many ways to determine whether or not you are infringing on the rights of others in your words, acts and deeds. The severities of the infringements are given names that indicate the seriousness: crime of misdemeanor, felony, malfeasance & etc.

You can experience or study the knowledge of particular instances of criminals, and their crimes, and learn from their mistakes. You can also take the advice of someone regarding the particular instance about what you may be contemplating. Either discuss your idea with them before you act, or, if you know their point of view already, let their way guide you. Just try to assure yourself that the guidance used is to practice goodness.

When you study your knowledge of the situation and come to understand, the wisdom from the understanding will guide your actions. Just be of a mind to do good. In other words, wisdom will guide your good intentions.

If you decide to use the guidance you receive from another individual. Assure yourself that the person who advises you is a good person. If he or she is not a good person, their advice may still be good, but you must look out for what they expect in return for the advice. Also, if you make an error, make a mistake or indulge in excess, however good your intentions, these too must be rectified. If you do error, make a mistake or indulge in more than necessary to balance the scale of injustice, find a way to atone before you are compelled to; or before your guilty conscious beats you up about your ill behavior.

You can find a way to atone wisely by studying whatever knowledge you may have about the fact that caused your act in error & etc. The understanding you get from study will help you to act wisely to admit and atone for any wrong doing.

INJUSTICE COMMITTED AGAINST
SELF IS ALSO OUT OF ORDER

Many good people who may be on the path, but who have not attained to a certain degree of mastery, may think that the only way one can commit an unjust act is against others. This is not so. We can also commit unjust acts against self [it will get deeper than the point we are making, but any infringement or crime is ultimately against self. This too may be dealt with. Maybe in this book: keep reading].

WHEN ARE WE UNJUST TO SELVES?

One can be accused of being unjust to self when they commit acts against their own self interest. This is against the natural order of the creation. One of the forces that will always cause this problem is when you have not used your spiritual powers in harmony with the physical.

Understanding of any situation will give you the wisdom to act in your own interest. When you do not, intentionally or unintentionally, the repercussions will be against self.

What are the reasons we do things against our own best interest? As we said above, fear of bodily harm can motivate one to do something against his own best interest. This is the means by which Black people became captives and enslaved to white people.

White people, essentially, bred fear into the Black race. Many of the processes used to do this job on Black people are well known - and documented.

For the sake of our discussion we will use only one of the many physical, brutal examples about how white people forced us to act against the best interest of self and kind. There is a "small mountain of knowledge" about the captivity we can study to understand other ways fear was inbred into Black people. Once we obtain a certain degree of understanding of the knowledge, the wisdom from the understanding will be used to throw off the oppression. This is generalizing it to the race. But understanding knowledge works just as readily for the individual man or woman.

Whether you concentrate on the removal of fear from self; or self and kind, you must get degrees of understanding about what it is you may fear. Understanding of fear will predicate your wisdom to deal with fear.

Fear evokes such a powerful emotion, wisdom will not only guide your desire to remove it, wisdom will also guide your desire to utilize the power in the emotion to turn it back to the fear monger. The example we shall use is that of a man who was so successful in mastering fear, he used his mastery to induce fellow chattel captives to overcome their own. Together they wisely used the derived energy to strike a mighty blow against white oppressors back on August 21, 1831.

THE REVOLT OF NAT TURNER AND THE BLACK LIBERATIION ARMY IN 1831

We talked earlier about Nat Turner. After he found his purpose for this life he studied what he knew of it. He got an understanding of the purpose and the wisdom of that, told him the nature of a way he could act to overcome the challenges to fulfill that purpose.

We will use the example of Nat Turner several times in this book. He is one of Black America's all time great heroes. He is especially revered by Black people, but the purpose that he set out to fulfill was so astounding and successful, his act against injustice is admired by freedom loving people all over our planet.

Since it was a physical act that was driven by his spirituality, Nat Turner overcame the white inbred fear. He also motivated an army of chattel slaves to overcome their fear to work to achieve a common objective. That is to free every Black human confined in captivity to white people in the United States of America.

We will look at how Nat Turner came to know his purpose; we will take a brief look at how he managed to harmonize his physical and spirit during the planning to achieve his purpose; and we will look at the balance he reached before he and the BLA acted. We will then examine how and why he decided to create an imbalance between spirit and physical.

As we know, or will find out, Nat Turner necessarily caused the imbalance of his spirit and physical self when he induced the visitation of some of the most brutal, devastating acts against chattel slavery, second-class citizenship, and other forms of oppression in the history of the world.

Nat Turner killed at least one, and gave the orders that resulted in the slaying of documented, as well as undocumented numbers of others. Nevertheless, when he went to this physical dimension, it created an imbalance to his spiritual and physical being. But the ability to maintain harmony between them allowed for profound success in achieving his purpose.

When he created the imbalance between the two by killing his so-called master it was made in the name of justice. We will also take a look at, even in attempting to free his Black people, he was mindful to keep the physical and spiritual selves in harmony to each other. But once he struck his sword against the head of Travis, the white person who held ownership papers on him: *was the imbalance between the physical and the spirit caused then?* Or was the fact Travis held ownership papers on Nat Turner unjust to the point that losing his life did not create an imbalance?

We will also look at the attempt to keep his acts in harmony, even as he agonized about having to do "the work of death."

THE WORK OF DEATH OF SLAVEHOLDERS: IN HARMONY OR IMBALANCED?

The story about Nat Turner may be too distracting for many readers. You may skip this portion if you don't want to read this example of how a black man overcame his own fear, induced others to overcome theirs and motivated them to rise up and kill their oppressors. It is a bloody story.

I realize it is a graphic example that white people, as well as some black people would prefer not be used. Nevertheless, I must record these words, using the examples that I believe will be more meaningful to the Black Youth of America. It is known for certain that the Black Liberation Army that Nat Turner organized was made up of Black Youth. It is also universally felt that the revolt by Nat Turner was a positive act to end chattel slavery in the United States of America: also the planning and leading of the revolt was a positive act by Black youth. Nat

Turner was only 30 years old at the time of the revolt in August of 1831.

It is also universally felt that Black Youth are particularly brutalized in the year 2009. The story about the Black youth who marched with Nat Turner may well be an inspiration to them to study the knowledge of Nat Turner. The wisdom from understanding that knowledge will give them some wise methods to act positively against white oppression today.

Without a doubt, I know that the spiritual message in my book will be useful for those who read it. By using the physical acts by Nat Turner with what we know about his spirituality, gives us a good example about how one Blackman harmonized the two.

I hope it is obvious that if the challenge against you is physical, at some point, you will have to take a physical act against it. But you must be mindful of the spiritual as well as the physical. Nat Turner was mindful. He balanced the spiritual and the physical before he acted.

Like achieving balance in anything, it will only last until you act spiritually or physical. The aim when you act is that you act in the harmony between the two. Let us take a look at the acts of Nat Turner to see how well he did.

Chapter Fifteen

NAT TURNER AS A POSITIVE EXAMPLE FOR EVERYONE

We will look at a well known, but little publicized example of how the fear that was instilled in a captive Black man in 1831 was overcome to strike a mighty blow against chattel slavery. This is the story about Nat Turner.

The fear of what white people would do if Black individuals refuse do their bidding began when Black people, for the most part, are babies. It is necessary for the oppressor to instill fear because he requires us to do some things that are in his own best interest rather than ours. Some individuals, including myself, say that this fear is still what motivate too many of us. Black people are still negatively impacted by the brutal ways of white people today. Back in "olden days" white slave owners used torture and brutality of every description to force our ancestors to do their will. Today the physical brutality is buttressed with mental anguish: the fact that all of the so-called "good jobs" that black people try to get are controlled by white people; when Black individuals are chosen to work the jobs they must cover the equivalent of two or three white workers; the gender of Black people working in so-called "good jobs" are Black women; the incarceration of Black males for minor crimes; the harassing of Black males; fraternizing with Black women; will not give Black youth a 'break" for fear of them, put us relatively in the same situation: or at the least it has the same result.

Black people fear the fact that potential employers will not give us a job unless we look and act like him. We know his likes and don't likes and we act accordingly [feminine acting Black males & Black women straightening and coloring their hair are the most pernicious].

Obviously Nat Turner also knew white people and their white supremacist slavery system. From his studies he found that fear is what white supremacist had used to establish the brutal system to take away the freedom of Black humans.

No doubt Nat Turners' first inclination, after understanding a certain degree of white supremacy, was to reclaim his physical freedom. This is natural. If you need something that you once had but which was stolen from you; and you see the criminal every day, it is natural to think of ways to get it back.

Since he understood the 'certain degree' about white supremacy, he didn't go directly against the people who had stolen his freedom. Because at that 'certain degree' of understanding of white supremacy in the 19th century, wisdom told him that "running away" was the only remedy for such a system.

And this is the action he made to reclaim his physical freedom. He ran away from the plantation where he was held in captivity. He successfully made his escape. He was gone for 30 days. But while he was away, he discovered that this was not the most important thing the oppressors had stolen from him and his kind. His physical body was free but his spirit was not.

Since I have written about the need for the human to balance and harmonize the physical and the spiritual, I hope it is not necessary to spell out the fact that Nat Turner realized he was not free just because he'd moved his physical body from oppression. But I will say that there are many things that the human must express physically to satisfy the spirit. The number one thing of course is the physical worship of the source of your creation. That is Allah in Arabic – God in English and any other good name that The Creator of the Heavens and the Earth is called, in whatever language. As I bring out in my book, "Melanin, Conscious Attunement and the God in I," after you attain to a higher elevation of spiritual degrees, you will understand that it is not necessary to worship The Creator in name. But wisdom will still let you know that so long as you are in this "earth suit," it must be fed spiritual food (which are what the rituals in physical worshipping are all about). After Nat Turner ran away from chattel slavery, his mind was free enough to study studiously enough to attain to a higher degree of understanding about chattel slavery captivity; which was the form that the experiment in white supremacy was practiced during that time.

With the attainment of the 'certain degrees' of understanding about white supremacy today, as it was in the 19th century tells us that the god white oppressors imposed on Black people was not the True and Living God. If so why would He permit such a thing? No doubt Nat also studied this dilemma.

Anyone with sense enough will try to understand why the Black Race is in such a terrible bind. The understanding that Nat Turner received gave him the wisdom to see that even the Creator of the Heavens and the Earth will only help those who help themselves.

In other words, The Creator has instilled every thing needed within us to break all binds that circumvent our human potential. There is nothing that is more backward, from the essence of who you are, than being in a situation where you are too fearful to worship and "love the Creator with all your heart . . .," there is nothing more backward [I repeat] than letting fear cause you to do anything that is not in your own best interest.

You have to answer the question of whether you really believe you were created in the image of The Creator. Fortunately for Black people Nat Turner, as well as learned men and women before and since that time answered this question by using their mind to study what they knew about their situation. As you probably know by now, the understanding gave them the wisdom to see chattel slavery, second class citizenship and other forms of oppression as a challenge they had to overcome to realize their human potential.

When Nat Turner studied the challenge of white oppression, as we said, he moved his physical body out of it. But one can move the body, and one can move the spirit. But this does not mean that both have moved. If you move one and not do things to move the other, this causes an imbalance. Using this premise, when Nat Turner moved his physical body, his spirit let him know that he had not fully overcome the challenge of white oppression.

The thirty days away from direct oppression *did* give him some wonderful time away from the oppressor. He used the time wisely as per the above assertion. His wise use of the time allowed his true purpose to come into view. It was not very clear, but it was clear enough for him to see that to fulfill it he'd have to return to physical oppression. And painful, as it must have been, this is what he did. What was the purpose his life portended? Turn the page, we are going to find out.

RETURNED TO RIDICULE OF FELLOW CAPTIVES

In the confessions of Nat Turner, he is quoted as saying, "I was too focused on the things of this world. The spirit appeared to me and said I should first "seek the kingdom of God and all things will be added." He quoted this well known verse from the New Testament. The "all things added" would be what was needed to fulfill his purpose.

After determining his purpose, Nat Turner went to work. According to his own words, he spent most of his spare time fasting and praying. He could have added planning for the revolt for this is what he was doing.

We know now that becoming a model slave was all part of his plan to physically attack white oppression. On August 21, 1831 he did just that. From the time that he returned to oppression, he was carefully planning for his attack. More can be read about Nat Turner in "The Confessions," Or "The Revolt of Nat Turner and the BLA of 1831." And I would advise everyone in North America to read both books.

But you must "read between the lines" in many places. The words spoken by Nat Turner are powerful words that are very instructive for Black people today. His careful attention to the spiritual side of self are especially important.

Some are surprised to find such attention given to the spiritual side of Nat Turner. We use material substance to feed the physical body. We take unseen substance for the good health of the Spiritual Body. We can say without contradiction that the fasting, praying and preaching was the food that Nat Turner fed his spiritual body. And yes, for good physical reasons, Nat Turner was also a preacher; and Community Organizer. He was extremely good in both roles – he helped people by finding way to serve them, even in the misery of chattel slavery Black community organizers or activist were useful.

SERVING PHYSICALLY IS THE EASIEST

The physical part of Nat Turner's planning was relatively easy. These plans centered around working in the fields as a slave; liberating some of the crops that he stored in the safe houses; and preaching the kind of interpretation of the bible that was above the head of the slave master. It is a message that, though the words say what the oppressor want to hear, the listener to the words are moved by feelings which the oppressor cannot feel. But it did engender trust in blacks, as well as the oppressor.

He used the trust to traverse Southampton County where he lived, as well as surrounding counties like Suffolk. I would guess that he knew the county like the "back of his hands." He set up safe houses and developed channels of communications. These served him well in recruiting and organizing trusted officers for the Revolt. No doubt he studied whatever possible about past revolts. By studying his knowledge of past revolts, and the knowledge he had from his own experiences and observations gave him the understanding needed to derive wisdom to USE THE KNOWLEDGE.

The study gave him wisdom about vital aspects needed for his plans. It doesn't take a wise man long to understand the nature of fellow humans. Since Nat Turner was born and raised in Southampton County, he knew who he could trust amongst the slaves. Military science appears to have been acquired naturally. But this too was likely a benefit from careful study and planning.

Since Nat Turner was a natural leader, he overcame the ridicule of others, by earning their respect. He had their respect at one time, but after returning to slavery after an escape for 30 days, he was scorned. But he won respect back by serving their needs. Since he could read and write he could help them with this. And his integrity was such that he would not engage in the main occupation of Blacks to "do for self." That would be the business of expropriation or liberating the property of the slave owner (this is called "stealing" if your intention isn't correct). [This brings us to a point where I could discuss ways and means that are employed to Reclaim, or take back what was stolen in the first instance from captive Afrikans, but will only point out, for now, when you take things from the oppressor with the wrong intentions, that is stealing; when you take things back from the oppressor with the right intentions, that is expropriation; when you demand that what was stolen be given back, that is Reparations.)

A CLOSER LOOK AT THE LIFE PURPOSE OF NAT TURNER

Let us look directly at the Life Purpose of Nat Turner. After he Ran away and effectively stayed away, he realized he still was not free. No doubt he studied the knowledge of this fact. And from this study came his life purpose.

Nat Turner concluded from his study about the white supremacist slavery system that the only solution to white supremacy is to destroy it. His Life Purpose was to strike a mighty blow against it. To do the job, he would need resources. The only place where he could get the resources was back on the plantation. So he returned to the plantation to secure some of the other things needed to strike a successful blow against the white supremacist slavery system. The things needed included soldiers, weapons, horses and other valuables.

REPARATIONS VS EXPROPRIATIONS

Captive Black people were fierce resisters within the white supremacist slavery system. They resisted in many, many ways. They ran away from the plantation during the planting of the crops; they ran away from the plantation during the growing of the crops; they ran away from the plantation during the harvest of the crops; and when they didn't run away, after the harvested crops were gathered and put into barns, they burnt the barns down; they poisoned the slave owner and his family; they spit in the slave owners food; and "played the fool" to avoid the wrath of the slave owner after a particularly effective move of resistance.

When all is said and done about Black history, it will be unveiled that the physical war plans of Gabriel Prosser, Denmark Vesey; and the enactment of the Revolt of Nat Turner and the Black Liberation Army of 1831 was only a tiny percentage of physical fighting Captive Afrikans planned and carried out in the efforts to liberate every Black man, woman and child that was held in captivity. Ours has been a gallant, noble liberation struggle. The resistance to the white supremacist slavery system was in the best interest of individual captives; and it was in the best interest of the Black Race.

But eventually, many would be Black warriors were turned against the best interest of their own and vested all their life fulfillment prospects, living at peace in the white supremacist slavery system.

This ends the example used to show how one man overcame his fear and turned this powerful emotion to strike a mighty blow against white supremacy. Unfortunately, not nearly enough Black people have studied our status as subjects of white supremacy to understand how pervasive it is. The immensity of white supremacy doctrine is a "fearful" thing that keeps on hurting Black people. With a certain degree of understanding of the immensity and just how pervasive it is, wisdom will lead to ways and means to destroy it once, for all and for all time.

Chapter Sixteen

WHITE SUPREMACIST SYSTEM JOBS BLUNT THE MAIN OBJECTIVE

In additional to the open, brutal assault on captive Afrikans, the slave master was also relentless in trying to convince Black people they were better off in oppression than they were in Afrika. Key to this was denigrating the continent to the extent that Black people wanted to have nothing to do with Africa. Meanwhile the land mass of Africa is the most valuable body of land on the Earth. But the captives had no other source of information, save the little they got from new captives, and "die hard" Black nationalists, whose legacy continues to this very day.

But the lying, stinking, bloody words of the Caucasian male predominated. He controlled the means to communicate in the land back then, even as he does today through mass media. His careful control of Radio, Television and the Internet is part of the brutal assault against Black people. There is a continuous assault on the mind about lifestyles in oppression. Working in "the system" is portrayed as the only way you can enjoy the lifestyles you see on television, hear about on radio, or experience in the virtual reality in cyberspace. Meanwhile, Black people live in the midst of power, influence and valuable material things that was stolen from or made possible because the theft of goods and labor.

It was probably not easy to do in the beginning of the captivity, but as the brutal assault took its toll, seceding generations forgot the value of what was lost. The jobs of Overseer, waiters and other kinds of "slaves" appear to be "good jobs."

Fortunately for Black people everyone did not forget. These men and women continued to fight the good fight against oppression. They wanted to defeat the enemy, reclaim what was lost and get as far away from the white man, if they couldn't kill him, as possible.

The brutality of the white supremacist slave owners was so relentless and cruel, over tens of hundreds of years the character of the resistance, in the main, changed. The enemy developed a body of Black comfort seekers within the Black community. For them, the objective no longer was to kill the slave master and get as far away from him as possible. For this segment of the Black community, the aim is to show and prove to the oppressor that we can be trusted within the confines of the systems of oppression: the white supremacist slavery system.

The black comfort seekers, loosely called "Uncle Toms," they wanted to be equal to the slave master, and in the white supremacist doctrine he'd devised to govern himself and his kind. And in time – with the hold out Freedom Fighters, still resisting and not compromising at all – the brilliant mind of Black people convinced enough white people to relent and make certain amendments to the constitution of the white supremacist slavery system: creating a new status for Black people within the confines of the white supremacist slavery system.

Over the centuries, by and large, the goals and definition of freedom changed from wanting to return home to staying in America to fight for equality under the white supremacist laws of the land. Our status became classified as Second Class Citizens. But the original people, Black people, is so brilliant of mind, that we have excelled in every area of white supremacy that we are given this second hand opportunity to compete. The Blackman is so dynamic that in 2008 one of us was elected President of the United States of America. And though Barack Obama will do an infinitely better job than any before him – benefiting captive Africans in the process – he is still only president of the white supremacist system. He will not, and cannot, even if he wants to, free Black people.

****

We will now look at some of the methods white people used to "bend the will" of Black people – causing them to short change their aspirations for Complete Freedom by covering up the facts about what it is; and of course, heavily flaunting the ill begotten advances they have made using the oppression of Black people.

We study the knowledge we have about the oppression to understand it to the DEGREE that the wisdom to destroy the oppression is in our hands: understanding knowledge = wisdom.

THE BRUTALITY AND MISEDUCATION OF THE NEGRO TOOK ITS TOLL

The Methods used to bend the will of the Blackman and woman came right out of the game plan of the devil. There was nothing white people thought they could do to control black people that they did not try.

Eventually just the threat or thought of white people was enough to change the mentality of most all Black people. Though the mere threat or thought was enough, the oppressor carried out the threats with such regularity that there was no way to predict where they would stop. The main threat was to do us bodily harm; second only to this was the threat to sell a member of the warriors family. This was effective. In fact, the second one was the most effective because it was against the love and feelings we have for our family. These are unseen things. Unseen things are properties of the spirit body. There is a book titled *Born a Child of Freedom Yet A Slave,* by Dr. Noreece Jones, this book documents various ways the slave master used to blunt the revolutionary moves of Black people. The Threat to sell a family member rank right at the top of things Caucasians used to keep Black captives on the plantation.

As we said, the threats were not a idle. The white oppressors had carried out the threats many, many times. So the threats coupled with their brutal use of physical force inbred fear into Black people. It is a fear that continues to this very day. We can get very technical so I'll try not to make my examples too clinical. But the fear was part of the trauma that caused a very recognizable disease.*

The disease is called "Post Traumatic Slavery Disorder (PTSD)." Like Post Traumatic Stress Disorder, it is a treatable condition. But the treatment requires that after a particular trauma that caused a particular disease, the victim must be "debriefed." Debriefed means counseled, redressed, medicated, cheered up, and other things to treat the disease. But up to the present day, Black people have not been debriefed about the traumatic event called The Transatlantic Slave Trade. There was such a traumatic experience that the United Nations has declared it a "Crime Against Humanity."

As the authors of a best selling book called *"Post Traumatic Slavery Disorder" Dr* Omar G. Reid, Psy.D, Sekou Mems, M.Ed., MSW, LCSW and Larry Higginbottom, MSW, LCSW, these medical professionals point out the fact that much of what Black people complain about and are often treated for, are ailments that are symptoms of Post Traumatic Slavery Disorder.

The reader is strongly advised to read some books on Reparations and others that analyze the problem. The conclusions in the books are parts of the efforts being used to give Black people tools they are using to overcome the oppression of white people today. We must especially take a deep, penetrating look into the fear we have for white people. The Honorable Elijah Muhammad identified "fear to displease white people" as the main fear of Black people.

When called on at a conference once, I was asked the question: What is the main thing that you got out of joining the Nation of Islam?

To answer the question, my brain computer researched all of the good benefits I'd derived from the Teachings in the Nation of Islam. My answer then was fear. Later in reading the book by Mr. Muhammad there was a statement by the Honorable Elijah Muhammad that "the greatest fear of the Blackman is to displease the white man." My answer to the question actually 'the removal of fear' as the most beneficial benefit I received for becoming a Black Muslim.

The fear of white people, by Black people is extremely important. We dealt with it earlier in the book by giving you a mantra that will help, if you follow the instruction that I also gave you. The mantra is THERE IS NOTHING TO FEAR. But much more is needed surrounding the entire emotion of fear that Black people have for white.

If you have too much, your fear will cause you to not do the level of work needed to liberate Black people, or for your individual success in life, if you possess too little, you are subject to be caught unaware when white people [generally] show what a lying, stinking brutal devil they really are.

One way to find the most productive level is to attain balance in words, acts and deeds before you make your moves. After attaining balance, when you do execute your will and enact word, act or deed, do them in harmony to each other: Muhammad told us that "Word is Bond!"

Elijah Muhammad is a man who found a productive and harmonious way to allay fear of white people. We will take a brief look at his approach to see how we "Black Muslims" were taught that resulted in fearlessness in the face of white people. "Black Muslim" is a pejorative term to indicate a certain orthodoxy belief and practice of the "Opinions and Philosophy" of The Honorable Elijah Muhammad. Using the term "Philosophy and Opinions," the title for the main text for the followers for Master Marcus Garvey is on purpose. It tells us at once that the main text that Black Muslims used and are using to build – especially develop the character that removes fear as a hindrance to advancing wherever we find ourselves in life. Or at whatever station in the progression and evolvement of our Spirituality. That main text is *The Message to the Blackman in America.*

THE HON. ELIJAH MUHAMMAD AND THE TEACHINGS OF THE NATION OF ISLAM

When The Honorable Elijah Muhammad said *"the greatest fear of the Blackman is to not please the white man,"* he was 100% correct. This fear in Black men will remain until we find ways to deal with the problem. White people are the problem. This is common knowledge. When you know the problem, you must analyze and study it.

Fortunately, individuals are not required to do all of the analyzing. Since the problem of white people have been with us for "these many centuries," white people have been analyzed, and thoroughly studied by some of the most gifted minds in history. But we dare say that none in history have had the success Black Muslims, under the leadership of the Honorable Elijah Muhammad have had.

What distinguished the programs of the Nation of Islam (Muhammad's organism) was the new information he brought. It appears that those before him had analyzed and acted on the facts as they found them. But the essential facts they found about Black people, to a large extent, were incorrect, or distorted. The three most important fact that were distorted or false that Mr. Muhammad corrected were: "Proper knowledge of self, Proper knowledge of The Creator and Proper knowledge of the Devil." Elijah Muhammad required that his followers study and accept the correct information about these three facts.

The correct information is unvarnished truth about these three basic reasons and purposes for building the Nation of Islam. Proper knowledge about the Creator [you can get stuck on the fact that he gave Him a name other than in an African language to your liking, but you will be the loser]. Elijah Muhammad taught openly that Black people are the Original people who came with the creation of what we see, touch, feel, smell and hear; and he also taught openly that our tormentors is just not a bad fellow – we knew that, which is why we fear him – but proper knowledge is he is the devil if ever there was one [white people have a history that they earned that proves conclusively who and what they are).

Once you accept Islam as taught by Muhammad, and study the unvarnished truth about the problem, the understanding will unveil the wisdom one needs to overcome the barrier of fear that was inbred. He will then use that wisdom to fight against white supremacy. The Black Muslims efforts will then be tempered by his degree of understanding what the wisdom also tells him he is capable of doing about this challenge to his human potential.

There is much admiration and respect for the accomplishments of the Muslims. These accomplishments could not have reached the level they did without leveling of the fear for white people. We will speak more about Elijah Muhammad and the programs of the Nation of Islam. It has been stated, "all programs have failed Black people save the Nation of Islam."

Many times the teachings of The Nation of Islam is not recognized by the non-Black Muslims. This is usually the case when word, phase or NOI idea is used by a fellow non-Black M Thisuslim. An example of this is the statement by Black men on the eve of the 10th anniversary of the Million Man March. As we close out this segment, I will record the piece that I wrote in the introduction to a book called "The Declaration of Dr. Kamau Kambon." It should be self explanatory in regard to why I say it was a statement by the collective gathering of Black men in Washington, D. C. They were there to celebrate the 10th anniversary of The Million Man March.

I'd discussed with several individuals my reluctance to gather a million Black men, once again, to prove we could be called into formation. To be successful, to me, we must take some kinds of actions to prove that our power can be disciplined and focused to act.

* * *

"The killing of Black people will continue until we plan to exterminate white people from the planet." This sentence effectively achieved the objective that I had in mind.

He made the remarks at the Pro-Black Media Forum, Howard School of Law, October 14, 2006. We were there to launch a National network that would be a medium through which the views of Independent Black Voices could be showcased to keep the National Black informed – 25-7, but especially during crisis or national emergencies...

Dr. Kambon achieved much notoriety for the statement. He published a little book in the aftermath called: "The Declaration of Dr. Kamau Kambon."

Chapter Seventeen

SOMETIMES ONLY WELL PLANNED DYNAMIC ACTION TO ACHIEVE A PHYSICAL RESULT WILL WORK

By "dynamic action" we mean acting physical, as in a war against captivity! Fortunately for the Black race, many captives in the United States of America, like Nat Turner, fought a physical fight against all forms of oppression, including chattel slavery, 2nd class citizenship.

From his birth in 1800 to his execution in 1831, Nat Turner was subjected to chattel slavery. Chattel slavery is the most cruel, criminal condition to which one can subject a fellow being. It is a physical claim of ownership over a man, woman and child by a fellow being: a violation of every human right that is bestowed upon human beings. It is a condition that one is duty bound to physically strive to break.

In fact, the only way a human can be subjected to chattel slavery, second-class citizenship and other forms of oppression is when he is dumb, ignorant and the oppressor is willing to use physical torment to the point of death, to keep the subject oppressed "dumb, death and blind." White slave owners have been willing to visit such torment on captive Africans in the United States of America.

On the other hand captive Africans have been willing to fight to break free of the captivity and other form of oppression of white people. As we obtained better knowledge we were more dynamic and effective in our fight to break free.

For anyone who doubts that 'knowledge is power' and 'ignorance is death' they should look at the extreme measures white slave owners use to keep knowledge from captive Africans. Moreover, extreme measures to "mis-educate" oppressed Africans are still carried out to this very day. But despite the extreme measures, Black people, by and large continue to break through. And everyone once in awhile a special Black woman or man gets superior knowledge. When they study the knowledge and understanding they receive superior wisdom. They use the wisdom to deploy superior dynamic actions against oppression. Nat Turner was such a captive African between 1800 and 1831.

At sometime in his life he received superior knowledge. He was getting increasing degrees of understanding of the knowledge. The understanding culminated in 1825 where the understanding gave him the wisdom to do the second most dynamic thing that a chattel slave could do: that is run-away from the plantation. Like many captive Africans who ran-away before him, Nat Turner continued to get understanding; the resulting wisdom caused them to develop ways and means to help Black people who were still in captivity.

UNLIKE OTHERS, like Frederick Douglas who helped from outside the confines of slavery; or Harriet Tubman who went back to rescue and guide captives out of captivity, he returned to captivity to go to war against slave owners. He returned because his study of his knowledge about the oppression. This was the problem. He derived certain benefit from study of the problem. One derivative was that only dynamic action would effectively free his fellow captives. His knowledge of white people told him that the only way they would free Black people was by physical force. He studied this as the challenge to his desire to free Black people.

His study of the challenge gave him the understanding to not only overcome the fear to resist the challenge of white supremacy, he induced others to do the same. Since it was a physical challenge a physical means was used in the rebellion to overcome it. It is documented that Nat Turner and the Black Liberation Army of 1831 killed scores of white in his attempt to free Black people. Killing scores of white people was not the most important service he gave to Black people. The fact that he found and successfully fulfilled his purpose is a everlasting legacy about the determination, courage and dynamic that the reclamation of freedom, justice and equality requires.

As much as I love and respect what Nat Turner was able to do in the era when he lived in the United States of America, we still must look subjectively at the fact that he didn't do the complete job. I am sure he hoped his actions would result in Complete Freedom for captive Africans.

On the other hand, I am satisfied in knowing his actions fulfilled his purpose. And less we forget, living to fulfill your purpose is the "whole ball of wax," that is the essence of life. When one find their purpose; studies it; understands it; and applies the derived wisdom to fulfill that purpose, THAT'S IT!

Everything about you [character, disposition, success & etc.] and your life branches and springs from the work that you do in life to fulfill your purpose. The more successful that work is in serving others, the more fulfilling, satisfying and peaceful your life will be.

When we find ourselves working mostly to find answers to who we are; how we are going to make a living; how we are going to get along with wives, children and others, rather than being the husband, father and friend that they need, our service is not at its optimum.

When your words, acts and deeds to attend to and serve the physical needs of others have been successful (you have dutifully secured a home; and you have raised your children), at some point the concentration and focus of your life must be on the evolvement of your own Spirituality. Up until the 'point' you will have worked to keep your physical and spiritual activity balanced; this has been a part of your duties and responsibilities to wife and children. Now that they are up, it is now time to re-order the concentration and focus of your life...the stories about Nat Turner is to give an example of how one extra-ordinary Black man focused and concentrated on achieving his purpose.

I have never lived in freedom in America: so I don't know how one carry forth with children after they have reached the age of maturity; of responsibilities to wife whose disposition cannot be expected to mirror her man, whether captive or free, but in captivity or in abject 2nd class citizenship and other forms of oppression, when the man spend an inordinate amount of time working to keep your loved ones physically happy and contented, something is amiss. *Inordinate in the use of this word here is when you have raised them in a secure home to the age of maturity, and they are still in great need of your physical support.* We should never stop loving our children and wife; never ever abandon our children and never stop being willing, if able, to give them all of the physical help they need to evolve their character. But at some point in the dynamic of the relationship they should derive their needs from the general service that we render to the effort to free The Black Nation. When one finds self in one of the inordinate situations, a careful study and plan to engage in service for the greater good is called for.

Something must be done to change the dynamic, for the cause can be but one of two possibilities: 1) You are not on your purpose. If you were, what you are doing with your life would be reflecting things that they need to find and fulfill their own purpose or 2) you are on your purpose, but your wives, children and other loved ones do not understand that life is purpose driven.

If they understood that life is purpose driven, they would have the wisdom to realize that the fruit of your work is for them; and it is their JOB to use the fruits productively to find and fulfill their own purpose. If your loved ones aren't able to get what they need, after maturity, from what you are doing in service to the Black nation, you are duty bound to help them. But you are not required to STOP working your own purpose to help anyone fulfill their own. This often happen, and when it does, it may be good for all concerned, but it is not required.

We could easily go into the many nuances when one person, *purposely* stop working full time at his or her own purpose to help someone else fulfill theirs. But we will use but two examples and they are part and parcel of each other:

a) when an Elder reach the age in their progression and the life force energy is obviously not such to continue working full time at their own purpose, they can scale back on life expectations or, b) they can let their projects in life go, or be in sub-service to the work and purpose of someone else, or c) they are young and have not yet found their own purpose. So they work by helping someone else who is fulfilling his or her own purpose [hopefully, the person you help is successful enough to pay what you need to maintain and take care of your duties and responsibilities).

It is good and ok to stop searching so hard to find something fulfilling to do, in order to help someone else who have already found their purpose – this is especially ok and good if the person who is on their purpose can pay you to help them do certain jobs [and you need money]. For if you are in need of money you have not mastered certain processes of life. More study is required to master them. While you are studying, help someone who is already on their purpose.

We will now return to the story about Nat Turner, with a personal, subjective look.

NAT TURNER LOOKED AT SUBJECTIVELY IN RELATION TO MY OWN LIFE

[*I know the above was pertinent, but a departure from our main topic: so we continue where we left off, hopefully with the discussion about purpose and responsibility to wives, children, and others in our lives more fully understood*].

But before looking at Nat Turners actions subjectively and personally, in my youth, back then I'd already accepted the benefits that the Black nation derived from study and understanding of his resistance to oppression. We had long ago accepted the fact that the challenge Nat Turner struggled against, was the exact same challenge that we face today – white oppression. I recognized it even though the truth about Nat Turner had been omitted or distorted and put into a false doctrine called White Supremacy.

When I got the truth: that Nat Turner was a powerful man who had the prowess to motivate self and hundreds of others to overcome their fear; the understanding gave me some of the wisdom I used to proceed with my efforts against the challenge that was contravening my own human potential.

I studied Nat Turner the man. It is known that he was a preacher. The enemy spouts that he was a religious fanatic. I am not a preacher. But I am a journalist. A Spiritual Journalist who have been called a religious fanatic.

What I found out about Nat Turners' life told me that he too was a spiritual man. This was confirmed when I read his own words in *"The Confession of Nat Turner."* Reading between the lines of his words, I was also convinced that his spiritual station was reached through the practice of a religion other than the one that was forced on captive Africans: so-called Christianity.

Remember, we are writing about the injustice that a person who does not act in his or her own best interest, rather he acts in the best interest of someone else. We are using individual members of the Black race as examples of this kind of injustice. Knowledge about how individuals are motivated by force to act against their own self interest is fairly well known. Since the main component (physical brutality) is still almost universally practiced against us. Misunderstanding of this fact yields shares the methodology that I used to build a life in resistance to white oppression.

Hopefully, examining myself will be of help to anyone so interested. When you study my effectiveness, or lack of same, the understanding will give you the wisdom to do a better job.

After understanding that Nat Turner overcame his own fear to establish his life in resistance, I looked for a way to do the same. I cross referenced my study with the study of other servants of African people. Denmark Vesey was one of the others that I studied. The Haitian revolutionaries Dessaline, Touissant, Boukman & etc. were others.

As I was studying how Nat Turner, Denmark Vesey and others overcame their fear of white oppression I came face to face with the teachings of a man in my own time. This man had motivated more men to overcome the fear of white people than any other in history. His was the Honorable Elijah Muhammad.

I don't know how much Mr. Muhammad studied Nat Turner. But I do know that Nat Turner said that during his ascent to his spiritual pinnacle he meditated and prayed constantly on the verse in the bible that invokes us to: Seek ye first the Kingdom of Heaven...." This told me that the primary source of his strength was spiritual. When I met the teachings of Mr. Muhammad I found that his success was basically because he required that his followers a spiritual path that was different than the religion of the slave masters.

In other words the first requirement of Mr. Muhammad was that you accept Islam as your "way of life". Islam is not the same religion as that of our oppressors. "Islam," as taught Mr. Muhammad, "is not a even a religion, rather it is The Natural Way of Life."

In more words, Elijah Muhammad taught that we should live the way we were intended to live when we were created. Any other way of life is unnatural. Millions who didn't accept Islam, still benefited and studied it to some degree. Since Mr. Muhammad hinged his Natural Way of Life on three things, this would be the degree of what their study got some understanding about:

"True knowledge of Self; True knowledge of Creator (Allah); and true knowledge of devil."

Remember, the reason individuals are forced to act against their own best interest is fear of what will happen to him or her if they acted otherwise. Mr. Muhammad worked on the fear we have for white people by giving us correct knowledge ourselves; correct knowledge about white people, as well as about our Creator.

Details about the teachings of The Honorable Elijah Muhammad can be read elsewhere. What I am doing is reviewing the methodology that was used by Mr. Muhammad and other men I found in the struggle. They had found effective ways to resist the same oppression I was of a mind to.

My understanding told me immediately that Nat Turner and the others built lives, and acted outside of some basic knowledge that was approved by white people. In other word they studied the knowledge but did not use it as white people wanted them to.

Not only did Nat Turner and the BLA [Black Liberation Army] plan and kill criminal slave holders, they also practiced a spirituality other than the one approved by the oppressors. They replaced the fear of the oppressor with the fear of their Creator. And once Nat Turner acted, there was no doubt at all that he was acting to overcome the challenge to his human potential. But first the fear was removed. With fear out of the way to protect against the main challenge/chattel slavery, he planned, attacked and killed as many slaveholders as possible. He did so with the best purpose in mind.

In summary, had Nat Turner not acted against slaveholders, he would have been forced to continue to act against the interest of self and kind. The fact that he overcame his fear and attacked the challenge to his human potential clearly shows that his life meant more to Black people than any others on the planet. This is one way we can estimate whether we are acting unjustly against self and kind, or not: Determine who is the primary beneficiary of your work or service. If it is not Self, Family or Black race (if you are black), change course.

In short, if you want to avoid acting against the best interest of self, get understanding why you would do, or are doing such a thing. If you find that you are acting against your best interest because you fear consequences from an outside force, you must find a way to overcome what it is you fear.

INJUSTICE AGAINST THE RIGHTS OF OTHERS

We have discussed ways to avoid injustice against self. We will now take a look at injustice against other people. Both are wrong.

In contradiction to the views of Machiavelli, we do not believe that the end justifies the means. Some will have you believe that the manifestation of a country called The United States of America justifies the oppression of Black people. Injustice is injustice regardless to who commit it. And also regardless to the reason it is committed. Or what was achieved by unjust means. At some point in time it must be requited. Another word for requited is compensated. In other words you reap what you sew. In more words, what goes around does indeed come around.

There is a peculiar thing about actions we carry out in life. It is inculcated in Universe Law. We said earlier that balance is a very admirable station to strive for in life. But it is not a station to aim to stay at the rest of your life.

Oh I know we are constantly told to be balanced. Or strive for the middle path. But I say that when you have both forces in balance in life, while it is a great peaceful feeling, life is such that at some point, at least in this life, you must act. The instant that you act, you will put yourself into an imbalance. It may be different on other planes of existence. But in this life, when you act, you must move against something. It doesn't have to be an act for justice, injustice, fast or slow, but when you act you create an imbalance.

What may appear to be a balanced act is really a harmonious act. You are acting in harmony with your other parts. So I say when you do anything in life, strive to do it in harmony with your spiritual self. Vice versa for the spiritual self, when you engage your spiritual self, strive to do so in harmony to your physical self.

Balance is the place that you want to start from; it is also the place to where you want to return, after your actions.

One of the difficult areas for Black people is reconciling physical acts to their spiritual acts, against white oppressors. As a whole, Black people are a very spiritual people. Our white oppressors have used this fact to keep us in subjection to them. It is well known that they supplanted our religion during captivity. After taking away our own religious practices, we were given a replacement.

Since the religion that was forced on Black people, as a replacement, is a false religion, any prayer made in the name of religion will be petitions to a false god. The false god is said to reward believers "in the by and by" and not in the here and now. In other words you must die before you receive your just rewards. The basic precept of the religion is that you believe in at god that supposedly "gave his only begotten son" for your sins.

Of course so long as the oppressors could convince Black people that their rewards would come after they die they could get away with stealing some of our vital rights on earth. One of those rights is to reclaim what is lost. When you lose anything by brute force you have a natural right to reclaim it "by any means necessary."

When anything is stolen from you, you have a right to get it back in whatever way will work.

If what was taken from you was through brutalization, intimidation, trickery or whatever, you can use power to employ any of these same means to have it returned. But using either method will cause a spiritual person to pause before they act. They will pause because, as stated above, when you do act you will create an imbalance – imbalances are not always enjoyable for the spiritual person when he or she must use violence to get back what cannot be gotten back in any other way. Using brutal, violent means to get back what was stolen will not be pleasant. But if you are successful end result will be satisfying.

Even though you can legitimately use brutality and violence when you have the right intention, you still must observe the limits when you employ physical force. But the white supremacist have been so brutal and violent against us that, with the right intention, we can be a violent and brutal for as long as it takes to get back what was stolen from us.

Meanwhile, the oppressor in the system of white supremacy would have you think there is never a good time to act physically to secure your freedom. But there is a good time to act; that time is when you acquire sufficient power and wisdom. That is, unless you just want to make a statement. Then you can act without any regard to whether you win or lose. In fact, making a "statement" (with the right intention) is a win-win way to fight in a liberation struggle.

The basic reason for writing this book is to share some ideals on how to acquire power. But more important is how and when to use it to secure the liberation of self and African people. The intention for words, acts and deeds governs all use of power. Whatever you are of a mind to use your power against, let your intention be for a righteous purpose....Please read on, there is more.

Chapter Eighteen

POWER IS ALWAYS WITH US: EVEN A BABY IS BORN WITH POWER

All humans are born through the womb of a woman. When the baby first arrives into the world, the first thing the doctor checks is to see if he or she has the power to breathe on his own. It is best for the baby if he cries. Healthy "babies air out their lungs." The doctor may not necessarily slap the baby on the butt to bring about the airing of his lungs, but he will not be satisfied until the baby uses his own power to cry or make some other sound.

THE HUMAN SELF

Every human is born with a Self. But it is necessary in this life to fight to evolve this self. When and where and how you fight will be determined by the character of your power. We all start out as babies. The power that a baby has is 'baby power." Then we evolve to toddler to adolescent, young adulthood, adulthood and so on. As self evolves it becomes more physically as well as spiritually powerful. Understanding of certain degrees of the process in the evolvement will beget the wisdom that will impact on the characteristics of the power of self. When you understand self, wisdom to use the characteristics of your power is fundamental. Wisdom of "when, where and how" to use it is like a neutral result from the understanding.

The natural evolvement of the human is necessary for the life we are given. Keep in mind that knowledge is power and is with us every step of the way. As we discussed earlier, just having knowledge is not enough. You cannot use it unless you understand it. If you understand a little, you will have a little wisdom in its usage. Understanding of knowledge is acquired by degrees

Unseen tools are used to acquire degrees of understanding. Your ability to "do the right thing at the right time in the right frame of mind" will be governed by the amount of degrees. The unseen tool that is used is your mind. It is the mind that uses the wisdom in the usage of power.

If you don't have enough mind power, or are not exposed to enough knowledge you will not be able to use the instruments that the mind uses to do what your self wants to do. One of the 'instruments' is called Will. Or will power. You need will power to implement decisions that the understanding of knowledge tells you that must be made. As we said, the wisdom to act correctly comes from the understanding of knowledge. The understanding will tell you the characteristics of the knowledge. The wisdom from this understanding will determine whether of not your power is sufficient to achieve the result that you are after.

Knowledge is actually not that difficult to acquire. It is the understanding of the knowledge that is difficult, but is necessary if you are to make wise use of it. [Keep in mind that "knowledge is power."] I realize that I am repeating myself here, as I am in many other places in the book. Hopefully the 'repeats' are making slightly different points about the subject matter. But it is so important that the reader understand the formula, I will repeat some things quite often. Understanding knowledge equals wisdom is one of these.

SOME HAVE TREMENDOUS KNOWLEDGE BUT DO NOT GET ANYTHING SIGNIGICANT DONE

I have lived long enough and experienced enough to know many, many individuals with tremendous amounts of knowledge. They have the knowledge but are constantly saying what they want to do, or be. Meanwhile, their actions belie the wisdom that is intricately within the knowledge. After much study and meditation on this phenomenon I concluded that IT IS NOT LACK OF KNOWLEDGE THAT HOLDS US BACK.

More times than not, it is lack of understanding of the knowledge that holds us back.

After coming to this conclusion, I searched for places in knowledge centers to see if anyone is stressing this. I have not found this to be so. So to me, UNDERSTANDING OF KNOWLEDGE EQUAL WISDOM

PROPERTIES OF THE MIND BEGETS WILL POWER TO ACT

Some students of life are convinced that the properties of the mind are the only power in the world. They feel this way because of one property that it possess. That is the faculty to think. As stated in my book: *Conscious Attunement*, "you can do nothing unless you first have the thought."

Will power, or lack of the same, comes in after you have the thought to do something. If you don't have a certain degree of will power it matters little how right it is to do a particular thing; or how strong your physical body is. Or how good it is for you; if you don't have will power you will have difficulty getting it done.

If you think this is overstating the case, observe the difficulty of breaking a bad habit like cigarette smoking; or the fear that black people have for cruel Caucasian people. The Honorable Elijah Muhammad taught that "the greatest fear of the Black man is to *displease the white man."* The fear is still there; the fear is a large part of why the black man doesn't do things in his own best interest. He may know what is right and in his own best interest but doesn't have the power to do right and reject wrong. Lack of power is one reason why we may do what is in the best interest of others rather than self. And yes sometimes we do something against self that is clearly not in our own best interest.

The science about smoking cigarettes is known. But more is needed to break the habit of smoking than knowing it is harmful: will power is needed.

OUTSIDE FORCES THAT CHALLENGE US

In the examples above, breaking a bad habit may be difficult, but it is done all of the time. There is a way to break any habit. The easiest way to break the bad habit is to be properly motivated. And that is one more reason why you must have the understanding so you can realize the wise thing to do is break a bad habit. The other thing needed is will power to act out your decision.

Wisdom tells you it is best for you if you give up the bad habit. Wisdom will also unveil the way to give it up – stop smoking. But if you don't have proper motivation you will not stop smoking. The bad habit will overcome your will to give it up. Of course if you have strong will power it is a different story. But even then you must be motivated.

You can get proper motivation in many ways. Understanding of smoking will give you the science about cigarette smoke. Science will tell you about cancer and other illnesses that smoking cause to your body. This motivates many. If this doesn't motivate you, some other things about this ghastly habit may do the job; it increase risk for heart disease, stroke, lung disease & etc. It is very expensive to smoke. Ok, you may have plenty of money so the two or three dollars of tax, per pack, still may not give you enough motivation.

When all else fails some people to give up bad habits, an outside force may do the job. The outside force can be pleasant or it can be cruel. If it is pleasant it motivates you to stop with an enjoyable reward. The reward is what motivates you to give it up. Doing so makes you feel good!

The motivation may also take the form of a punishment. This is when something unpleasant is given when you smoke. You will stop smoking of something is going to hurt you real bad.

If the outside force uses cruelty, like cruel Caucasian people who motivated Black people to slave for them, they killed, hurt us real bad or sold our mates or children. These are some of the ways Black people do things that are not in their best interest. He uses fear from the outside. He also motivates from the inside. In fact his favorite way to you is through deception. We will get to that later, but he deceives you into thinking that doing it in his best interest is best for you.

With all of the above said about outside motivation that causes one to do things against his own best interest, power is required to overcome the motivation. As stated, this is the easy part. Since knowledge is power, get understanding about why you do things as your do that help others more than it does for self and kind. Certain degree of understanding will give you the desire to change the behavior. More or deeper degrees of understanding will give you ways to change.

OUTSIDE FORCE

The greatest motivating force for a non-believer is the threat of bodily harm. Second to that, for most of us, is threat of bodily harm to a loved one.

When we first hear the statement by Messenger Elijah Muhammad regarding our "greatest fear," we are usually taken aback. You will not want to believe this. But upon closer examination, during which you obtain more understanding of knowledge of what white people did to subject us to their white supremacist doctrine; their reasons for it, and our difficulty in overcoming his reasons for being so cruel, we will understand why it is so hard for Black people to build our own societies. The Oppressor motivates us not to act in our own best interest.

INSIDE CHALLENGES

Tools to overcome physical challenges (outside force) or mental challenges (inside) can be acquired or increased by evolving your mind power. As we stated in our little book called "Melanin, Conscious Attunement and The God In I," there are certain physical exercise one can do to increase will power.

The Creator, Allah Almighty created us with the tools needed to fight challenges as an interval part of our being. But we must use them. If you don't know how to use them then you must get an understanding about the knowledge of the challenge. From this understanding you will get the wisdom about how to use the tools of your mind.

We have much knowledge about the increasing the powers of your mind. Increasing your mind power is the exact methodology we use to increase the power of our physical body: we exercise the part of the body that we want to strengthen. We mustn't confuse large with power. You can have both, but unless you have will power it doesn't matter how large or strong your physical body is.

We are born with a certain gene pool. If the gene pool has you programmed to be a giant seven footer, that's what you will grow physically to be. If your gene pool has you programmed to be a nitwit, or dummy, that's exactly what your mind powers will reflect. Understanding of this evolvement will gain us the wisdom to meet challenges we face as a tall person or a small person.

There may well be challenges that you must overcome to grow to be a seven-footer. But to overcome the challenge to growing to your physical size will be relatively easy. For that seven-footer to evolve to his potential as a human being will be more difficult. As stated, the first fight is to realize that you have the potential, say, to be a basketball player in the NBA. This will be "self discovery."

Or there may well be things that can be done to mitigate your mental prowess. Whether the struggle is inside or outside, they are parts of the packages of our lives. They are built in, or born in. If one is going to stay alive, challenges must be overcome. They must be overcome in a specific way if we are to not only stay alive but also thrive in overcoming the major challenges in our lives.

As it is with the overcoming of the challenges in regard to other things in the 'package' of our lives, like Sex, the ultimate benefit in overcoming challenges is the building of our character. Of course the ultimate benefit for having overcome challenges that are specific to having Sex is to have a baby, or to procreate. We will not get into any other specific challenges in the package of our lives at this time. But it doesn't take much thinking to name some in any life. But the challenges that must be overcome to procreate are things that you must do to have sex.

PURPOSE FOR THE CHALLENGES

Many feel that character building is actually the only real purpose for living. So the Creator of All built challenges to prepare His creatures to, yes, meet other challenges. We must overcome one challenge after another in order to stay alive. The methodology that we use in overcoming the challenge shapes our character in like manner.

He made it very enjoyable to procreate. The sex drive in men and women is second only to the will to be free. The drive for sex is close, for it is known and documented that the sex drive will cause a man to suppress, or betray his will for and drive for freedom. But if he strives to overcome challenges necessary to win his freedom, the development of his character will help him to overcome anything to become free. In Other words, it takes a strong character to overcome the challenges to win your freedom. While you are confronting the challenges your character is being developed to withstand anything that may threaten your goal.

The Creator also made character building automatic. If you overcome challenges in a good way, you will build a good character. If you overcome challenges in a not-so-good way, you will build a character that is not so good.

WHAT IS THE BEST CHARACTER?

The best character is like the Character of the One Who created you. The Honorable Elijah Muhammad told us that the "proper name" for the creator of Black people is Allah. What ever one calls his or her Creator, when you understand that you were created in The Creators Image, it seems to me that His character would be the most desired.

Now there are challenges for Black men and women to develop as per the image of their Creator. First of all, when we were brutalized and robbed, as a people, our identity was stolen. When you lose your identity, you also lose the identity of your Creator. Losing the identity of The Creator is losing Proper Knowledge of Him. It was necessary for the criminal to try to take everything possible from Black people. We say try because it was a failed attempt. All was never lost, but that what was lost had to be found before we would ever be able to exhibit the character of our Creator.

The idea of freedom was one of the things that the devil, or slave owner tried to take from us but failed. He did succeed in taking away our physical freedom. But the ideal of freedom is also Spiritual. He tried, but failed to take away our spirit. And many will say that it is the use of our spirituality that allowed us to overcome the challenge that tried to kill our spirit. Another way to look at it is seeing our spirit as the cause that let us survive long enough to get proper Knowledge about our Creator. With Proper Knowledge we strive to identify with the image that we have of Him. The Image has zero tolerance for injustice. Anything of an injustice nature takes away rights we were born with: our human rights. Tolerating injustice diminishes our efforts to be pleasing to The Creator.

When we face up to and strive to overcome the challenges to change our condition from oppression to freedom, we build a strong character. When we don't face up to the challenges of white supremacy, we cannot overcome the challenge so we develop the kind of character that is not strong enough to win our freedom. This means our characters will reflect that fact. A walk through any black neighborhood will show the kinds of character that we have developed in white supremacist societies. This will change when we realize what the major challenges in our lives are. We say that if you truly believe that you were created in the image of the Creator. The ultimate challenge to you will be to overcome anything that is preventing you from reflecting the Image of the Creator. And since we know that white supremacy is what dominates our lives. Our ultimate challenge is to overcome white supremacy. The main devastation that white supremacy visits on us is the circumvention of our potential as human beings.

What is the major challenge in your life?

LIFE PURPOSE

When you believe in Allah, or whatever you choose to call The Creator, you soon learn that you are not an accident of nature. There is a purpose for your being created. It is not one of Allah's secrets. And it is not a secret as to how one can find out what their life purpose is. That is the main reason why the devil took away our identities. *When you obtain proper knowledge of yourself, your Life Purpose will be unveiled.*

When I personally obtained proper knowledge of Self, it was unveiled that my Life Purpose is to "make my maximum contribution to the liberation struggle of black people."

Every Black person born will have at least one challenge that will be related to the status of his race. All black individuals will have the challenge to overcome the challenge of white people that we are inferior to them. This challenge is the lie upon which white supremacy doctrine rules the world. The challenge to free Black people from the oppression of white people is called The Liberation Struggle.

We will shed some light on the Liberation Struggle of Black People from the above perspective. We will attempt be analytical to the degree of seeing all challenges attendant to our noble struggle as tasks that must be overcome. This is because of two imperatives:

1) *Whether challenges are looked at spiritually or physical they are no more or less than life challenges that must be overcome to realize our potentials as individual human beings*

2) *We will try never to lose sight of the fact that we are in a material world: so to overcome the challenges to us as human beings they also must be overcome by material means. That is, balance the Spiritual with the Seen in order to achieve a material result. To me that material result is the Complete Freedom, The liberation of Black people.*

Since the major challenge to black people is to overcome challenges that cause us to be a race that is suffering oppression. We must use means at our disposal, or use, to overcome white supremacy. It is the practice of white supremacist doctrine that subjects us to oppression. It is why Black people are on the bottom rung in every society in the world. The physical rung, that is.

In consulting history, we understand that people who suffered oppression have overcome that oppression in two basic, over arching ways: Political and War. Of course politics and war are part and partial of the same thing. However, they are thought of, in general terms, of one fighting and drawing blood. The other is working to win the fight, utilizing the means of the systems which are doing the oppressing.

This book is spiritual and political. Political in the sense that "in the struggle" is a phrase that is usually used to identify a way of life for Black people who are conscious of the need to resist white oppression in whatever guises it manifest itself in life. There is not one facet of the lives of Black people where it does not show. The places where black individuals breakdown in life challenges, places where their success mean more to other races of people than it does to their own, is that nobody have told them how to meet life challenges in ways that benefit Black people more than it does any collective group of any other people on the planet. This book proposes to help with that need.

In most instances we have tried to point out the material aspect when we make a spiritual point. And vice versa. The places where the point is not clear, hopefully the side that is not pointed out will be so obvious that it will not be necessary. On the other hand, if the spiritual or physical side is not easily seen, this will present a challenge to the reader to see that particular side. I still may be able to help, so contact me, or read more of what I have written in trying to fulfill my purpose.

Remember what we said about the benefits in overcoming challenges. When Black people overcome the challenge of white supremacy, we build a character that is deserving of the freedom that we will win. This kind of character understands the value of what was lost when we became captive people. Understanding the value of what was lost will derive the wisdom that we will not be made whole until we get all of our possessions back. The wisdom derived also unveils ways to win it back.

The character that reclaims his freedom will also have the courage and determination to work through whatever challenges necessary to win.

IT IS EASY TO SHOW NEED TO FOR PERSONAL STRUGGLE

While it is easy to show individuals the need to struggle against the challenge of personal demons, Demons that confront our efforts to be successful in life, it is not so easy to show that as a people, our race must overcome the challenge of white supremacy to be successful, as a race. So we began by pointing out some basic things about the need to overcome the challenge of white supremacy. And we did so with the understanding that anyone reading this book is free of any doubt that white supremacy is the bane, or major challenge that Black people must defeat to become a free people.

If you happen to be an individual who does not think Black people have to overcome white supremacy, what I am writing is not done to convince you. No, this message is for those who understand the nature of what oppress Black people to a certain degree. When you reach that degree, there will be no doubt that defeating white supremacy is the major challenge of your life.

We are not trying to diminish the need to overcome personal faults that "hold us back." What we are saying is that when you identify the main challenge and struggle to overcome it, your character flaws will be made whole. If the reader continues to read for understanding, rather than to be convinced, he or she will derive the wisdom to execute words, acts and deeds to win the victory.

THE CHALLENGE OF WHITE SUPREMACY REQUIRES BLACK CONSCIOUSNESSES

Defeating white supremacy is a challenge that will require a degree of Black consciousness, if one is going to be successful. Remember we stated above that one who is "in the struggle," must be black conscious. How do we become "black conscious?" Becoming is an easy state of mind to attain. All one needs to do is be black in a white dominated society. Being so, you will quickly become conscious that you do not have the same access to the common good that is created in any society, as do white people. You will become black conscious or be in denial of the fact. Being in denial of the fact and NOT confront this challenge, you will build a "not so good character." Some have a little. Some have a lot. Some think that the more you have the better off you are. Some think that the less you have the better off you are because white people prefer as little as Black consciousness in black people as possible.

It should go without saying, but I will say it anyway since we're going into the ending of the book: There is a wide degree of black consciousness in our people.

Unfortunately the preparation for the challenge of white supremacy does not begin in the normal manner. Nor is it the determining factor in the amount of Black consciousnesses that you have. But over coming the challenge of white supremacy does manifest in a normal manner.

The manifestation occurs in our lives when we try to be successful in the use of our God given talents. White supremacy is established on injustice. It violates individuals to the achievement of their full potential as human beings. When we try to use our gifts, or prepare ourselves to use them, white supremacy surfaces as a challenge to us that must be overcome – especially when you ply your talent, in ways that will benefit your people more that it does white people, or any other people. As we stated in Real Afro-American History, Vol. in 1975, *"There is an order in which you donate your services to. If you have something to give, first you take care of self, then you take care of family and then you take care of nation, or race."*

I believe there is a particular order that pervades everything that we perceive to do. That order is the natural way. Anything that blurs your ability to see the natural way is itself, unnatural. The natural way is to take care of self as this is "self preservation." Family should be taken care of next for obvious reasons. Then come benefits to your own people, or nation. Ask yourself 'who benefits the most for what you do in life? If your answer is not in the order of the above 'natural order,' you may not be able to stop and change immediately. This is not required. What is required is that you plan to change course.

* * * *

IN THE BEGINNING

Even before life officially begins, the sperm must overcome severe challenges to become the one that fertilizes the egg. The fertilized egg becomes the embryo. In the mothers womb the embryo must soon begin to breathe on its own. Breathing, on its own presents its own set of challenges to the embryo.

First of all he or she is breathing air that is part of the earth; Earth is populated by humans with certain habits that pollute the atmosphere of the air we breathe. That is a challenge. Politically speaking, the breath that the baby must inhale is the challenge that Black babies must deal with, if they are to survive. As they go, life in the seen will present certain challenges that must be overcome – white supremacy – if they are to have the chance to realize their full potential as human beings. Please note how selfish the individual must be in the beginning. The sperm on its journey to fertilize the egg will not help any other along the way.

When the baby grows up, his journey may find him helping others along the way. Some babies grow up to be good humans; others grow up to be not so good. The 'not so good' ones do not help but will hinder the ignorant, helpless, innocent and others less powerful than themselves. They will represent challenges that can be overcome in many ways. Many times this happens when a more powerful individual intervenes and help the less powerful against the not so good people.

Just as the pollution of the air is overcome by the baby when the mother filters it, until the baby develops its lungs and etc. This can be seen as the overcoming of challenges in life until we get the power to defeat the challenge ourselves.

It is extremely important to have correct knowledge about the challenge. Once you have correct knowledge you must then understand it. When you understand it degrees of wisdom that reflect how much you understand can be applied to the challenge. When you do not have enough power to overcome the challenge, wisdom will tell you ways to overcome the challenge that will reflect the amount of power you do have. This is important when the challenge is a major, brutal, heartless one that benefits some of those 'not so good humans' we spoke about. Let us take a look at the central challenges of Black people in the United States of America.

THE CHALLENGE OF WHITE SUPREMACY BEGINS EARLY AND STAYS LATE

The reason why a baby easily overcomes the challenge of polluted air is easily understood. The reasons why humans do not resist evil was covered through this writing. However, we will say at this point that resistance to evil is a must when the individual is determined to realize his potential as a human being. If he doesn't find a way to resist the circumvention to his potential, he will continue to grow, but in a retarded and unnatural way. It is important to his well being that he struggles to overcome the challenge to his potential as a human being. We previously discussed the residual benefits to your character development whether you are successful or not.

THE WHITE SUPREMACY IS POTENTIAL

White Supremacy is only 'potential' when manifested and practiced in the world. This is because it is a demonic philosophy that brutalizes everyone it comes in contact with.

Many think the brutalization stops at the devastation of any non white people who live in it – its victims, for the most part. But white supremacy brutalizes and destroys the potential in all humans that try to live within the societies that it dominates. It is an unnatural philosophy. And like all unnatural conditions it will not last. White supremacy is a demonic philosophy. Another name for demonic is devil. The devil is powerful until you find a way to resist his power. That makes it 'potential.' And that potential will only be there so long as you don't resist it.

It is not demonic or evil because it is unnatural. There are some unnatural philosophies that aren't demonic. They will not last either, but they are not demonic or evil because they may be harmless to humans who try to abide in its unnatural states. In fact, when the sincere individual tries to abide in an unnatural state whatever it may be, in order to stay, there are rules that you must live by. In trying to live your life in an unnatural way you will soon see it has limits. You may still live within the confines of the unnatural state and accept the limitations. But once you reach the limits that you must, if it is unnatural, you will look for ways to get around the limits. Some may say "to expand the limits."

If the systems, or states that it causes you to be in are not evil, there will be ways within its makeup to expand its limitations. It may easily be changed or even be replaced by a better system. That is, again, if it isn't built with evil intent. Of course the devil, who is the ruler of evil systems, operates his systems by evil means. So he too may expand the evil system when it is obvious that his game is up. But before his game is up he will use his evil means to visit much brutality, harm and death to those who resist his evil ways.

WHY THE DEVIL CHANGES SOMETIMES BEFORE HIS GAME IS UP

Let us take a brief look at some reasons why it is not always easy to resist evil. Or in the example we are using, white supremacy. And also, why the devil changes some times before his game is up?

There are many reasons why one doesn't resist evil. But ignorance and fear are the primary ones. Fear because they are afraid of what will happen to them if they act against evil. Ignorance, because they don't understand "there is nothing to fear." If they understood they would have the wisdom to act on the knowledge that there is always ways to resist evil.

Once you know something is evil you must resist it or suffer the consequence. The consequence is you will never live up to your potential as a human. And when you are circumvented from living up to your potential and don't act to overcome the challenge, you become less than a man or a woman.

On the other hand, if you aren't physically resisting a known evil (white supremacy), to avoid the ramifications of being less that a man or woman, you must resist spiritually. You must never give into fear and not resist a known evil. As a minimum you must plan, or be on the look out for ways to overcome the evil.

In the case of white supremacy, you must never allow yourself to believe that since it is such a pervasive and powerful system, you must give in and live as best you can within it – forever. Since we all know how evil and brutal white supremacy is, we know that we must be careful. But if it is evil, we also know that that it will not last and there are ways to resist it. And this is where your wisdom comes in.

The wisdom is in the understanding of the knowledge that it is only fair seeming, will not last and there are ways to resist it. The understanding will give you the wisdom of how to resist it.

So if you KNOW it is evil. You must not try to accept it. Study to UNDERSTAND why you know it is evil. This understanding will give you the wisdom of how to resist it.

IT IS ALSO HARD TO CHANGE HARMLESS SYSTEMS

It is said that the only constant in life is change. All things must change, or stagnate. And die. So whether a system is evil or harmless when you try to change it, resistance to change will be natural. The means by which changing things is resisted will determined the severity necessary to effectuate change.

If evil means are employed to resist change, it still must be confronted and overcome. If good means are employed to resist change, it still must be resisted and changed. But when evil is employed to resist and beat back change, then the ones the evil is used against must use physical means to overcome the evil. The challenge to the initiator of the change is to not be tempted to use evil methods to achieve its objectives. We live with the understanding that there is a right way to do anything. This understanding gives us the wisdom to look for the right way in whatever we are of a mind to do.

This does not mean when physical acts are used against your efforts to overcome evil, you cannot use physical means to overcome their ways and means. But this is the challenge, more often than not, that delays methods that could legitimately be used to effectuate correct change. Or destroy evil.

Black people have been tricked and brutalized in every way that the white man could conceive. One of the ways we were brutalized was, we could be killed just on the accusation of a white person that we were "militant." The doctrine of white supremacy protected the criminal who falsely accused and killed us. This was in "olden days." In modern days, the brutalization is not as insidious. This is a case of the devil changing his ways to achieve the same objectives. Today, the police will provoke the young Black man to defend himself. Then beat him to a pulp, or kill him. This tells us that if you are put in a situation where you must defend yourself, don't let emotion overrule your understanding that you don't have to do it at that moment.

How did we survive without becoming an Uncle Tom, or give in and try to become like the criminal? The Black race or nation is replete with heroes and sheroes that resisted the evil of white supremacy. I have named some above. How did they do it?

In order to survive, the wise Black man hid his true feelings and intent. So there were rebellions and plans to rebel going on all the time. When Nat Turner and Denmark Vesey couldn't resist white supremacy immediately, they made plans to resist. And they did resist. They knew white men and white women were evil so they worked on the understanding of that knowledge. The knowledge they understood gave them the wisdom to not be provoked by the evil things they witnessed. The saw wives and children sold away from home. They saw friends and loved one beaten and killed. But they had the wisdom to know that if they came to the rescue of their loved ones, or friends, there was no chance of successfully overcoming the challenges. So they hid their feelings and planned. Hiding feeling and planning are spiritual or unseen acts of resistance. But one day they physically acted.

The fear of white people is a state of being that has been beaten into us for centuries. They used so very many ways to inbreed fear into us that an entire book could probably be written just recounting ways and means they carried out these crimes. But wisdom is such a great attribute that when you put it to good use it is used to turn the tables on the evil doer.

One means the white people employed to inculcate fear into our psyche was his viciousness when a member of the race came to the assistance of another. It could be wife, husband, child, sister or brother, but if you saw said person being brutalized, wisdom told you to not come to their rescue. Coming to the rescue of a loved one was met with unmerciful acts of brutality by the devil. That meant instant death for the would-be hero. In fact, when a punishment was administered to a captive/slave, they would call all of the slaves to the sight of the crime. The devil would force the people to witness what he was doing and sort of dare anyone to come to try and save him or her. It was not long before we had the knowledge of what would happen if we did try to save one of our members. Yes, we would be brutalized. What we had to do was study the knowledge of what we knew. Studying this gave us the wisdom to know not to do anything. At least not at the time the crime was being committed.

There were some who allowed the fear to cause them to contract a disease called Post Traumatic Slavery Disorder. And this disease so crippled them mentally that they became too fearful to resist. Knowledge of the same crime gave others the wisdom to not resist at that time because they too would be destroyed. But resist they would because they the understanding also told them that there is always a way to resist evil. And the wisdom from the understanding guides the ways and means by which they carried out the resistance to evil acts.

Some captive Africans planned and ran away. Others planned and actually killed the criminal slave holder – poisoning was a favorite method. Others would wait for the best opportunity to present itself. Sometimes this opportunity would not come until the end of the harvest when the crops was already gathered and put in the barn. But one day the barn would suddenly go up in smoke – burned down by a wise slave who knew what he had witnessed was evil. His resistance to evil was to strike a match and burn up the crop.

But the rewards of white people to docile Blacks was so consummate that as the centuries came to past, the militant Black man and woman became less and less. In fact, in the actual breeding of Blacks for chattel slavery, the number one trait they tried to breed out of us was the anger and fight in us. So over time, for many, fight was bred out and fear was bred in. And as any introduction to Black history will teach, the use of religion was used to pacify the captives. And the endless distortions in the Religious books were essentially designed to replace the desire to win their freedom by defeating and killing our enemies.

We will get back to the kind of balanced writing that many readers like. *Maybe I'll win one of those Caucasian literary prizes.* But before i go there, I will give a few words about the kinds of characters that was bred in as fighting was bred out.

The breeding of the most useful captive Black men and women defeated the designs of the breeding of slaves. We know very little about them, so when you do hear about Nat Turner, Denmark Vesey, Gabriel Prosser you must affirm in your mind that they are only the tip of the iceberg. Not only that, they were the most skillful at adapting to the ways and means that would be the most successful in resisting evil in the most effective ways. That is finding the way to kill their oppressor. And free as many captives as possible.

The most important thing that had to be cultivated and learned was to not show how much they hated the oppressor. So the emotion of anger had to be mastered "to perfection," as Brother Lumumba used to say. Brother Lumumba was my Black Nationalist mentor in Harlem, N.Y. He lived to the ripe old age of 83 years as "an uncompromised Black man in the Stolen Land called the United States of America."

The only good white man to Brother Lumumba was a "dead white man." When he said "to perfection," that means the white man didn't know how the Blackman felt about him until he could feel the knife between his ribs,

As the reader may remember, or should know by now, the reason why Nat Turner and the two other warriors named was successful is because they planned their revolts in secrecy. They planned in secrecy and killed the slave masters as much as possible in secrecy. Of course the ability of Nat Turner, & etc. to adapt to the necessary ways to fight the enemy was counter balanced by the legacy of Right wing negroes of today.

Uncle Tom characters were bred directly from the pacifist slavery teaching of the slave masters. But uncle Toms were so close to the state of being an imbecile that even the slave holders had no use for a lot of them. The most useful slaves were the ones who took the religion called Christianity to heart. That is, they were taught that no matter how hard things were in their lives that Jesus "loved them." And Jesus would show that love and they would receive their just rewards after they die and go to heaven. In short, too many of our people, even if you leave the fear equation out of our liberation struggle, were ones who believed that the way to defeat your enemy is to "turn the other cheek."

I don't have much doubt that this quote is in the New Testament. For it is a perversion of a spiritual law: the Just Law of Compensation. What goes around does indeed come around. But the coming around, or working out of the great law, only means it will come around to you if you over step the bounds. In other words, you are permitted to even the score. And white people have been so brutal and murderous that Black people can do a lot of killing before they even approach the get even point.

In short, the change necessary to break the bounds that white people have on black people is to get even on all of the brutality that has been visited upon us. It is possible that millions of white people will be killed to bring about the condition necessary to change the state of white supremacy domination.

I am actually reluctant to say it here, but since this is a spiritual book, there is a way that white people can avoid the wholesale killing of millions in their race. I will go deeper into it when I write specifically about Reparations because this is part of what they will have to do to avoid their doom. It is only a part of what is required of them because whatever they do or do not, Reparations must be paid. But they can avoid much of the killing of their members if they both make amends and pay the Reparations. But with a history they are living out, there is nothing on the historical ledger to indicate any chance that they will make amends. Certainly not before millions are killed as they are forcefully brought to justice and made to pay reparations.

NECESSARY CHANGE
 IN A HARMLESS SYSTEMS

We will end this chapter by saying a few words about the methods that one engages in to bring about necessary change in a system that is harmless, or there by mistake. The rulers may be well meaning but just don't know how to bring about the necessary change. Since it is so hard for almost all change, there will be resistance to change a system that is harmless, or just there because the rulers of the society could not come up with a more perfect system.

In this case, there is an orderly method within the system that can be used to bring about the change. And that is the way that change should be brought about. The greatest danger to using this methodology is that rulers over the system are men or women. As such they will likely want to maintain the status quo: keep things as they are. But more times than not, the laws on the books can be used to overcome their reluctance to change. Of course human nature being as it is, someone is bound to consider breaking the law to stay in power. So whoever is the agent of the movement for change must be strong and prepared to defeat him also.

But by and large, the one who need change the most is the one that is under the subjection of the status quo. Sufficient change will not be rendered by the ruling authorities. Change must come about by the actions of the subject people.

In short, this is exactly Why we Struggle and Why we Fight. As a subject people, we are under the domination of an unjust system that is ruled by white supremacy doctrine. It is an evil system. Evil is demonic and wrong. How do you overcome evil, demonic and wrong situations? You must struggle against them. This is why we struggle and this is why we fight.

CHAPTER NINETEEN

ON RAISING CHILDREN

As the world knows, when I write or say anything that is designed to impact the world - in which Black people are the underclass, the word or thought is meant to be applied to the condition that we are in. But as the reader should also remember, I have said that all challenges in life are just that: a challenge to the individual to do what is in their own best interest – without hurting the interest of anyone else. Of course you are allowed to defend yourself because it is in your best interest not to be abused, killed or otherwise taken advantage of. Reclaiming possessions criminally taken is also permitted. If someone has denied you your rights, it impact negatively on your character. Reclaiming your rights or your property will be necessary before you reach whatever goal.

This is more evidence that character building is the dominant reason why we are in the world in the first place.

Each experience shapes our character to be the best representative of the goal that you are striving for. The challenges are the tasks that must be overcome to get there. Besides being challenges to bring you to your goal, they are developing, or building the character that will be best suited for your representation when you reach your goal.

Since I am a Black Muslim I believe Black people were created by an All Power Supreme Being. The Supreme Being is The Creator of everything in existence. He is called by different names, in many different languages: Allah in Arabic, God in English, Jehovah in Hebrew, so on and so forth. The Creator has certain Characteristics: as I strive to overcome challenges to reach my goals, my character will reflect the attributes of The Creator.

My Creator is "Most Merciful" and "Most Gracious" and other stellar characteristics. My characteristics will reflect those of my Creator when I reach my goals. My work in life, my life challenges are opportunities to build such characteristics.

We have individual goals in life. We also have collective goals – and what I term, overall goals. The individual goals are to overcome challenges to achieve success that benefits the best interest of self and family.

Second to the best benefit or interest for self and family is for your own particular race. And the third goal is to have that success benefit all of humanity.

There is a particular order that The Creator designed us to build within. When you build within the order, your work will reflect the harmony that is prevalent any time that you are pleasing to The Creator.

"Everything is in Divine Order." This is true. One of our Internal Challenges is to find this order in whatever we engage our wills to do in life. When we find and have enough character to stay and do our work in Divine Order, "All is well." When you don't work in Divine Order "all is NOT hell," but you will have to do the work over again. Of course sometimes it is "hell." Or feels like it.

When we look at the condition of Black people, we can clearly see that as a race "we are in really bad shape." It is the same when we are looked at individually: some of us are "in bad shape!" In life we are always presented with choices. Whom will we help first, in any particular situation? If you, the individual is in need of what you get your hands on, you take care of self and family first, then family and race. We think this is in Divine Order.

There is a Divine Order that we must work within to overcome our individual challenges. When the individual is working within the Divine Order his efforts will reflect good benefits for those of his own race MORE than it does for any other race on the planet.

For those who don't see the wisdom in the above, but are interested in seeing it, you must first examine self. The examination should give you a good understanding of that self – yourself. The understanding of the knowledge of self may unveil the fact that your race is not the primary beneficiary of your work, or the success that your work has achieved. The wisdom will also unveil the ways and means by which you can change that fact.

Many will say, and have said, "Success is success." And I will readily agree that this is so. But what character are you reflecting with that success? Is it the character of an All Powerful Creator that created you in the race as a Black human being? If so what are His Characteristics?

I have had many persons tell me that it doesn't matter. They are saying that it doesn't matter whether they are conscious of being Black or not. But it does matter. If it matters to our Creator it matters to us.

It matters if you are Black or White because as a race, Black people are suffering oppression. Our challenge is to overcome that oppression. We will overcome the oppression when we conquer the Internal Forces that challenge us to be successful. Understanding the Inside Forces will unveil the fact that an external Force is unjustly circumventing your potential to live as a human being. The individual who says that it doesn't matter that white people benefit from his success more that Black people will be part of the challenge that must be overcome by

Black people who know this is not in Divine Orders. "No man was created to be under the oppression of his fellow man." "All are created with the desire to be free to realize his highest potential.

Any success for black individuals that is based on the needs of white people is only fair seeming. It is not real because you are not loved by either race. So the peace and harmony that should come with success eludes you because you don't reflect the characteristics of The Creator.

But the most important part of the dilemma that you are in is that your success is based within a doctrine of white supremacy. When white supremacist doctrine is understood, it unveils the fact it is based on injustice to other people. Since everything is in Divine Order the injustice will be rectified.

* * * *

The questions arise constantly in the mind of any conscious Black person. What is the goal for the individual? Will my achievements as an individual suffice the ultimate goals of my race?

The answers to the above questions are easy to answer if you accept the rule and authority of white supremacist doctrine. When you accept the doctrine of white supremacy, you are saying that your potential as an individual was not contravened by white supremacist rulers of "the system." This answers the first part of the question.

The second part of the question must be answered likewise: your answer must reflect the fact that you feel that white supremacy did not circumvent the potential of Black people. You will feel that it is ok for Black people to be the under class in every society where we are in the world – yes even in Africa. In Africa you must feel that the best way for Black citizens in Black countries to attain to our goal is to use the same ideals that white supremacy uses.

The above thinking cannot be termed unreasonable.

Of course when it is termed unreasonable by anyone, it will be because they have not found the motivation to think outside of the white supremacist system. When you do get a certain degree of understanding of the knowledge, about white supremacy it will cause you to conclude that your potential is contravened. At this point you'd be compelled to overcome the challenge. That is, if you desire to do what is best for Self.

Remember we said that when you know what is best for self but don't act, you must convince yourself as to why not. For if you know but don't act in your own best interest, there must be a reason. Lack of will power? Fear?

Whatever the reason is, your mind must be convinced or lied to.

I don't generally put Black people, who do not think out of the box, of white supremacy down. Only someone ignorant of white supremacy would do so. Us who have studied the white supremacist system understand how devastating it has been on Black people. We have been victims for a wicked system. Rather than "put down" a fellow Black, we try to induce them to study white supremacy.

THE EXCEPTION TO PUTTING DOWN INDIVIDUAL BLACKS

The exception to the above is if they have a very limited knowledge about "the system" and are spreading their ignorance, or they have attacked and put down those of us who have studied the system and concluded that this system is not best for self, nor good for the race. For when the system is understood it becomes clear immediately that we are in the condition we are in because our potential was contravened by white supremacy. The question then becomes what to do about it. How do you think outside of the system?

If you are thinking within the system of white supremacy, the ultimate for your life will be to reform the system and exclude the aspects about it that are contravening your potential as a human being. As I said, feeling thusly is not a reason for a Black Freedom Fighter to put someone down because they don't agree with them. This should not be taken to believe that I have any tolerance for white supremacy.

The kind of freedom I strive for has no reconciliation with white supremacy. No accommodation whatsoever in the same space. The system of white supremacy must be broken down and destroyed: Done away with and replaced with a system that is based on the Divine Order of the Universe. Since it is a challenge to strive to build a just, Divine system that is based on MAAT, the striving to achieve it must be done in the same manner that you strive, struggle or fight for anything else.

You may choose your own words to describe the barriers that must be overcome to establish a just system. But in white supremacy, the challenge, or barriers are already before you, both internal and external. To achieve your goals you must use, basically, the same methodology as described throughout my writing. That is, understand the knowledge of the challenge that you struggle to overcome [this is pre-supposing that you know something is wrong at the present time]. The understanding will give you the wisdom to act correctly. However, if you have not engaged your internal struggle first, when you get the wisdom, if you have a certain degree of understanding, the wisdom will tell you to get more knowledge of self. Getting knowledge of self is a spiritual pursuit. Then the two are balanced; after the balancing of the physical and the spiritual, then you act to effectuate change in the status quo.

In the striving to achieve, your character develops into what it should be just system that you have built. Remember now, you are striving to build based on the Divine Order of the Universe. Your character must reflect that.

If you are in the white supremacist social system, you have already developed a certain character to still be alive – especially if you are a Black person, and even more so if you are a Black man. When you study knowledge of self, you will discover some parts of your character that will likely not be very flattering.

One of the first things that I found out about myself, that was not to my liking, was the fact that I was required to take all my orders from white people to earn a living. This would not be bad in itself except that the white supremacist system was made and is run to the best interest of white people. And, without a doubt, every white person learns sooner or later that it is in their best interest to keep Black people in subjection to them and their race. So I became uncomfortable with having to take orders and do work for white people. But as a young Blackman with a lack of deep knowledge of self and kind, my uncomfortably played out in life in that even to this day it is hard to describe.

WHAT WAS I THINKING EARLY IN LIFE IN WHITE SUPREMACY?

The best I can describe it is that I was in a kind of zone. It was a zone that was aware that white people had enslaved my people and we were living as second-class citizens in the aftermath. I knew there was something wrong with this situation. Now when a human being determines that something is wrong with a particular thing, or situation, he or she must react to it in some way. And I did.

As I said, before I found proper knowledge of self, I was in a kind of zone. So when I say how I reacted to a situation that I was born in that I knew was wrong, since my understanding of it was limited, my reaction to it was in a limited way.

Somehow I felt that I would overcome the unjust situation by being better than my peers. I mean a better athlete, better speller, and I guess a better physical fighter. Somehow I thought that I would just get there by living my life. For example, I was a good baseball player. I knew I was good and somehow I expected to become a professional baseball player. But I didn't allow myself to really engage in the kind of practice and mindset that would give me the best chance to get there. If someone had advised me to study to understand my situation and my talents I have not doubt that I would have made it as a professional ball player.

White supremacy surely impacted my making it or not. And also without a doubt, my reaction to the impact of white supremacy shaped a part of my character. I didn't even see white supremacy as the challenge to my future. And there was nobody in my life to guide, teach and advise me that if I studied what was challenging me, I would be better off. In fact it would be many, many years before I even heard the phase "white supremacy." When I finally began to study and understand my situation (and of course the situation of my people), it still took awhile before I could get proper knowledge of three of the most important things that constitute life. The three things are proper knowledge of self, proper knowledge of the Creator and proper knowledge of the devil.

But the opening of my eyes came as I first got rudimentary knowledge of Black history. The understanding that I got of that gave me the wisdom to, first of all, pursue more knowledge. Since this is not my memories I'll skip over much of the details about my own self discovery. But please indulge me just few more words.

As I grew and evolved through my early years as a man, there came a time when I had enough understanding to question "the system." I asked why is it that white people own so much and Black people, relatively, own so little? I found out that the basic wealth of white people was built with unpaid Black labor. Studying this fact, I finally came to understand that Black people are built into the system as a permanent underclass. There is no way any intelligent Black human being can accept the status within a system like this.

Later I found that there is, in fact, a class of otherwise Black humans who readily accept that status.* But even they know that "the system" is an unjust way to govern people. The live as Blacks who enjoy the privileged white people give to their servants. They are called "Boulé" they readily accept their status as second-class citizens.

There is no doubt in my mind that all Black humans know the system is unjust. But yet some still accept it as a legitimate government to invest all of their socialization needs as humans. But deep down in every human lies a natural aversion to injustice. That aversion compels them to resist the injustice in some way or rationalize, or lie to self that there is no need to change the status quo.

The rationalization for being at peace with the system takes many forms. The number one form it takes will be based on some kinds of hatred of self. The number basis of self hatred is ignorance, which translates as a lack of proper knowledge of self and kind. Second to self hatred – which may be part and partial of number one – is fear.

The basis of fear what will happen to them if they live in ways that white people don't like. They may obvious injustice, but will do so in way that meets the approval of white people. This is a legitimate fear for the ignorant.   But how long can an ignorant person use it as an excuse? If he begins to use his own ignorance as an excuse, it will not longer be a legitimate excuse to accept white domination. That is unless he is not only ignorant, but is also an idiot!

IT IS LEGITIMATE TO FEAR A PEOPLE WITH A BRUTAL VIOLENT HISTORY

We have said that the fear of the people who built "the system" is legitimate. It is legitimate but it is NOT a reasonable fear. It is legitimate because white people who built the system have demonstrated many times over what they will do to you if you resist injustice [in ways by means that are not approved by them]. Of course at the foundation phase of building the white supremacist system, when you employed means to resist injustice, they would kill you out right – right away.

Later on they have various degrees of punishments to meter to your person if you resisted in ways that was not approved by 'the system. Today, when the white rulers of the white supremacist system don't kill you outright, they hurt you real bad. During the foundation phase they would hurt you real bad or sell you, your wife, children, or loved one to some other bad place.

Fear of white people is real but is not a reasonable fear. It is not reasonable because we have such a rich history of resisting the brutal behavior of white people. Black history recounts time after time when our ancestors resisted white people at every turn. Black individuals in 2009 have no excuse when they don't resist fear. If our ancestors found ways to resist as chattel property, what kind of Black individual refuses to live a life in resistance to the brutality, oppression in white supremacy? Only an ignorant or cowardly one!

In discussing resistance to white supremacy we are not suggesting any particular method of resistance: It can be in the mode of Dr. Martin Luther King Jr., Minister Malcolm X, The

Honorable Elijah Muhammad, The Great Marcus M. Garvey, Harriet Tubman, Nat Turner, David Walker, Denmark Vesey, Paul Cuffee or Gabriel Prosser, etc. But to think that all there is to life is as a subject to white people is a form of insanity. When you decide that since you have become a good functionary in "the system;" it pays you well, you live good, you have a beautiful wife and children, live in a nice home & etc. you don't feel theirs is a need to resist white supremacy, something is wrong with you. Everything about you is subject to the best interest of white people. You have power, but that power is subject to be used in the best interest of white people. Black resisters to oppression throughout our history would not accept this status – regardless to how well off they were. They worked to change the status quo, not use their power and resources to become part of the status quo. There was a time when it was extremely hard to get proper Black history. But not today; today Black history has been researched thoroughly by Black people. The only logical conclusion one can come to when our fellow Blacks are not living in resistance is lack of correct knowledge of our history; they are in a planning mode [as per Nat Turner when he returned to the plantation after 30 days and became a model citizen).

History represents knowledge; knowledge is power: so when the knowledge is understood, wisdom to resist fear will be yours. Once you wisely face up to fear, it is neutralized. Once it is neutralized it can be used to your advantage.

Using fear to your own advantage is possible because your knowledge of Black history has empowered you. Understanding of the power will give you the wisdom as to what extent it can be used, from where you are in the "here and now" to neutralize use it to your own advantage.

FEAR MUST BE OVERCOME BECAUSE THERE IS 'NOTHING TO FEAR'

There is a predictable characteristic in anyone who fears to act against injustice. Here again is an opportunity presented to build ones character. Remember we said that when you have a goal, doing the things to get to that goal will require that you overcome certain tasks. In doing things to overcome the tasks you will automatically be building the character that that is commensurate with the goal that you are reaching for.

When you are of a mind to resist injustice in a white supremacist system, how you resist the injustice will shape the character that you will have when you reach your goal.

If you only work within the approved means of "the system" to achieve your goals, your success in resisting will be circumscribed. Resist a lot and you will evolve a good, strong character.

Anyone can see by the condition of Black people that it is going to take a lot of resistance to achieve the status of Freedom, Justice and Equality.

As I continue to wind up this book, we are going to move quickly though discussions about current happenings in Black America. Hopefully the reader will apply some of what I have written up to this point to the challenges in the here and now.

CHAPTER TWENTY

> **THE LAST QUARTER:
> THE ENDING OF THE BOOK**

ON ADVISING BLACK YOUTH TO STOP DISSIPATING BLACK POWER LOOKING FOR WORK IN "THE SYSTEM!"

A PROPOSAL TO BLACK YOUTH TO EVOLVE A LIFE STYLE THAT DOES NOT REQUIRE GIVING UP YOUR BLACKNESS TO LOOK FOR WHITE PEOPLE TO GIVE YOU A "GOOD JOB."

I have stated previously that we must raise a generation of Black youth who are not educated [or as Dr. Carter G. Woodson stated 86 years ago, *mis-educated] and* prepared to work in "the system." Too much of their time and power is wasted and dissipated pursuing a fantasy j.o.b. For the most part Black youth don't find out there is an alternative to the fantasy of a *good system job* until after they have been mentally and physically diminished, in the system. The alternative is to work for self to take care of duties and responsibilities as humans.

I know *not* working in the system is already the case for the mass majority of Black youth in the year 2009. But their lack of positions in 'the system" is not by design, by self. We want to cultivate and design systems that will give them the tools to "do for self." That is, as entrepreneurs or someplace that is clearly in the best interest of empowering Black people. Their first hand knowledge about how difficult it is to find a job will be a tremendous asset in turning them from a mindset that both saps their strength/power and frustrates their ambition to live a good fruitful successful life.

When they make up their mind and do for self, they avoid two of the most debilitating things that we face in white supremacy (1) having to ignore numerable insults on the job, or be in a perpetual state of anxiety to stay employed (2) getting laid off or fired because you have protested being passed over, or will be passed over for a promotion that you know you deserve. Of course most Black youth don't have to worry about these because they are not working in the system. But rather than start out creating jobs for self, they spend too much energy and time looking for a job. As for those who are working, they will eventually be diminished mentally and physically to some degree, dissipating and scattering their power as individuals.

THE REASON OUR CHILDREN ARE NOT GAINFULLY WORKING

Presently, The reason Black youth are not working in corporate America is because corporate America doesn't like them. But Black youth are still being mis-educated into thinking a "good job" is working in America for a *good white man.* The thought that there is a "good white man" who will give them a "break" to succeed in life must be disabused in their young beautiful Black minds.

They must be told from the "cradle to the grave" that white people don't like them; they don't like them because they fear their Blackness. But also tell them, even though they fear you and don't like you, they may still give them a "break" if they deny their blackness. You enhance your chances to get a "break" when you evidence very little of your Blackness, and are willing to work for less, or in menial vocations beneath your qualifications. Or when there is not a white person available who can do the "good job" half as well as you can for far less money.

WHY WHITE PEOPLE FEAR OUR BLACKNESS

They fear your Blackness because of the pain, suffering and turmoil they historically perpetrated against Black people. It is pain, suffering and turmoil that caused injuries that continue to fester down to this very day. They are guilty of a documented crime against humanity. A crime that will not be restituted until we raise a generation of Black youth who will use their power to get into a positions where they can hold white people accountable for the injuries. This will not happen if you are giving up your power to make him stronger in the positions of dominance that they now enjoy in society; societies that are based and operated on a doctrine of white supremacy.

    We clearly state to our Black youth that working white supremacy jobs require that you accept inferior positions to them, not because they are superior but because they are white. Black people were first captured and forced into inferior positions. The force caused both mental and physical injury. The mental injuries resulted in Post Traumatic Slavery Disorder (PTSD). And of course the physical injuries run the entire gambit: from broken limbs to death by lynching (police brutality).

    The abuse and injuries continues because they are necessary to maintain the status quo in white supremacist systems. However neither can be treated in whole until we receive our reparations. And you will not receive your reparations until you are able to back up your demand on the guilty.

So working in the system is a two-fold threat to white people: (1) if you are conscious of your Blackness and refuse to give it up they fear that one day you will understand that they owe the debt of reparations (2) Your understanding will give you the wisdom to properly use your power in your own best interest and act to reclaim what is rightly yours.

When Black youth don't work in the System they have (1) not wasted a lot of time looking for a job they will never find; and if they do find on close, it will be because they have diminished themselves in some way, or will be when they work around white people for awhile and find out what they are really like (2) doing a good job for corporate America strengthens the doctrine of white supremacy. White supremacy pre-supposes the inferiority of Black people to white people. No Blackman or woman can put up with living in this lie without becoming mentally deficit in some way.

THE WORK OF BLACK COMMUNITY ORGANIZERS AND MASTER TEACHERS IN THE AWAKENING OF BLACK YOUTH

Meanwhile, as we struggle to awaken Black youth, we find the injuries we incurred are playing out in every sociological way imaginable. Our Master Teachers and Community Organizers, including those who evolve to be the would-be-liberators, as died in the wool Black nationalist Freedom Fighters - have lived and recorded clear statements and terms that confirm the injuries we sustained living in doctrines of white supremacy. They have also served up ways about how to heal the injuries.

Since the injuries continue to fester into today's Black youth, they manifest into some ill behavior that is exacerbated when they waste an ordinate amount of time and energy looking for a white fantasy "good job." Even if they find a job, it may be good but the environment where the job is worked is not in good surroundings.

By the time they reach the age of reason society and their "bio rhythm" cause black youth to know they must now take care of their own duties and responsibilities as human beings – heretofore they will likely to have been raised and "mis-educated" into some bastardized notions of making it in an oppressive White Supremacy System. Only at this time will they come to know they were mis-educated: They will not have proper knowledge of self; and they will not have proper knowledge about the fact that white people do not like them. Yet they will vainly go through many different changes that are inappropriate to proper knowledge of self and kind; all in the effort to make some white person like them and give them a break.

MIS-EDUCATING IS BRAINWASHING

Mis-education is what Dr. Carter G. Woodson, one of our Master Teachers, called the universal scope of brainwashing of Captive Afrikans. The fact that his analysis was correct is played out today in the education of Black Youth. But Dr. Woodsons teaching cannot be missed, bastardized mis-characterized, and distorted in other ways, as it once was subject to be. This is because he recorded his teachings in a series of books. His seminal book is one of the all-time best selling books in Black history: it is titled *"The Mis-Education of the Negro."* Parents and guardians of our youth can go along way towards the neutralization of the mis-education by introducing the work of Carter G. Woodson to them early in life.

The *Mis-Education of the Negro* must become essential teaching for Black youth from the cradle to the grave. The book must be broken down and fed to them while they are still babies. The Mis-education of the Negro should be required reading by the age of puberty, as well studied intensely in secondary, high school, under-graduate, post graduate through graduate school. If it is not, as the great Hoyt Fuller said: *"...if Black people don't not know that the white man is the devil, everything else he knows will only confuse them."* [this is a paraphrase of Mr. Fuller, whose profundity of intellect is indicated by one of his celebrated students, Dr. Frances C. Welsing].

When Black youth, or any human is given a graduate degree, that portends mastery, without having thoroughly absorbed them in the *Mis-Education of the Negro,* their "mastery" will manifest in some ill defined, various notions of a man or woman – depending entirely on the level of degree they have been exposed to and studied the universal scope of how Afrikan Captives have been brainwashed and trained in White Supremacist Systems of oppression.

We have already estimated and extolled the virtue and the sheer past mastery of the universal scope of Captives Africans by The Honorable Elijah Muhammad. As the recipient of Supreme Wisdom directly from The Creator, "Who Appeared in the Person of Master Fard Muhammad," the Messenger delivered the message he was given so profoundly and dynamically that it became at once the base knowledge that any number, manner and character of Black Master Teachers and Social Scientist appropriated to awaken Black youth to the reality and poison of white supremacy.

Some of the Master Teachers received the treasured X that indicates they were exposed to the full measure and scope of The Supreme

Wisdom [it is possible to have all of the knowledge but there is absolutely no substitute to the direct teaching one receives from a master of any particular knowledge]. Yet all of the most outstanding of the Master Teachers paid, or are paying homage to the body of work of The Honorable Elijah Muhammad.

In a book subsequent to this one: *"The Acquisition and Proper Use of Power*, I shall, InshAllah, give my views on the great benefit for individuals, like myself, who did not complete the processing to receive the X – thus, the direct teaching from officials to whom Mr. Muhammad directly prepared to teach Black people. And of course he taught some in particular to deliver the message directly to the Blackman and Woman in America. Minister Malcolm X and Minister Louis Farrakhan comes readily to mind in this regard – there have been none on a par with these brothers, regardless to the accomplishments of the aforementioned Master Teachers: so this is yet another book that I intend to share, if it be the will of Allah. For now I will only say that one of the most important benefits one can derive for Afrikan Captives, if you did not join the Nation of Islam is that you are free of the application of the law: man made laws, that is. With this freedom you can explore more fully the far regions of the scope of the Universal, or Natural Laws that governs the entire Creation – at best, all man made laws, rules and regulations are replica of these. We know of a certainty that depth of The Supreme Wisdom that was given to The Messenger included the total universal scope. But the light of understanding this fact, and the wisdom itself is only by the Will of The God.

We will write our estimation of the above one day, or codify them into some of the other work, as we work hard at 69 to consolidate positions into Black life in the here and now.

Given the above, one might think that Black youth will have been exposed and taught, at least the rudiments of white supremacy. When they continually expect white people to give them a "break," as they look for a "good job," it belies this conjecture. For reasons we hope we have covered in prior words, in this book, we shall not go into the myriad of reasons why in 2009 they still don't know that white people don't like them, as another of the Master Teachers, Sister Shahrazad Ali told us in one of her books: *"Things Your Parents Should Have Told You."*

Black youth parents have not told them the truth because many times they themselves did not understand the truth. This is the case though the truth is readily available in the books and other documentation of the Master Teachers. Why some parents did not study and pass the teachings, let alone the Message of the Messenger, to their children are known quantities. But to explore them here will take us beyond the scope of the words to awaken and instruct Black youth to stop looking for work in the system.

Without being overly bearing in singling out their parents, Black youth must personally study the body of work by the Master Teachers [Amos Wilson, John H. Clarke, Na'im Akbar] and etc. For now, you can measure where you are by connecting the following themes to the individuals who will be bio'd later: *Developmental Psychology of the Black Child, Menticide, Afro-Centricity, Post Traumatic Slavery Disorder, Post Traumatic Slavery Syndrome.*

Let us continue now with our instruction to Black youth to stop looking to work in white corporate America.

BLACK YOUTH STILL LOOKING FOR A GOOD JOB IN WHITE AMERICA

Given the above, yet Black youth, like their parents, still feel there is no other alternative: When we want a "good Job," we think about working for corporate America. Meanwhile, few ever get the "good job" desired; some of the reasons why go beyond white racism. But white racism is the paramount reason. White racism still mentally cripples Black people in general but Black youth in particular.

If we can guard the minds of our youth by limiting their exposure to this desire for white supremacy work, we can grow healthier young Black men and women. I hope I am placing enough emphasis on protecting them "from the cradle to the grave." Let us now take a look at some of the ways to protect them against the dangers in white supremacy.

PROPOSED DESIGN TO POISON BLACK YOUTH AGAINST PLACES AND SITUATIONS THAT INJURE THEIR MINDS

We propose to "design," or prepare Black youth to live without the desire to get a "good system job." We want to poison their desire to work in corporate America. We know almost every Black youth in America would run to a job, if they could get one in corporate America. We want to teach them against corporate America as we teach them against all dangerous experiences in America. If there is danger, we tell them to stay away from it. Depending on their ages, we may force with threat of physical punishment if they partake of the danger against our instructions.

Fortunately, no Black youth meets the main qualifications to work in corporate America. In white supremacy the main qualification is that your skin not be Black. And if you are Black, you must not be born in the United States of America. It is estimated that up to 75%

of young Black males, in America are unemployed, or under employed, including the in prison or have given up on finding a "good job."

The Caucasian himself says that 32 to 50% of Black youth are unemployed. But they don't take into consideration the "under employed. Moreover, many Black youth have qualified themselves by the highest possible standards that white America say is necessary to get a good job. But since it is impossible to meet the main qualification, however well qualified they are in other ways, they will always be handicapped to some degree in white corporate America. The "handicap" equates to discrimination in social sets that assists greatly in promotions. The handicap equates to gross insults by any number or ranking of whites, co-workers or otherwise; the handicap equates in less pay for doing the same, but in most case, more work than white co-workers. Since knowledge of these facts can be documented with our own personal experiences in white supremacy, understanding of the knowledge will give us the wisdom to properly use them to make working in corporate America NOT a desirable place to be. They will then be more likely to listen to any alternatives to entering the danger zones in white corporate America.

We know that the unspoken qualification that you be white of color is not factored into equations to explain the high unemployment statistics for Black youth. But as a Black man of almost seven decades - living in racist white supremacist America, I would be a fool to omit this factor. I am also a parent of five Black youth. Four have graduated from four year colleges. Of the four with college degrees, none, as in – 0 – are working in careers for which they studied in college; in fact, each of them is working far beneath the level of their education. My fifth child is a Junior at a four year institution.

Admittedly, using my own children as examples may not be typical for Black youth. For to some degree, they were oriented in their preparation for the America workplace by a father who was never "gainfully" employed by white America. When I say this I am not counting four years in the USAF, or the four years as an apprentice to master the production of the printed word: yes, I am a Master Printer by trade. And I did air traffic control in the military. But other than that, my life has been one of "doing for self" in business. But of course like all Africans, I came to the age of reason thinking that one day I would have a good job in white corporate America. And also like us all, I looked intensely to find a job. Moreover, many of character flaws can be traced to things I did to protect myself to survive in white supremacy based corporate America. The reason I am recounting personal experience here is because my examples are good aids to use in a book that is designed to instruct the reader in how to acquire and properly use power. For I am certain that had I been taught about the danger in white corporate America I would have done either one of two things, #1 I would not have spent an inordinate amount of time trying to get to a place that I had been told is dangerous and hurtful #2 If I had been told about the danger, but went into the hostile environment anyway, I would have been better prepared to guard against some of the challenges I had to defeat to get the skills to become a master printer.

It should be understood without me saying it, but without having to overcome the character flaw challenges, I would have been a more loving and caring husband; and better prepared as a father to raise my children. Yet, with the above said, striving to overcome the challenges has shaped my character to be what it is; and from the indications of folk that I meet, I have achieved a great measure of success in trying to be the best Khalifah on planet earth [Khalifah means Representative of The Creator in the Kingdom on Earth]. The most wonderful thing that I like to be called today is Uncle Brother.

Yet, if I had thought of the idea to educate Black youth to NOT work in the "system," I would have taught my own children directly, as I am advising young parents today. For if I had, perhaps my own children would not have wasted so much of their time looking for, filling out applications, interviewing for and being rejected for work in corporate America. And they would have been better prepared to follow into their own fathers footsteps.

TOO MUCH TIME WASTED LOOKING FOR A BREAK FOR CAREERS THEY WILL NEVER GET

We must take advantage of a clear opportunity in this era. The opportunity is to break the cycle of Black youth who think the way to succeed is to find a "good job:" Most soon have to face the fact that there is nothing in the "system" that can be called a "good job." They continue to look, but the experience of looking for a job in white America is so debilitating that their psyches are scarred for life: when they realize that their dream is not only "deferred," they are dreams, for the most part that will never see the light of day. With this being the case, the mass majority lower their career sights and begin looking for work as generation, for the most part, did up until the 1960s in America. That is, back then when we went job hunting we just looked for any work that would pay us – beneath our education, demeaning, insulting, shameful and humiliating as they were, these were incorporated into our characters. And the energy derived from the pent up anger was either played out into determination that "our children will be better employed than us." Too many of our really great youngsters must still make dream killing decisions. Even today, most Black youth will apply for any job that is advertised.

Meanwhile, some stop looking for work. They support themselves by their "wits." Many of these go into petty crime that plays right into the hands of the criminal, white supremacist "system." They are eventually killed or maimed by the police or by fellow brothers and sisters. Most wind up with criminal records and in jail. Others become violent, cruel and heartless with absolutely no visible signs of the little babies and children who happily told us what they "want to be when they grow up."

Today, when the scene of "what do you want to be when you grow up" is played out, we must disabuse them of any indicating of ambition to work any job in corporate America.

THE CYCLE OF BROKEN BLACK YOUTH BE STOPPED BUILDING A SYSTEM TO FREE BLACK PEOPLE

It is possible and in the interest of everyone that the potential in Black youth have a chance to be fulfilled. But it is only possible for the cycle of criminality in white supremacist America to be broken by Black people: the following discussion is a frank one about ways and means we can apply our power to do the job. We know today that "programs" in the system will not work for the Best interest of Black people: so the following should be read as a contribution to the building of a system to free Black people.

START EARLY IN THEIR BABYHOOD

From the time our children are babies, we must teach them the nature of Black existence on planet earth. Since it is an existence that is dominated by the oppression of white people, we must teach this, along with teaching them Black history, to respect their parents, respect their elders, how to read and write, how to be a productive man or woman and etc.

None of the essentials things that our children need to learn about life should be taught in a vacuum. So teaching them never to expect to find "a good job" in "the system" should not be taught in a vacuum either. In other words, if you teach children to respect their parents and elders and they are not taught the reasons why, at best there will be a delayed benefit to the teaching. Too much proverbial "water may have gone under the bridge" before your teaching kicks in. Too much of the water, in this case, means they may already have wasted too much time finding out why you taught them as you did – some of the mistakes made may have been fatal, so the great potential in many Black youth will never have gotten a chance to be fulfilled. Others, whose potential was circumvented to a lesser degree will not be able to recover from the debilitating experience to fulfill little of the potential that was evident in their youth.

To get the best results, we must fill the vacuums with direct teaching from the time they are babies: they must be taught that doing right and rejecting wrong is the best, most fruitful conduct for human beings. Let them know there is a great reward for practicing right conduct. Introduce The Creator into their life here, at the place you teach the choices of right and wrong.

Doing right and rejecting wrong is ordained by The Creator. When you obey you are rewarded [Blessed] for such conduct. Tell them this: you are rewarded when you do right. And it is right to work among your own people; or start a business to serve your own community.

When they are very young, we can insure they are rewarded for such conduct. When they do right, we must praise and show abundant love. Teach them directly at a very early age that it is right to respect their Elders. We should also give them toys or some 'thing' else that will make them joyful when they exhibit righteous conduct. They will grow up with good times associated with doing things like respecting Elders; and doing other good deeds.

TELL THE TRUTH ABOUT THE SYSTEM EARLY IN THEIR LIVES

In preparing them NOT to expect to get a "system" job, it should be done in the same way. Tell them who dominates the system. And tell them why. When you teach them to be respectful to patents and elders, you should also let them know who you are and why they should respect you. In teaching not to expect or want a system job, teach them who control the "systems" and why they have such dominance and control over your lives: it is easy to point out to them who controls the schools, churches, libraries, stores, recreation centers & etc. Let them know that there is great danger working in corporate America. Teach them it is just simply NOT a nice place to be.

THE *DON'T TOUCH THE HOT STOVE* ANALOGY

Teaching your children about the danger in corporate America should be taught as simply and clearly as teaching them they should not touch a hot stove, or other things that will harm them if they violate what you are teaching.

As it is the nature of young humans, and others who have not learned from the experiences of others, when they are away from you, it is quite likely they will 'test' what you tell them not to do. If they test a hot stove, this will likely be the only time in their lives when they will violate this particular teaching: *touching a hot stove is a self re-enforcing experience.* If we do the job with our children, if they ever get a job in corporate America, it too will be a re-enforcing experience.

What is right and wrong, good and bad can be ingrained into the young inquisitive mind, as per the hot stove experience. [For the older, ignorant, dumb, fearful, especially "bootlicking, cheese eating uncle toms, I am afraid I personally do not expect you can learn easily from what I am writing. But it is never too late]. And for Black people who are sincere in wanting to live a life in resistance to oppression, rather than to 'go along to get along," as a life style, if you are sincere, your opportunity to succeed in achieving such a desire is almost as great as the possibilities with the Black youth. But it is with the Black youth that holds the greater possibility.

To effectively teach the Black youth the above, the rewards from each lesson must be made very clear: When you do what is right, you will get love from me and a joyful reward. If you don't do what I teach will still get the love from me, but only after you receive scorn or a punishment rather than a reward – the scorn and punishment will depend on the degree of the violation of the wrong.

TEACHING BLACK YOUTH

WHAT TO EXPECT IN THE SYSTEM

Teaching children what they will receive if they work in the "system" as opposed to "doing for self" can be done on the same principle and basis as the above: Tell them what to expect when they are looking for a job; and teach them what they can expect if they happen to find one. Since "experience is truly the best teacher," you must tell them the truth, and make it as plain as you did about the hot stove. For like the hot stove, regardless to what you teach, they are likely to look for a "system job" anyway. But the experience will likely give them enough disappointments, regardless to their qualifications, to reinforce your teaching about such. And if they happen to get a 'good system job,' what you teach them about what to expect on the job will also reinforce what you teach them. The insults, the hurtful words, the racist attitudes & etc. is what they will find in their white worker colleagues.

Since what you have taught them is based also on the principle of "experience is the best teacher," there'll be no danger of contradiction for such teaching because the history [experience] of Black people in the United States of America is so clear. Just have your facts together – along with your own personal experience.

TEACH BLACK CHILDREN THAT WHITE PEOPLE DON'T LIKE THEM; AND NOTHING THEY CAN DO WILL CHANGE THEIR MIND

Sister Shahrazad Ali, one of Black America's all time best and most effective writers, wrote a book called *"Things Your Parents Should Have Told You."* The very first thing she says we should have told our youth is that "white people don't like you." If they grow with this understanding, they'll not be expecting white people to do anything for them. Expecting white people do give them a "break" is the source for much disappointments for our youth. The unfounded prejudice against Black youth is the source of the majority of their ill behavior.

Children should be taught that "the system" is not fair to them because it was made to be unfair, on purpose. And that it is controlled by people who benefit from the unfairness. Tell them when they work in "the system" it helps to sustain the unfair system.

Remember, when you are teaching children, you are hoping they will hear and obey without delay. But since this isn't likely to be the case, you teach it anyway because when they taste, or try what you are telling them not to do, or what to expect if they try, they'll have the same experience as putting their hands on the hot stove when you told the baby not to. If you teach the truth about white corporate America, their own experience will play the part in the self full filling.

KNOWING RIGHT vs DOING RIGHT: PARTS AND PARTIALS OF SAME DECISION

Knowing what is right and doing what is right are parts of the same right decisions that we make in life. Knowing what is right is yet another way to see the major challenges to the human being after he is born into the world. Doing what is right is the best way to overcome the challenge [we have already discussed reasons why we don't always do things in our own best interest]

Since the primary job of parents is to prepare their children to solve problems and overcome challenges, if the parent was properly prepared he and she will properly prepare their children. Only ignorant parents teach their children to do wrong rather then to do right. Unfortunately there are some parents who teach their children exactly that. But this is because they never understood themselves: you can't teach what you do not understand. You may well teach what you know. But if you don't understand it you will not have the wisdom to share ways and means to teach others.

ALL WHITE PEOPLE ARE NOT CHARGED

We will not charge all white people of teaching their children that it is alright to be unjust to Black people. But we do know of a certainty it is parents who pass on the benefits they have gained from an unjust system. We also know that Black parents who work in the system receive benefits that are less, so they have less to pass on to their children.

We don't know what white people tell their own children about the disparity between the two people. But Black people do not enjoy the luxury to NOT tell our children why white people have so much more wealth than Black people.

We must let our children know as part of their education that white people suppressed Black people and stole much of our wealth. We can explain the disparity by pointing out that white people enjoy all of their own wealth/power as human beings. And they are wealthier and more powerful than Black people because they have their own wealth as well as the wealth they stole from Black people.

We must teach our children that we will never be whole human beings, individually or as a race, until we get our wealth/power back from white people. When our children are taught this fact, it is then easy to tell them that when they work in the system it makes the system/white people stronger. They will develop and grow with the understanding that somebody has something that belongs to them: so knowing this is a fact, we let them know who has it and the ways and means that can be employed to get back our possessions.

We teach them that there are several ways to get our wealth/power back from white people. Some ways are better than others. All ways require proper use of power. The better ways will take less time to get the job done. But will require a greater power. But the less time it takes, the less pain and suffering you and your people will continue to endure. But if you understand this fact; and what you must do to acquire the great power necessary to do the job they will go to work without delay!

We point out that working in the system is not one of the preferred ways to acquire the power to do the job. But it is one way, maybe the best way, depending on your will power. Your will power must be a match for the contention that working in the system brings to bear against the best interest of Black people. Working in the systems, as per the reasons why Nat Turner became a model slave, in the system, is the only correct mindset to have. That mindset is to acquire power to get back what white people stole from Black people. Study the methodology of Nat Turner – especially how he paid close attention to the evolvement of his Spirituality, even as he did his job in the here and now [how he managed to balance his spirituality and physical bodies before he acted have been gone over previously].

We must teach our children how to acquire greater power by using the power they already possess. Once you have and awareness of your power you can use that power to get back what was stolen. First you demand that the criminal who stole it, return it. If this doesn't work, you use the power to build a system to back up your demand.

Our children must be told to not come out selling "wolf tickets" or bluffing. You must give them knowledge about Black history, white history and how it is played out in the here and now. Try to ingrain into their minds the importance of UNDERSTANDING history. The understanding will give them the wisdom about ways and means to use their power [we have also discussed this at length]. The wisdom will let them know what they can expect to be able to accomplish with the power they have – and the ways and means to acquire more.

Everything is about power and the proper use of the power.

LAST WORDS

I have had my way and say about what I want to share in the *"Acquisition and Proper Use of Power."* And I have spent a good portion of this book applying what I am advising.

I have written with Black Youth as my target market. Whether I have been successful in conveying my thoughts and feelings will be proved out over time: maybe in the near time.

I have developed a great love and appreciation for Black youth and Black women in particular; and of course, in general, I feel Black people have lived up to the greatness that is evident in the accomplishments of our ancestors.

I dare say, that in coming generations, some Black people in my own time will also be singled out and declared to be worthy of respect and praise for our accomplishments. I hope my words will be included in the "small mountain of information," as one of my mentors (John Henrik Clarke stated it), which is the body of the work of contemporary brothers and sisters.

It is not always easy to see from within ones own life experience. But in estimation, in the here and now, my generation more than held our own. The fact that we have survived having come through so much to get this far is truly remarkable in itself. And had we not the tenacity, audacity, determination and will to survive, we would have perished long before this day. But against all odds we did survive with enough of our temerity, tenacity, audacity, determination, as well as capacity that we have vouchsafed to pass on to generations to come.

On January 17, 2010 at Khalifah Estates in Southampton County, Virginia: the reputed birthplace of Nat Turner, www.naturnertrail.com I have an unyielding belief and faith in the destiny of Black people: for I have some good understanding of the knowledge of where we are; how much power we arrived here with, the wisdom from the understanding tells me in unreserved measures that we are headed for Freedom Day.

What that Afrikan Freedom Day will look and feel like is certain: we shall not be encumbered by an enemy with the capacity to employ a discredited, bastardized evil doctrine of white supremacy to blunt our potential as human.

We will have been paid our due Reparations because we brought enough of our power into manifestation to back up our Just Demand for Reparations. With the resource of Reparations, we will be free to employ the expertise to begin the healing of our people.

The Reparations will have given us clear, credible choices of our own choosing: *1)*

Take our Reparations, or any part our collective will moves our wisdom to allot, and move back to Afrika of elsewhere 2) Take our Reparations and remain in the United States of America, still within the domination of a white supremacist, capitalistic system but with the financial equity to be free of debt and to heal our Post Traumatic Slavery wounds 3) Take our Reparations and move into the territory of the deep south where the RNA (Republic of New Afrika) have identified as a land mass where Black people enjoy the resident majority – and work to enact a Plebiscite to establish a republic as "free as Canada."

IN THE HANDS OF BLACK YOUTH

And finally, our destiny is in the hands of Black youth: they will be beneficiaries of previous generations that have equated ourselves well to the task in our time. And there is no doubt in my mind, whatsoever, that Black youth of today are ready to take their turn in delivering Black people into the era for which we have been struggling and fighting for this long.

We will win the war because it is a righteous war. We will win it righteously and we shall live and enjoy our power righteously. So it is ordained, so it shall be.

End of Text
What follows next is self explanatory

SONG OF PRAISE

PRAISE BE TO GOD
THE KING OF KING
PRAISE BE TO GOD
FOR EVERY THING

PRAISE BE TO ALLAH

PRAISE BE TO ALLAH
IN ALL HIS GLORY
PRAISE BE TO ALLAH
WE TELL HIS STORY

PRAISE BE TO ALLAH
PRAISE BE TO ALLAH

UNUNUNUNUN
UNUNUNUNUN
UNUNUNUNUNUNNNNNN
UN!
UN!
UN
[all rights reserved]!

[The following is reprinted from the Spiritual Manual of UBUS. We have emphasized through the text of the book, the necessity of balancing the physical and Spiritual: this manual will help with that]

THE MYSTIC ORDER OF UBUS
A NON-DENOMINATIONAL, NON-SECTARIAN WHOLISTIC SPIRITUAL EXPRESSION OF RIGHTEOUS STRIVING PEOPLE

WHAT IS OUR MISSION? OUR INDIVIDUAL MISSIONS ARE TO FULFILL OUR PURPOSE AS CREATED SPIRITUAL BEINGS. THE THINGS WE DO AS SPIRITUAL BEINGS IN OUR EARTH BODIES REFLECT OUR DEGREES OF SUCCESSFUL WHOLESOME, ENJOYABLE EXPERIENCES WHILE STRIVING TO ACHIEVE OUR PURPOSE IN THIS LIFE. OUR PURPOSE IS FOUND WHEN WE UNDERSTAND PROPER KNOWLEDGE OF OURSELF; PROPER KNOWLEDGE OF OUR CREATOR AND PROPER KNOWLEDGE OF ANY DEVIOUS MIND, OR DEVIL WHO THINK IT PROFITS HIM OR HER TO CIRCUMVENT OUR POTENTIAL AS A HUMAN BEING.

OUR UNITED MISSION IS TO BUILD A STRONG RIGHTEOUS ORDER OF HUMAN BEINGS. WE UNDERSTAND UNITED WE ARE STRONGER

AND MORE POWERFUL THAN ANY ONE OF US ARE AS INDIVIDUALS. THE PURPOSE OF OUR RIGHTEOUS ORDER OF HUMAN BEINGS IS TO SERVE THE BEST INTEREST OF THE WHOLE. THE WHOLE IS THE TOTALITY OF ALL ENTITIES OF PERSONS, PLACES AND THINGS IN CREATION.

THE WHOLE EQUALS ALL OF THE PARTS AND IS STRONGER THAN ANY ONE IN THE ORDER ARE AS INDIVIDUALS. OUR UNITY BUILDS A COMMON GOOD THAT EACH SINCERE PERSON USE TO ASSIST IN ACHIEVING THEIR INDIVIDUAL PURPOSE. WE STRIVE TO USE THE COMMON GOOD IN HARMONY TO THE WHOLE IN THE ACHIEVEMENT OF OUR INDIVIDUAL GOALS.

AS A UNITED ENTITY, COMMON GOOD IS CREATED; IT REFLECTS THE WILL OF OUR RIGHTEOUS ORDER, THE MYSTIC ORDER OF UBUS (MOOUBUS). THE WILL OF THE MOOUBUS USES THE COMMON GOOD TO ACHIEVE SPECIFIED AND UNIVERSAL PURPOSES [SOME ARE KNOWN OTHERS ARE MYSTERIOUS AND UNKNOWN].

METHODOLOGY

1. Our methodology is to be as Righteous in our Words, Acts & Deeds as we can. We understand we were created by a Supreme, Wonderful Creator for a Divine Purpose. Being righteous in words, acts & deeds in planning and working to fulfill our purpose pleases the Creator. When we are pleasing the Creator, we are in harmony with the rhythm of the Universal Laws that govern the

Creation. Being in Harmony and Rhythm with the Universal Laws makes the work within processes necessary to achieve our Missions purposeful, wholesome rewarding experiences. That is PEACE!

a) We understand that our best, most advantageous efforts to fulfill our Purpose is to accept right and reject wrong at each instant in the execution of our will. Our wills are expressed through our words, acts and deeds. We understand that the things we do in the expression of our words, acts and deeds reflects the execution of the number of the 360 degrees of our consciousness, on the level of our success in the attainment of our Missions, in the fulfillment of our purposes.

b) We understand that The Creator unveils the Best Course of action at our every decision; we strive to see, accept and act with exact precision on the Best Course unveiled each time we make a decision to execute our will. Each decision we make is an opportunity to advance the degree of success for the attainment of the Mission we are on.

e) We understand that the peril in the execution of our will to express our words, acts and deeds are errors, mistakes and excesses. With this understanding we wisely pray to avoid errors, mistakes and excesses. But when they happen we strive to see, accept and obey the lesson they portend and embrace the infusion as enhancement to our character evolving into the Image of the Divine Being that created us.

c) We were created as unique Spiritual Entities within the Grace and Truth of The Divine Creator. The unique Spiritual Entity is called our Spiritual Body and is our only Reality. It is the only reality because it is the only portion of the Divine Spirit within our human body.

In our Reality, as created spiritual beings we brought into manifestation the Physical Body in similitude to the way that we were created. The Creator included Thou Divine Spirit as the Essential Portion of our Spiritual Body to achieve Thy Purpose. We included our spirit as the essential portion of the earth body that we made and strive to be within in Life to achieve our purpose.

Our Spirit is a portion of The Divine Spirit and was breathed into us through the Power of the Word. We entered into the physical Body that we made via our inhaling/breathing. If the earth body that we made had not the ability to intake the Spirit of The Creator within us, the life of the body would cease to exist and the properties from which it was made will return to the essence of the material part of the earth (from whence it was made).

Our spirit would then return to the Unseen from where we came. *[The Unseen is the Essence from where we came, made and placed ourselves into our physical body. When we return to our Essence in the Unseen we may well create another entity; but since that is after this life, which is death, we will not know of a certainty until that time.*

We do know of a certainty that Successful Attunement with the Creation, in this life, gets us to a wonderful place in the hereafter. This being the case, we strive to achieve our Mission – being righteous in words, acts and deeds as our chosen methodology. Being righteous puts us in harmony with the Creation. That is Success Attunement!].

END OF PART 1

NOTES:

HOW MUCH DO YOU REMEMBER?

PART 2

ATTRIBUTES OF THE UNIVERSAL WHOLE
The Model for the human being

The Universal Whole is governed by Natural Law. Each Natural Law is administered through a component part of the Whole. The component parts are called Attributes. The Attributes use the Natural Laws in governing the Creation. When we master a Natural Law we have learned how to administer, or apply the Universal Law in question for the benefit of self, in harmony to all of the component parts of the Universal Whole.

The component part called Spiritual Being made the body from the created entity called earth. Another name for earth is humus (the source for the word human). The Human body was made in similitude to how we were created. A portion of the Creator was placed in the human body – making it a Human Being. Humans are made as replicas of the Supreme Being: Making it a Human being.

DIVINE ATTRIBUTES

We will now discuss some of the component parts of the Universal Whole. They are commonly called *Attributes.*

THOUGHT IS THE MASTER ATTRIBUTE OF OUR CREATOR: it is activated by thinking by the Mind of the Supreme Being. Thought is also the Master attribute of human beings. It is activated by the made human brain by thinking.

THE POWER OF THOUGHT: THE MASTER ATTRIBUTE

Physical Attributes are properties of the physical body that we made. Some of the attributes are arms, legs, hands, fingers, toes, brains & other physical things that are essential parts of the unique human body that we made . . . [we pause here to address the question of concern that is likely to enter the minds of all who Love the Creator. That concern is the flat statement regarding *"the physical body that we made."* We are taught all our lives that The Divine Creator – the name of which is usually the best name in the language of the individual who may be referring to The Divine Creator, Sustainer and Cherisher of All Things, Persons & Things, Who Created everything.

Now we are saying without hesitation that we made the physical body within which we reside on earth: So there will be absolutely no question about #1. Why I say we made the physical Body and #2. Who is the We who did the making? We will share some more from the basic text we wrote more than 35 years ago. A book called *Melanin, Conscious Attunement and the God I.* Hopefully the following will clear up all concerns that may be in your mind about questions 1 and 2.

*There is One Divine Spirit that constitute the whole of existence
I am existing: therefore I am a part of the Whole
The Divine Spirit in me is the only real part of me that I am
My physical body is the vehicle within which the real me manifest
in this life, Within the Whole of existence
My body is not really me, just as the car within which my body rides is not really the body which I am within at any place or time in life
My body uses the car to travel from place to place in life
My real self uses the body to travel from place to place in this life*

Gasoline, put in the car is the substance that keeps the attributes, or parts of the car operating in approximate unity, harmony and rhythm resulting in the movement of the motion that you Will

The finer tuned the parts of the car are coordinated to each other the better the car will operate and the more efficient and faster it can run

Breath, inhaled into the body is the substance that keeps the attributes of the body operating in approximate unity, harmony and rhythm resulting in the movement of the motion that you Will

*The finer tuned the parts of the body are coordinated to each other
The better the body will operate and faster it can run*

Tonight I consciously identify my real self with all the other parts of the One Divine Spirit pervading existence...we are One

Hopefully the above meditation will clear up any questions of concern about who I am talking about when saying we made the body. Yes, we created beings made the human body. And it is a portion of our spirit in the body that keeps it alive. When we remove ourselves, the body will die and return to the essence of the earth of which it is made.

As for that other concern, where we appear to be rivaling The Divine Creator - for things rightly taught that only He is capable of Creating; notice I did not say the Divine Creator is Making anything. The Creator creates and we make things out of what was created. That is all.

The Creator created us as beings in His own Image by imparting in us the Essence of The Divine Spiritual Being that He is [yes, the Spirit of The Creator exist]. The Creator is the Supreme Being; He is a Being with a Divine Spirit. He imparted a portion of the Divine Spirit that He is into the beings He Created in His Own Image, us spiritual beings.

When we impart our spirit into the human body that we made, the body becomes a human being. A portion of our spirit in a human body. We have not made a body that we can incorporate all of our spirit within. We would like to do just that; and that is what we strive to achieve – have what we made become one with our being. We try to guide it but it doesn't always listen and obey.

Though we cannot impart all of our spirit in the human body, we can impart portions as the attributes of the body are capable of utilizing the spirit in harmony and rhythm to each other [attributes].

When the body is only able to utilize a small amount of our spirit, in the execution of its words, acts and deeds, it will have little spirit. But when it is able utilize a lot of our spirit in the execution of its words, acts and deeds, it is said to have a lot of spirit. If it is lacking harmony and rhythm with some of the other attributes, it may be said: "he, or she has a lot of spirit but he can't run NOR jump."

But when the attributes of the body are working in harmony and rhythm to the attributes that govern running or jumping, then it will be said, "he has a lot of spirit and he can also run and jump."

THE NATURAL DESIRE OF THE CREATOR IS TO CREATE: The Natural Desire of the Human Being is to Make

Since it is the natural Desire of The Divine Creator to Create, He imparted within created beings the ability to replicate, for example, a kind-of-man and woman. If we can make a kind-of-man, everything else should be easy to make. And we can make a kind-of-man because we have knowledge [knowledge is power] of how to make our bodies in similitude to how we were created.

All that is needed to achieve this, and all other tasks we conceive are within us in the form of knowledge. All the knowledge is power we can use when we understand it. Knowing this, we study to get understanding of the knowledge – the understanding gives us the wisdom to achieve what we perceive, but only to the degree of our understanding.

We gave the physical body attributes of brains, legs, arms, ears, and etc. We use them to build according to the wisdom we derive from the understanding of the knowledge that is within us.

We strive to use the physical attributes of our material body to benefit our entire being. When we are successfully using them to benefit the whole body, a good percentage of the attributes will be working in harmony to each other. This equates to peace and power for the Physical Body. We don't know if any body has ever been made that attained oneness with the being that created it. For our body to come into oneness with its maker it must successfully master all of the attributes to the extent that they worked in complete harmony to each other. But we know about some that appear to have come close. Very close. So close that it is said that The God "came in the Person" of that particular Human Being.

CLOSING THE GAP – MAKING THE PARTS WORK IN COMPLETE HARMONY TO EACH OTHER

The ways you are able to close the "gap" between making the attributes, and have them work in complete harmony to each other, are so plentiful that we will not single out any of the ways right now. What the seeker of understanding of what I am saying will find in my work are synthesis of a multitude of other Spiritual Disciplines, religions, Black Muslims, Yogas, martial arts, masons, Muslims, Elks, Black Hebrews, and etc.

The mission of the Mystic Order of UBUS is not to lead the way; or to point the way, it is to explain The Way. The "explanation" is for a reason: that reason is to impart understanding of the Knowledge of THE WAY. From the understanding come Wisdom to act, to build, whether the building is a house or a Good Character it is building Right On.

In this use of the word WISDOM, it will assist you in adapting your life to other disciplines that are simply parts of the One Way [all of the different religions, orders and such make up the One Way: all are further from the straight and narrow Path than The Creator would have us on. He could put us on the straight and narrow path if he wanted to; but since overcoming challenges to find the straight and narrow is the surest way to develop character and strengthen the Human Being – it is what it is. And what it is, is one way to build character and advance by degrees in this life.

In short a certain degree of understanding of any path will beget the wisdom. The Seeker is then required to act accordingly. The closer he or she works in their own best interest, while not fringing anyone's else Natural Rights as a human entity, the more successful they will be as a Human Being.

THE ONE WAY

The fact that MOOUBUS work with the little known fact that there is only One Way, is why we are called Mystics. It is not generally known. The reason it is not generally known is for a very good reason: to use this knowledge effectively one must have mastered previous attributes, less he or she mess themselves up while trying to dress themselves up.

I hope the above clears up the question about the "We" and the attributes we made for the physical body to function in this life. We will now take a closer look at the entity that The Divine Creator, created. It too has attributes – Ours are replica of the Divine Creator.

But before we leave this section let me say: nobody knows how we made our human body; or how we imparted a portion of our spirit into it. These are some of the mysteries of life.

As I said, mystery simply means unknown. Understanding of the mystery of any thing equates to your degree of master-hood.

There are many other mysteries that constitute life. And until the mysteries are known, we evolve to positions of belief about particular mysteries by studying the knowledge we have of the facts that they do exist.

Understanding of this knowledge is the basis of the wisdom we have to say we believe this or that. Then we wisely act on the knowledge of things we believe in; with a little bit of understanding of what you say you believe, you will achieve a little bit of success in using the knowledge. And vice versa!

END OF PART 2
NOTES:

HOW MUCH DO YOU REMEMBER?

PART 3

FACTS ABOUT THE ATTRIBUTES OF OUR CREATED SPIRITUAL BEING: THE BASIS OF OUR BELIEF THERE IS ONLY ONE GOD

Our Divine Creator created our unique spiritual body (being, entity) with Attributes and Spiritual Things that are Unseen. We understand that thought is one of the Unseen Things that was bestowed upon our Spiritual being.

We also have other Unseen attributes, hearing, taste, sight, sound are examples. All of our attributes are governed by Natural, Universal Laws through the activation of our thoughts.

We understand Thought is the Master Attribute of the Spiritual Being that we are. Thought is the master because without thought the physical attributes of our body cannot be used. Nor can the Spiritual Attributes of our Being be used.

Some attributes are used by our conscious thoughts; others are used by our sub-conscious thoughts. Whatever the Attributes are called, they are unseen – making them attributes of our Spiritual Being.

We bestowed the powers of our Spiritual Attributes upon the physical body by making it dominant. We made and enabled a physical attribute for the physical body. That attribute is the human brain. The brain is used to overcome challenges for success in life.

If we empowered the brain directly it would "blow up," so to speak: we wisely created an intercessory. The intercessory is called The Mind, of course there are several divisions of the mind (which we will discuss later). The thoughts from the mind, too, must be mastered for the attributes of the body to be in complete harmony with the whole body. The human brain (an attribute of the physical body) is empowered to tap into the Mind of the Spiritual Being. The "tapping" is called thinking. This is the method used to find the right answer.

We strive to Master all of the attributes that are bestowed upon us. Our degree of mastery is reflected through the words, acts and deeds of the human (also called physical) body that we made.

Mastery is achieved by obeying the Universal Laws that govern the attributes [Gravity is an unseen attribute, governed by unseen laws that can be understood, quite readily. You learn and obey it, or bear the consequences when you violate it.

As we know, Ignorance of the law does not excuse consequences for breaking it. With more Understanding of the law of Gravity we beget more wisdom about how to use it to achieve our objectives. Understanding of the knowledge you have about gravity means that you have a degree of the wisdom about the natural law that governs the unseen attribute called gravity. Repeat: *Wisdom is using my knowledge of the law that governs gravity to achieve my purpose.*

Since gravity and other unseen attributes are governed by Universal Law, when we understand the Universal Law we use the wisdom from the understanding to Master and use the attribute.

In the example of the Law we are using called Gravity [What goes up comes down because of the law that govern gravity]. Our degree of mastery is reflected in our words, acts and deeds in using the law that governs gravity.

It is important that we know about certain Natural laws. For if you don't know about the Law you are subject to violate one. But you will be subject to the consequences of the violation whether you know or don't know about the law.

But when you know you can study, or examine what you know. Studying what you know will get you the wisdom to use the knowledge. And it is in the use of the knowledge where processes are evolved to master the attribute of our Spiritual being that governs the Law of gravity, or whichever.

SOME PROCESSES TO ATTAIN MASTERY

The processes to attain mastery is the same as in the use of Universal Laws that govern other Attributes that The Creator, in all Thy Wisdom, bestowed upon our Spiritual Body. Remember: Our spiritual Bodies were created by our Divine Creator out of the only Substance that was available in the Beginning. *"And in the Beginning was the Word. And the Word was The Creator..."*

This being the case, and understanding that the case is spiritual and is governed by Universal Law, we strive to understand Universal Laws. Wisdom from understanding Universal Law gives us the ability to use the power of the knowledge of the Entity that we are created from - the One Entity that was at the Beginning. We understand that the Master attribute called Thought is The Word brought into manifestation. How, why, when, and where, is a Divine, Ever Unfolding Mystery. We call the "Ever Unfolding Mystery" Life.

We use the properties, attributes and such, that were bestowed upon us by The Creator, through the use of the physical body that we made. The attributes that we incorporated into the composition of the physical body is the means by which we use our physical, as well as our spiritual Attributes. We are forever striving to keep them in attunement to each other. When they are in attunement all that is conceived in harmony to the Universal All is achieved. This is where "miracles" are born.

Pause here, and just reflect on what you just read. It is simple by profound.

END OF PART 3

PART 4

MYSTICISM – SUFISM

MYSTICS WE ARE

We refer to ourselves as Mystics, or Sufis and other such names in the languages that we utter as words from our Physical Body. We are mystics because we strive to master the Universal Laws within the Divine Mystery. *Our attainment of degrees of mastery of the Universal Laws makes Unfolding the Divine mystery a Wholesome Rewarding experience. [the word Sufi is introduced here, briefly, because we shall not take any space in this book to give a history about Sufism, as we know, understand it. What we will say is that as a Black Muslim (my religious practice), I have a better foundation to understand mysticism as practiced by the Sufi's (Mystics) that accepted Islam. Yes, there are Mystics, or Sufi's in all religions).*

Understanding the knowledge that unveil-unfold the facts that the Creation originated from The One Creator is the greatest knowledge we have. Understanding this knowledge gives us the ability/wisdom to uncover/unravel the mystery called life. The state of our existence in Life is governed within the Universal Laws.

Science is based entirely on the Universal Laws. This mean science is our most reliable aide to physically understand the mystery called life.

It is our understanding that any uncovered Attributes, claims of manifested degrees of mastery of Laws that governs life can be proven with the use of the Science we call Mathematics. This is a Natural fact that is True, Right and Exact in our states of Being.

Our Degrees are estimates of the amount of mastery we manifest of the 360 degrees of the attributes of the Creation. In other words, we understand each degree of the 360 represents an attribute that we strive to master – that is All!

AGAIN, HOW DO WE ATTAIN MASTERY?

We attain mastery by using the wisdom derived from our understanding and practice of the Law that governs the attribute. The degree of understanding is the amount of wisdom we receive to practice what we think the law portends. We say think because often in practicing we "go into error, make mistakes or indulge in excesses," which is why we pray for protection from the ultimate cost for all such behavior. We strive to learn the lesson that is in the error, mistake or excess we commit, or such that is committed by others. Then we try again.

Ideally, we learn from the errors, mistakes and excess of others. This is one of the most invaluable of the multitude of duties and responsibilities of parents:

We strive to raise our children to avoid the errors, mistakes and excesses we have made; or that we learn from the ill behavior of others. I told my children many, many times *"If you don't learn from your parents, your teacher will teach you; if you don't learn from the teacher, the police will teach you; and if you don't learn from the police, they will beat you up real bad or kill you to force you to do things their way."*

Each lesson learned and mastered is an attainment of one of the 360 degrees of the Whole. You will know you have mastered the degree when you are capable of consciously using it in service for the greater good of the Whole. Of course True Masters do not concern themselves with such, the estimations of the amount of degrees of a master are made by a Task Master. A Task Master is one who have mastered many tasks, which equates to several equivalents of the 360 degrees of life.

A True Master understands the enormity of the challenge, so he or she will not stop at any of the perceived degrees of attainment. In fact, he or she is so busy enjoying the processes, that any distraction from his work to overcome challenges may be resisted .

[since there is absolutely no time in our existence when every one of the 360 degree is NOT in use, in harmony, in rhythm and in love, the level of our understanding of this fact/knowledge gives us the wisdom to practice

the use of the attributes. The practice – via our words, acts or deeds – are opportunities to master the attributes. Mastering the attributes builds and develops our characters into the divine entities that we are. That is Good].

THOUGHT ACTIVATES THE ATTRIBUTES

We strive to use our thoughts to activate the other attributes to live successfully in this life. We understand that living successfully in this life prepares us for Wonderful Places in the Hereafter. Everything we do in life is precipitated and activated by thought. We think before we act; the mastery we have over the attribute called thought will determine whether it is a thought that was activated by our individual portion of Divine spirit or not. That is the Right Way to have our physical body act in word, or deed. Reflect the characteristics of the Divine at all time: the reflection is through the power of your words, acts and deeds.

END OF PART 4

PART 5
THE MASTERY OF THOUGHT

MASTERING THOUGHT

Past Masters strongly advise that we carefully, diligently and determinedly strive to "master" Thought. In fact, mastery in regard to thought is a misnomer. Thought cannot be mastered but it can be controlled and directed to achieve the objectives of the will of the being doing the thinking. In other words, when thought arrives, we accept or reject them according to our own states of mind.

In more words, when thought does happen with us, or around us, we have the power within us to master how we react to it. Mastery is achieved in the same manner we master everything else in life: it is achieved through practice; we understand that practicing righteousness in our words acts and deeds creates the desired states of being in the processes that leads to mastery.

From this understanding we receive the wisdom to be aware, or conscious of where we are, and our positions and dispositions in relation to others in our experiences at that particular time.

If we are at desired states of being, good thoughts are attracted. Less than good thoughts are rejected! They bounce away, or they boomerang and return to the sender – depending on the intention of the sender. To help with in this phase of the processes, I will share some of the words that work nicely for me:

* DETACH YOURSELF FROM ALL EARTHLY DESIRES IN THE SUPREME SPIRIT OF INMOST SINCERETY

- BE PATIENT IN PURSUIT OF JUSTICE
- PERSEVERE TO BE SINCERE
- FORSAKE YOU LOWER NATURE
- CONTROL YOUR EARTHLY DESIRES
- LOVE POWER IS THE SOUL POWER, WHICH IS ACTUALLY THE SOLE POWER

IN OTHER WORDS, IT IS REALLTY THE ONLY POWER THERE IS – AND YOU CAN INCREASE ITS MANIFESATION THROUGH YOU ACCORDING TO THE SINCERITY THAT IS EXPRESSED IN YOUR WORDS, ACTS AND DEEDS

BE SINCERE AT ALL TIME. SINCERETY IS THE KEY THAT UNLOCKS THE DOORS TO THE HEARTS OF OTHERS. IT VIBRATES A SPIRIT OF FRIENDLINESS AND WARMTH TO EVERY HEART THAT IT CONTACTS

"Make me enter a Truthful Entering
Make me go forth a Truthful going forth
And Grant Me from Thy Presence
An authority to help me"
(Holy Qur'an)

PART 6

THE PREDICATION AND ACTIVATION OF THE POWER OF THOUGHT

Since everything in life is precipitated and activated by thought, you want your thoughts to be as correct in their activation of your other attributes as possible. Mastery of thought will cause your words, acts or deeds to be done in your own Best Interest. So if you act from a thought that does not come from you, you may well be acting on the thought of some other entity in life; and that entity may have you uttering words, acts or deeds in their own Best Interest. Not Yours!

Our thoughts are used by our Spiritual Body to direct the attributes of the physical entity that we made – our Physical/earth Body. We direct our earth body in similitude to the ways and means The Creator directs the spiritual entity that was created – our only reality. The Creator is Unseen but is Omnipresent – meaning always with us. Our spirit is unseen but so long as the body is functioning in the seen we are always within it. When our spirit is no longer in the earth body, the physical body is dead. In fact we began to leave it long before it died.

When we are attuned to the Vibration of The Creator, all is well with our Spirit(ual) Body. When our physical Body is attuned to our Spirit, all is well.

Our Physical Body is made of the earth and is called Human. When the Spirit is in Attunement within the human, the entity is called a Human Being. Human Being implies that we are in Conscious Attunement with our Spiritual Body.

When we are in-human, we are working with little of our Spirit in the Human body. Still a Human but to a lesser degree. When the spirit leaves altogether, the body returns to the essence of which it is made. That is the earth. And we move on to continue our evolvement to obtain mastery.

THE UNITED POWER
OF SEEN AND UNSEEN ENTITIES

Humans who unite their bodies manifest entities of power that are self evident because they are groupings of people (Nations, organizations, social clubs & etc) that can be seen in congregation. The power is manifest because of the collective will of the individuals that constitute the organization. The individuals do not give up their own will, but they unite it to others to make a united entity – the unification creates a common power that is good, or bad gradations of the two that are created in common. The power that is created in common can be used in its fullness when the majority of the individuals in a grouping support a common objective. This happens when the collective will of the organization is executed for a particular purpose.

The individuals in organizations agree to limit their use of the common power that is created by the group. But all who are parts of the organization control a portion of what is created. When this knowledge is known, the individual only needs understanding of the knowledge to gain the wisdom to use his or her individual portion. Of course the wisdom from the understanding will also tell the individuals uniting his or her portion with other portions will give that entity more power in the use of the common power that is created in common by the group.

Humans who unite their Thoughts manifest entities of Power that are Unseen – like the power of gravity. Unseen, but nevertheless is there. You can use it consciously or subconsciously from your own thoughts, randomly, or from the thoughts of others. We understand it is best to use it consciously. Just as power in common is created by physical organizations of individuals. The attribute, or "thing" called thought can also be united to create power in common. Understanding of this knowledge will give you the wisdom to use the power that is created in common; or your own individualized portion of the united power. This is in similitude to the Divine Power of the Universe of The Creator. All individual beings, places and things that Thou did create have access to Thy Power with their individualized portion of the Totality of All.

We consciously unite our thoughts to create a common Power Source for our individual and collective use at 8 am daily. Understanding that 'thoughts are things" makes it so. Understanding of the Natural Law that governs unification allows us to be in conscious attunement with the Creation. The unification magnifies our individual power.

We strive to stay in attunement with our manifested entities through our Human Body in similitude to the ways and means of The Creator does with our Spiritual being. We understand that the closest attribute we have to do this is through the power of thought. With the activation of thought in word, act or deed, we are able to use the attributes of the physical body. This is good!

We know not how The Creator does it, but we know Thought is an attribute that is always at our disposal. The power of thought is conditioned only by our understanding of it. Our understanding of thought gives us the wisdom to use the attributes of the physical body to achieve our missions and fulfill our purposes. The Law that governs thought determines how, when and under what conditions we can use the common power that is created by united thoughts.

d) We understand that the duality of our Spiritual Body and our Human Body is our manifested Presence in the life of our consciousness. We understand that we made a Human Body that has some wonderful attributes for our use in life [Brains to think with, similar to the mind that the Spiritual Being thinks with, The Divine Mind. Our thoughts utilize the physical attributes of the human body (Arms, Legs, Heart, Lungs & etc].

We as Spiritual Beings have some wonderful attributes for our use. The Spiritual Attributes are Unseen [thought, hearing, seeing, tasting, etc]. And they are used potentially as The Creators Attributes are used on our behalf. [What are some of the Attributes of the Creator?]

Many of us assume the Attributes as names for our human bodies. When the name is chosen wisely the individual indicates he or she want their character to reflect the attribute. When the name is chosen for the individuals (babies, or whatever, the individual do not control the power to make his or her own decision.

PART 7

OTHER THINGS THAT WE HUMAN BEINGS DO: THE UNITED POWER HOUR OF MOOBUS – 8 A.M.

In summary, we understand that the Attribute called thought can be organized into a United Power Entity: "Thoughts ARE Things." The collection, or unification of particular "things" manifest a Mystical Power Source that can be utilized by all sincere individual contributors to building the Power Source..

We MOOUBUS Unite our Thoughts at the Power Hour of 8 a.m. It is good to stop what you are doing and engage your mind to send sincere thoughts to 8 a.m. There they unite with thoughts that have been sent by other humans. When humans are in unity there is a physical chain of strength. When thoughts are in unity there is a spiritual chain of strength.

But we understand it is not necessary to stop what you might be doing at the time to be a part of the United Expression at 8 a.m. Sincere Thoughts that are created and sent to 8 a.m. represents sincere desires to be in Unity with us. The thoughts are received, incorporated and United with ours. The united expressions have created a power base that is spiritual in nature because it is unseen.

We understand that Thoughts that are insincere rebound to the sender. We constantly thank/think The Creator for the Universal Law that makes it so!

e) We understand that our Human bodies are personal entities that are MADE by our Spark of Divine Mind as physical entities; as is automobiles. We purchase physical entities called automobiles that are MADE by other Humans for use by our Human Body attributes in our earth lives. We MADE our Human body for use by our Spiritual attributes to use the properties of our Human Bodies. We also make physical entities that are purchased by others for their use in this life.

The question we pose to the reader now: what are you building in this life? Is it preparing you to serve, and be served? Will it end when your physical body ends? Is it preparing your being for the Hereafter?

Are you doing Proper work within your reality on earth? If you are Black, you must determine whether or not you are doing the Proper work for the role that your race is playing in the Experimental System called The United States of America. It is "Experimental" because, among other things, chattel slavery was purposely incorporated within it at its inception. This is wrong, unjust and they (Founding Fathers) knew it was at the time. We don't know what their ultimate plan was. But we see what they are doing today; and have done in the past: Black people must act accordingly.

NOTES
HOW MUCH DO YOU REMEMBER?

PART 8

*IN ALL OF THE MOST MERCIFUL,
MOST GRACIOUS, MOST WONDERFUL, MOST
PRECIOUS MOST POWERFUL, MOST BEAUTIFUL,
MOST BOUNTIFUL CREATOR, SUSTAINER &
CHERISHER, OF ALL MINDS, ALL THINGS
ALL PLACES WITHOUT AND WITHIN THE
HEAVENS AND THE EARTH
ALL PRAISE TO THEE FOR BLESSING
US TO BE WITHIN THY GRACE
AT THIS TIME IN THIS PLACE
IN OUR SEVERAL STATES OF MIND*

*THANK YOU ALMIGHTY CREATOR OF MY
ANCESTORS, MY FATHER MY MOTHER, MY
SISTERS, MY BROTHERS, NEAR RELATIVES
MY CLOSE FRIENDS, ASSOCIATES AND THOSE
SINCERE MINDS WHO MEDITATE AT THE HOUR
OF EIGHT A.M.
ALL THANKS AND ALL PRAISE TO THEE
FOR BLESSING US TO BE
CONNECTED IN SPIRIT AT THIS TIME*

*BLESS THOSE WHOSE THOUGHTS ARE IN
HARMONY WITH OURS, BLESS THE ONE WHO
HAD A UNITED SINCERE DESIRE TO BE AND*

THANK YOU FOR THE ONES COMING INTO OUR EXPERIENCES RIGHT NOW!

WE ARE BUILDING WITH OUR UNITED THOUGHTS- CREATING A UNIFIED SOURCE OF SPIRITUAL, DYNAMIC ENERGY - SERVING OUR INDIVIDUAL NEEDS, OUR COLLECTIVE NEEDS
SECURING FREEDOM, JUSTICE & EQUALITY FOR FELLOW HUMAN BEINGS WE MADE TO ACHIEVE OUR INDIVIDUAL AS WELL AS OUR COMBINED PURPOSE IN THIS LIFE

OH ALLAH, OH ALLAH
HAVE MERCY ON OUR INDIVIDUAL AND UNITED EFFORTS BLESS OUR WORD, ACTS AND DEEDS THAT ALL THE GOODNESS THOU HAS DECREED MAYBE SEEN, ACCEPTED AND UTILIZED -
THAT ALL MANNER OF INJUSTICE AND OPPRESSION BE REMOVED FROM THE CIRCUMVENTION OF OUR POTENTIAL
AS BEINGS IN THE HUMANS WE DID MAKE IN THIS LIFE
ON THIS DAY AND FOREVER
KEEP US SAFELY WITHIN THY KEEPING
IN ALL THY MOST SINCERE, ENDURING AND EVERLASTING NAMES
- Imin -

INDEX

THE HONORABLE ELIJAH MUHAMMAD
DR. AMARI A. OBADELE
MINISTER LOUIS FARRAKHAN
ATTORNEY CHOKWE LUMUMBA
BROTHER MAHMUD RAMZA
YAHYA ABDUL KARIM
DR. AMOS N. WILSON
BISHOP LEON A. BYNOE
DR. OMAR REID
BROTHER LUMUMBA ODINGA
RETHELLA RASHANNAH KHALIFAH
ADMINISTRATOR ROBERT HARRIS
JOHNITA AZENA SCOTT
MR. KOFI BROWN
DR. LLAILA O. AFRIKA
MINISTER JAMES 5X GROOMS
DR. JOHN HALL
SISTER AMUNTYT KHALIFAH
SISTER SHAHRAZAD ALI
DR. TONY MARTIN
DR. NA'IM AKBAR
DR. KHALLID MUHAMMAD
RAS KEIDI AWADU
MINISTER AKBAR MUHAMMAD
MR. HANNIBAL AHMED
PROF. PRESTON WILCOX
MR. MUNIR MUHAMMAD
MINISTER BARASHANGO

DR. MOLEFI ASANTE
DR. MUATA ASHBY
DR. KAREN ASHBY
DR. LENORD JEFFRIES
MR. PAUL GUTHRIE
DR. KAMAU KAMBON
SISTER MUYIAH KAMBON
ATTORNEY OPIO SOKONI
MALIK AREEB SHABAZZ
MR. LUTHER WARNER
BROTHER NATI
MR. ERIC GIFT
PRESIDENT JOHN JERRY RAWLINGS
MR. HENRY LARTEY
DR. FRANCIS C. WELSING
DR. E. CURTIS ALEXANDER
BROTHER ALI
MR. CAROL BARNES
DR. RICHARD D. KING
MR. ADIB RASHIED
MR. ELIJAH KARRIEM
NANA EKOW BUTWIKU I
ELDER JAMES MAGEE
ELDER LAVINIA MAGEE
SISTER BARBARA ORANGE
SISTER JANETTE CRAWFORD KNIGHT
SISTER MARGARET HOUSE
MR EUSTICE CRAWFORD
SISTER ISA LEE HILLS-KNIGHT
MR. LOUIS E. KNIGHT

MR. JAKE KNIGHT
MR. ROBERT L. KNIGHT
BROTHER JESSE KNIGHT
MR. ALFRED KNIGHT
SISTER ELLA KNIGHT
SISTER ELIZABETH KNIGHT
BROTHER EMANUEL L. KNIGHT
BROTHER LARRY KNIGHT
SISTER GLORY JEAN KNIGHT
SISTER BEVERLY ANN KNIGHT
SISTER MARY KNIGHT
SISTER MARTHA KNIGHT
SISTER LULA B. EDWARDS
MR. MARVIN CLOWNEY
BROTHER MAURICO
MR. SENGHOR
MR. ASAD
MR. OMAR TYREE
MR. THUTMOSIS POWELL
MR. ROBERT T. DAVIS
BROTHER ALI
BROTHER MARK MUHAMMAD
SISTER MARY SMITH
IBN H. KHALIF KHALIFAH
KHADIJAH AMINA KHALIFAH
TAMUREDAH RAUSHANAH KHALIFAH
ALIKE HAZZIEH KHALIFAH
NADIRAH UHURU KHALIFAH
MR. PAUL BANKS
WAR CORRESPONDANT DEL JONES

MINISTER NEAL JACKSON
SISTER DIANE JACKSON
STELLA & SYSVESTER BATTLE
SISTER AHYANNA RETHELLA KHALIFAH
SISTER DEJA JENKINS
BROTHER TARIK MUHAMMAD
SISTER RHONDA MUHAMMAD
SISTER QADIRAH MUHAMMAD
SISTER AMIRA MUHAMMAD
BROTHER HERMAN FERGUSON
SISTER IYALUUA FERGUSON
BROTHER GEORGE WELCH
BROTHER NATHANIEL BRACEY
SISTER KHADIJAH BRACEY

REVIEW
&
PREVIEW SECTION

Index

CHAPTER 1
THE ACQUISITION AND PROPER USE OF POWER

* CHARACTER DEVELOPMENT
* BLACKS ARE SUBJUGATED TO ALL
  OTHER RACES ON EARTH
* THE RESULT OF THE IMPROPER
  UNDERSTANDING OF OUR SITUATION
* KNOWLEDGE IS POWER

CHAPTER 2
THE CHALLENGE OF WHITE SUPREMACY

* A BRIEF LOOK AT BLACK HISTORY
Vs. WHITE PEOPLE
*OPPORTUNITY FOR AFRICANS WHO ARE NOT YET
  MATERIALLY SUCCESSFUL IN WHITE SUPREMACY
* COMFORT IN THE SYSTEM
* POWER PROPERLY USED: COMFORT IN
THE SYSTEM *CAN* LEAD TO REAL HAPPINESS
* THE USE OF BLACK POWER IN WHITE SUPREMACY
* UNDERSTANDING THE SPIRITUAL BODY

CHAPTER 3
Brief Overview of the encounter of Black and White People

* THE PRIME REASON FOR STRUGGLE
* COMPLETELY OVERCOMING WHITE SUPREMACY
* HARMONIZING THE SPIRITUAL
  AND THE PHYSICAL BODIES
* YOU AND YOUR MIND ARE IMMORTAL
* IGNORANCE IS DEATH
* THE GENERATING OF POWER:

DOING THE THINGS TO GET POWER
* FREEING THE SPIRITUAL SELF
* ULTIMATE SUCCESS

Chapter Four

SUCCESSFULLY OVERCOMING SUVIVAL REQUIREMENTS WHILE FOCUSED ON THE LIBERATION OF BLACK PEOPLE

* THERE IS ALWAYS ENOUGH POWER
TO OVERCOME CHALLENGES
* STRUGGLING FOR & PROPERLY
USING POWER ON THE PHYSICAL PLANE
THE PLANES OF EXISTENCE ARE ILLUSIONS
* THE ACQUISITION OF POWER AND
PROPER METHODS TO GET AND USE IT
* THE FIRST THING TO OBTAIN IS PROPER
KNOWLEDGE OF SELF AND KIND
* ALL BLACKS ARE SUBJECT TO WHITE
PEOPLE IN WHITE SUPREMACY SYSTEMS

CHAPTER 5
PROPER AND IMPROPER USE OF POWER

* IMPROPER USE OF POWER
* THE PROPER USE OF POWER
WHILE LIVING WITHIN OPPRESSION

CHAPTER 6
NO ONE ASPECT OF LIFE NEED HAVE THE POWER TO CONSUME OUR LIVES

* WHITE SUPREMACY: USING POWER
IN THE BEST INTEREST OF OTHERS
* I MAKE IT A POINT TO
NOT TELL ANYONE NOT TO
SERVE AS A PHYSICAL FIGHTER
* USING BLACK POWER WITHIN
WHITE SUPREMACY

Chapter Seven
EFFECTIVE WAYS OF POWER THAT ARE NOT CONFRONTATIONAL TO THE ENEMY

* YOUR FEELINGS AND REALIZATION
  OF A NEED FOR CHANGE IN YOUR LIFE
* THE FEELINGS ABOUT THE NEED FOR CHANGE WHEN YOU HAVE LITTLE SUCCESS TO SHOW FOR YOUR LIFE
* THE ESSENCE OF LIFE
* HOW TO OBTAIN
  PROPER KNOWLEDGE OF SELF & KIND
* THE SAME THING SAID ANOTHER WAY

SUMMING UP PART 1

CHAPTER 8

* OTHER WAYS TO ACQUIRE POWER
  AND USE IT PROPERLY
* MORE WAYS TO ACQUIRE POWER
  AND USE IT PROPERLY
* CRIMINAL USE OF POWER TO STEAL
  HUMAN POTENTIAL IS OPPRESSION
* LOOKING AT TASKS & CHALLENGES
* ACQUIRING POWER
  BY USING CRIMINAL MEANS
* WHAT IS THE ORIGIN OF WHITE PEOPLE?
* THE PRINCE
  BY NICCOLO MACHIAVELLI
* NATURAL ROLES
  IN OPPRESSIVE SYSTEMS
* THERE IS A DIFFERENCE
* THE SPIRITUAL AND PHYSICAL
  STRUGGLE AGAINST OPPRESSION
* THE SECOND MAIN WEAPON OF
  WHITE PEOPLE USE OF DECPTION
* BASIC, SEEN AND UNSEEN,
  KNOWN FACTS ABOUT THE HUMAN

* EATING NUTRITIONAL SPIRITUAL FOOD
* 'WHY' WE DO NOT ALWAYS ACT
IN THE BEST INTEREST OF SELF
* THERE REALLY IS NOTHING TO FEAR
* IGNORANCE ABOUT THE TRUTH
CAUSE US TO ACT IN OTHER THAN OUR
OWN BEST INTEREST
* TRUTH ABOUT BLACK OPPRESSION
IS WRAPPED UP IN OUR SPIRITUALITY
* WHY WE ACT IN THE BEST
INTEREST OF OTHERS
* BRUTALITY FORCED BLACK PEOPLE
TO ACT IN THE BEST INEREST
OF OTHERS

Chapter Nine
69 YEARS OF EXPERIENCE IN OPPRESSION:
LIVING IN RESISTANCE AS A DUTY

* THE BLACK STRUGGLE IS FOR POWER
* BLACK YOUTH ALWAYS IN STAGES
OF DISCOVERY ABOUT OPPRESSION
* IT IS TIME TO BEGIN TO PREPARE OUR
CHILDREN TO WORK OUTSIDE
OF THE SYSTEM
* WAYS TO PREPARE OUR CHILDREN TO
RESIST OPPRESSION AS A LIFE STYLE
* WHAT I AM DOING TODAY
* RESISTANCE AS A DUTY
* OUR MAIN IMPEDIMENT AS HUMANS
* PHYSICAL FIGHT – SPIRITUAL STRUGGLE
* THE DIVINE UNFOLDING MYSTERY
OF LIFE (DUMOL)

Chapter 10

THE NATURAL DESIRE TO KNOW YOUR SELF
AND PURPOSE

* HOW MUCH UNDERSTANDING
OF KNOWLEDGE DO YOU HAVE
* EVERYTHING HAS A PURPOSE
* THE TRUE CREATOR
* THE SUPPRESSION OF OUR TRUE SELF
* THERE IS NOTHING TO FEAR
* TRUE SELF AS WELL AS
THE CREATOR IS FOUND WITHIN
* WAYS TO FIND GREATER TRUTHS
* IT IS NATURAL TO WANT
TO KNOW WHO YOU ARE
* HOW LEARNED MEN AND WOMEN GUIDE
 OTHERS TO AVOID ERRORS AND MISTAKES
* LEARNED MEN AND WOMEN GUIDE
 OTHERS TO AVOID ERRORS AND
 MISTAKES RESTRAIN FROM EXCESSES
* ELIJAH MUHAMMMAD, BLACK MUSLIMS
AND THE NATION OF ISLAM
* CORRECT KNOWLEDGE: NOTHING
 CREATED WITHOUT MEANING AND PURPOSE

Chapter 11
THE STRUGGLE IS TO OVERCOME CHALLENGES

* DIVINE ORDER IS A STATE OF PEACE:
PSYCHIC POWER IS IN THE PEACE
* HOW TO CONSCIOUSLY INCREASE
YOUR WILL POWER

Chapter 12
RAISING CHILDREN THE NATURAL WAY SHOULD BE TAUGHT IN OUR YOUTH

* IN THE NATURAL ORDER DADDY
IS PRESENT AT BABYS BIRTH
* WHEN FATHER IS HOME AND THINGS

STILL ARE NOT ENOUGH
* WE ARE CREATED OF
SPIRIT AND MATTER
* PROPERTIES OF THE FORCES
* EXTERNAL FORCE AND HOW WE
DEAL WITH AND BALANCE THEM

Chapter 13
THOUGHT IS THE COMMON
DENOMINATOR FOR HUMANS

* PHYSICAL POWER – POSITIVE AND
NEGATIVE FORCES –
* THE TRUE VALUE OF BALANCE
* HARMONY AND BALANCE ARE TWO
DIFFERENT STATES OF BEING
* DISAGREEMENTS BETWEEN OUR SPIRIT
AND PHYSICAL BEING: CONSEQUENCES
* WHY BALANCE IS NOT THE
END GAME

Chapter 14
THE FIRST LAW OF NATURE:
YOUR FIRST STRUGGLE

* WRITING TO EMPOWER OTHERS
* WHEN ARE WE UNJUST TO SELVES?
* THE REVOLT OF NAT TURNER AND THE
BLACK LIBERATIION ARMY IN 1831
* THE WORK OF DEATH OF SLAVEHOLDERS:
IN HARMONY OR IMBALANCED?

Chapter 15
NAT TURNER AS A POSITIVE
EXAMPLE FOR EVERYONE
* RETURNED TO RIDICULE OF
FELLOW CAPTIVES
* A CLOSER LOOK AT THE LIFE PURPOSE

OF NAT TURNER
* REPARATIONS VS APPROPRIATIONS

Chapter Sixteen
WHITE SUPREMACIST SYSTEM JOBS BLUNT THE MAIN OBJECTIVE

* THE BRUTALITY AND MISEDUCATION
OF THE NEGRO TOOK ITS TOLL
* THE HON. ELIJAH MUHAMMAD AND
THE TEACHINGS OF THE NATION OF ISLAM

Chapter 17
SOMETIMES ONLY WELL PLANNED DYNAMIC ACTION TO ACHIEVE A PHYSICAL RESULT WILL WORK

* NAT TURNER LOOKED AT SUBJECTIVELY
IN RELATION TO MY OWN LIFE
* INJUSTICE AGAINST
THE RIGHTS OF OTHERS

Chapter 18
POWER IS ALWAYS WITH US: EVEN A BABY IS BORN WITH POWER

* SOME HAVE TREMENDOUS KNOWLEDGE
BUT DO NOT GET ANYTHING
SIGNIGICANT DONE
* UNDERSTANDING OF KNOWLEDGE EQUAL WISDOM
* PROPERTIES OF THE MIND BEGETS
WILL POWER TO ACT
* OUTSIDE FORCES THAT CHALLENGE US
* INSIDE CHALLENGES
* PURPOSE FOR THE CHALLENGES
* WHAT IS THE BEST CHARACTER?
* LIFE PURPOSE
* IT IS EASY TO SHOW NEEDS
* IT IS EASY TO THE SHOW NEED
TO FOR PERSONAL STRUGGLE
* THE CHALLENGE OF WHITE SUPREMACY
REQUIRES BLACK CONSCIOUSNESSES

* THE CHALLENGE OF WHITE SUPREMACY
BEGINS EARLY AND STAYS LATE
* IT IS ALSO HARD TO CHANGE
HARMLESS SYSTEMS

* Chapter 19
ON RAISING CHILDREN
* THE EXCEPTION TO PUTTING DOWN
INDIVIDUAL BLACKS
* WHAT WAS I THINKING EARLY IN LIFE
IN WHITE SUPREMACY?
* IT IS LEGITIMATE TO FEAR A PEOPLE
WITH A BRUTAL, VIOLENT HISTORY
* FEAR MUST BE OVERCOME BECAUSE
THERE IS 'NOTHING TO FEAR'

THE LAST QUARTER:
THE ENDING OF **THE BOOK**

* **ON ADVISING BLACK YOUTH TO
DISSIPATING BLACK POWER LOOKING
FOR WORK IN "THE SYSTEM!"**
* THE REASON OUR CHILDREN
ARE NOT GAINFULLY WORKING
* WHY WHITE PEOPLE FEAR
OUR BLACKNESS
* THE WORK OF BLACK COMMUNITY
ORGANIZERS AND MASTER TEACHERS
IN THE AWAKENING OF BLACK YOUTH
* MIS-EDUCATION IS BRAINWASHING
* BLACK YOUTH STILL LOOKING
FOR A GOOD JOB IN WHITE AMERICA
* PROPOSED DESIGN TO POISON
BLACK YOUTH AGAINST PLACES AND
SITUATIONS THAT INJURE THEIR MINDS
* TOO MUCH TIME WASTED LOOKING
FOR A BREAK FOR CAREERS THEY
WILL NEVER GET
* THE CYCLE OF BROKEN BLACK

YOUTH BE STOPPED BUILDING A SYSTEM
TO FREE BLACK PEOPLE
* START EARLY IN THEIR BABYHOOD
* TELL THE TRUTH ABOUT THE SYSTEM
EARLY IN THEIR LIVES
* THE DON'T TOUCH THE
HOT STOVE ANALOGY
* TEACHING BLACK YOUTH
WHAT TO EXPECT IN THE SYSTEM
* TEACH BLACK CHILDREN THAT WHITE
PEOPLE DON'T LIKE THEM NOTHING THEY
DO WILL CHANGE THEIR MIND
* KNOWING RIGHT vs DOING RIGHT:
PARTS AND PARTIALS OF SAME DECISION
ALL WHITE PEOPLE ARE NOT CHARGED

POST SCRIPT

The P. S. is to acknowledge the work of Dr. Imari Abubarkari Obadele. I will share my Tribute to him. It is not that he was more important in my life than others, for indeed, my biological, Great, Solid Surrogate Father, from the age of nine years old died in the same month as Dr. Obadele: January of 2010. His name was Louis Edward Knight. But Dr. Obadele was one of the Greatest Servants of Black people in the 20th century to all Black people.

I worked with him in the forming, building and work of N'COBRA (The National Coalition of Blacks For Reparations in America) to achieve it first priority mission, during the 1990's. He was all that the history books say he was, and more.

I never worked personally with The Honorable Elijah Muhammad or Minister Louis Farrakhan, but I did with Dr. Obadele. Hopefully the following gives you a some estimation of what he meant to the Liberation Struggle of Black people.

TRIBUTE TO A GREAT MAN

As I looked for a way to pay Tribute to Dr. Obadele, and express my love, admiration and respect for the man and his work, the words that Attorney Chokwe Lumumba spoke at the pre-sentencing of one of our most dynamic, functional, effective, but now incarcerated Freedom fighters, Mutula Shakur rang out in my mind: *"We have been here before,"* opened Brother Chokwe.

"We first stood before your jurisdiction as chattel property that you were not bound to respect. And did not respect" end of quote.

Today we stand in UTMOST RESPECT AND HONOR, as Dr. Imari Obadele join our ancestors...and we say, as Brother Chokwe Lumumba said to the white supremacist dog, in the NYC courtroom in August of 1988: and I quote Chokwe again, *"his memory will not go away. Others will take his seat, and when they get to know him, will glad to sit there.*

"We will teach our children. This will ensure a future resistance. If it is anything like we perceive, this

government is in trouble." **Ended Chokwe Lumumba. And ends my Tribute to Dr. Imari Abubakari Obadele.**

However, as an aside to our surviving Freedom Fighters; as we have done with other Fallen heroes, and sheroes, we collect our dead and wounded, we honor their service to our Noble struggle; we then return to our positions, redouble commitments, more determined, more sure of the righteousness of our Cause...AND WE ARE MORE CONVINCED than ever, that decisions we made to stay the course that cause us to live life styles in resistance to White Supremacy systems - subjecting us to the vilest form of ridicule from family, friends and foe ALIKE is the healthiest way to live on planet earth.

Give me time to read my commitment and I will be done. It is what I learned, more than anything else, from Dr. Obadele.....

PLEDGE TO THE CAUSE
If I never see another sun
If it never rise again
If the day of celebration of black liberation never begin If my state of being today never end
With good as my shield I shall never give in

"FREE THE LAND!"

THE LAWS OF MAAT

We have tried to address the main problem, in my estimation, the main challenge for the Liberation necessities of Black people. That is the acquisition of necessary power; power across the entire spectrum of earth life. And we have done so in as simple language and style as possible.

While we are comfortable with the mixture of Spiritual and Physical power of The Book, the four years in the writing allowed time to receive and utilize some concepts and precepts that are not expressed to the extent that I have grown and benefitted from them. However, I dare say that a re-reading of my book, before publication convinced me that the teachings, and recordation by our ancestors are saturated within my text.

As I try to do in all of my writing, this is meant to be a "living document:" meaning, it is useful in the life of the reader in the here and now.

And as I did in my earlier book: *"MELANIN: Conscious Attunement and the God in I,"* I invite anyone of a mind to, to visit me at The Nat Turner Reference Library in Southampton County, Virginia www.natturnertrail.com.

I strongly advise that you call first if you want to assure a meeting and greeting with me. But this is certainly not necessary to partake and vacation, or other kind of visitation to this hallowed, historic place.

Call 434-378-2140. Or email khalifah@khabooks.com

MEDITATION FROM THE TREE OF LIFE

As Ausar, I vibrate from the spheres of the Tree of Life
The Tree of Life is within the Context of Thee
I speak, act and Live Free of All manner of Strife
Spheres of the Tree of Life Vibrate to the only Reality

Master of Ausar, inclined to be with others that I Am
Generating thoughts, visions, and dreams as I Am wont to be
Reflecting the Peace in all complexity of Divine Reality
Understanding experiences applying wisdom to
 master the Law Tehuti

Master of Tehuti the Sphere of Wisdom that I Am
Living word, act and deed in the Way of Ausar
Vibrating Divine Teachings, being in heaven
Answering righteous just call as the Master of Sekher

Using the Law of Sekher, caller in Law in the Spirit of Divine
Loud in harmony with other Spheres of the Wonderful Tree
Ra hear my calls for it is on behalf of the Universal all
Awaiting the justice in the sureness of the laws of MAAT

Master of MAAT as my disposition portend
Loving in the totality of Devotion to the end
Reaping the reserves that are held for the few
Staying the course through others to get to Herukhuti

Master and understanding the Law of Herukhuti
Applying the wisdom to mete justice
Where justice is due
Willing the Divine Laws of Master Heru

The Master Heru demands justice for all
Willed to obey or be subject to Fall
To learn lessons in the Law without end
Free to imagine within the Laws of Het-Heru

Master Het-Heru offer the way to dance
Singing into the spirit in Divine Reality
Accepting immortality through Love and romance
Into the sure circumstance of the sheer power of Sebek

The Master of the Law of the Spoken Word
The Right Way will surely be Righteously heard
For Sebek communicates by any means necessary
To find the way to Receptivity in the Law of Auset

As Master of the Law of Auset
I Am receiving an Abundance of all Things yet
Needed to manifest all Spheres to Serve Humanity
I have no selfish ideals as to how I am to serve almighty Geb

Master of the things of the Good Earth
Is giving fulfillment and Righteous Birth
Awakening my Spirit into the manifestations
 of Divine Supply Blessing me to Receive all that I need
As I move infinitely on into immortality

040817-100-4-60W